Allegheny City

May 24, 2013

Carol Peter

All the best!

Dan Rooney

US Ambassador

Allegheny City

A History of Pittsburgh's North Side

DAN ROONEY
and
CAROL PETERSON

With a Foreword by
BRIAN O'NEILL

UNIVERSITY OF PITTSBURGH PRESS

Published by the University of Pittsburgh Press, Pittsburgh, Pa., 15260
Copyright © 2013, University of Pittsburgh Press
Manufactured in the United States of America
Printed on acid-free paper
10 9 8 7 6 5 4 3 2 1

Library of Congress Cataloging-in-Publication Data

Rooney, Dan, 1932–
    Allegheny City : a history of Pittsburgh's North Side / Dan Rooney and
Carol Peterson : with a foreword by Brian O'Neill.
        pages   cm
    Includes bibliographical references and index.
    ISBN 978-0-8229-4422-5 (hbk. : alk. paper)
        1. North Side (Pittsburgh, Pa.)—History.   2. Pittsburgh (Pa.)—History.
3. Manchester (Pittsburgh, Pa.)—History.   4. North Side
(Pittsburgh, Pa.)—Buildings, structures, etc.   5. Pittsburgh (Pa.)—
Buildings, structures, etc.   6. Manchester (Pittsburgh, Pa.)—
Buildings, structures, etc.   7. Historic buildings—Pennsylvania—
Pittsburgh.   8. Neighborhoods—Pennsylvania—Pittsburgh—
History.   I. Peterson, Carol. II. Title.
    F159.P66A448 2013
    974.8'86—dc23   2012047727

CONTENTS

FOREWORD

Brian O'Neill

ASK DON "RED" LIVINGSTONE about Pittsburgh's North Side, and old stories tumble from him as easily and as naturally as kids once tumbled down Monument Hill. Red was one of those kids back in the 1940s. That's when his slice of the North Side was a real neighborhood known simply as "the Ward" because it had been old Allegheny City's First Ward.

Now it's an entertainment complex, "The North Shore," with Heinz Field, PNC Park, a couple of museums, and lots of bars. It had none of that when Red was a kid—except lots of bars.

Times change. Cities change. People don't change much. Red, a retired Teamster, now lives on Mount Washington, across the rivers from the North Side, where folks can literally look down on his old neighborhood. Not that people ever needed a hill to do that.

There are at least eighteen distinct city neighborhoods north of the Allegheny River and east of the Ohio that, taken together, form the North Side. Taken as a unit, this is Pittsburgh's largest neighborhood and one that long has suffered a bad rap from outsiders.

Red's wife, Joanne, will tell you that when she was a young woman, her grandmother told her, "Whatever you do, don't marry an Irishman from the Ward."

The Irish flag that hangs from the Livingstone porch is evidence that Grandma Rice's advice didn't take. She may have seen too much drinking and fighting in the Ward when she and the twentieth century were young, but Red saw it, or at least remembers it, as a slice of heaven. "This neighborhood—it was like a movie set," he says. "You know if the Ward would ever come back, I would move back."

The North Side is coming back. I've lived there since 1990. (That's so long ago that the Pirates were good.) My wife and I are raising two daughters here, and they have grown up walking to the Carnegie Science Center, the National Aviary, the Children's Museum, the ballgames, the rivers, and more. There are few affordable places in America where a family has all that within a ten-minute stroll.

Yet the rap on the North Side hasn't changed all that much since Red was a kid. Even as it experiences something of a renaissance, a local joke has it that the North Side is like soccer: it's the sport of the future—and always will be.

This book tells the Allegheny/North Side story from the days of canals and cotton mills through the present day. Dan Rooney, who grew up in the neighborhood, left, and returned to his boyhood home with his wife, Patricia, has joined with Carol Peterson, a tireless scholar of Pittsburgh's history, to coauthor this essential story.

Dan is, of course, the owner of the Pittsburgh Steelers and was the US ambassador to Ireland. But like his father, Art, who founded the team, he has an appreciation for the down-home joys of this quirky city neighborhood that no amount of fame or success will ever shake. I've bumped into the Rooneys often at the 8:30 A.M. Sunday mass at Our Lady Queen of Peace (sister church of St. Peter's, which once served as the cathedral of old Allegheny City). I've also chatted with them waiting for an "icy ball" from Gus Kalaris, the vendor who has parked his orange cart by the West Park tennis courts every summer "since your dad was a lad."

Red Livingstone can vouch that this always has been the Rooney way. A little room on the second floor of his home is his man cave, filled with photos and memorabilia of his youth. Take, for instance, the vintage Steelers jersey and tube socks. They once belonged to a punter named Pat Brady who played in the early 1950s. The uniform is so basic it wouldn't be worn by a junior varsity team today, but it was pro gear then, and the Rooneys gave that stuff away so neighborhood teenagers would have something to play in.

When he was even younger, Red played on the "Little Rooneys" football team, and he was among the boys from St. Peter's grade school who played in the Rooneys' backyard in the afternoons. On Sundays, they'd pile into Art Rooney's Buick station wagon, ten kids or more, to go to Steelers games.

"Everybody go to mass this morning, boys?" Mr. Rooney would ask. They could always affirm their attendance honestly. This may have been due less to their devout faith than to their knowledge of what the nuns would do to them in class Monday if they didn't attend church on Sunday.

Red and his mother moved from apartment to apartment when he was a child, but never left the lower North Side. Downtown was a mystery, and other city neighborhoods were rumors. The Ward was all.

Livingstone left the neighborhood in 1949, and slowly and fitfully, the old neighborhood left the city. For years after moving up to Mount Washington, he would get out his binoculars to see if anyone was playing baseball or softball on Monument Hill. If there was a game, he'd hustle down and play. But as the years passed, those binoculars would show less and less of what he once knew. He himself would drive the tractor-trailers that brought the concrete walkways to Three Rivers Stadium, which opened in 1970 only after his neighborhood was leveled to make way for it.

Not surprisingly, Red doesn't like all the changes. "If they'd have left Federal Street alone, it would be ten or fifteen times what Carson Street is today," he said, referring to fifteen blocks of night spots that line the South Side's main corridor.

He and his friends often talk about tracking down the guy whose idea it was to level old Allegheny City's downtown in the 1960s to make way for Allegheny Center Mall. That mall died before the twenty-first century arrived, and if Red and his childhood buddies could just find the planner's grave, they'd leave something on it—and it wouldn't be holy water.

We can dwell too long on the past, though. Families of the early twenty-first century are forming memories as strong as Red's. Some they share with previous generations—skating on Lake Elizabeth, getting ice balls from Gus, watching the fireworks that Pittsburgh is forever sending skyward. Others are new—wandering the Children's Museum, the Science Center, the Andy Warhol Museum, the Mattress Factory art museum, the stadiums, and the Water Steps, a very cool riverside fountain in all senses of the term.

When Red walked me to my car after an afternoon of reminiscing, I couldn't help but notice the Federal Street sign in his Mount Washington backyard. I asked him what's so special about the North Side that he'll never let it go.

"The people and the things that happened there," he said.

That's what I love about the North Side, too, though I'm not thinking of the same people or all the same things. Fortunately, Dan Rooney and Carol Peterson don't seem to have left anyone out, from the time the Pennsylvania General Assembly created a three-thousand-acre reserve on the northern bank of the Allegheny River for veterans of the Revolutionary War, through the heyday of the steel barons, and on to all the urban makeovers, good and bad, that have made the North Side what it is today.

If you have any interest in the way American cities evolved, and if you have a particular interest in Pittsburgh, this is *the* book for its largest section, the North Side.

ACKNOWLEDGMENTS

We would like to thank Beth Reiners for her assistance with historical research and Sam McUmber for translating Pittsburgh German newspapers to English.

Allegheny City

CHAPTER 1

Beginnings in Wilderness
The Colonial Era to 1840

I N 1783, at the close of the American Revolution, the area that later became Allegheny City—and even later Pittsburgh's North Side—was a wilderness, home to perhaps a few hardy white squatters and an uncertain number of American Indians. Within view, just across the junction of the Allegheny and Ohio rivers, the village of Pittsburgh bustled with commerce. It was already known as the "Gateway to the West," and its population was growing steadily.

While its population was sparse, the area that would one day be Pittsburgh's North Side had long been home to Seneca Indians, one of five tribes of the League of the Iroquois, who by 1748 had established a village near the river, at a location between present-day Allegheny Avenue and Federal Street. By 1783 a dirt path—a former Indian trail—cut through the land north of the rivers. From an Allegheny River crossing at Herr's Island, this path ran along present-day East Ohio Street, West Ohio Street, Western Avenue, and Beaver Avenue. In 1799, Allegheny County would take charge of this path and designate it the route to the town of Beaver, in Beaver County.

During the colonial era, George Washington and Christopher Gist were among the travelers who used this dirt path. In 1753, Virginia sent the twenty-one-year-old Washington, with Gist as his guide, to warn the French away from the Forks of the Ohio, land that England (and Virginia) claimed. Gist accompanied Washington on his almost-fatal crossing of the Allegheny River, near the present-day Fortieth Street Bridge. The French ignored Washington's message, and Washington returned in 1754, his journey eventually leading to the world's first global conflict, known as the French and Indian War in the United States and the Seven Years' War in Europe. Washington confronted the French, first at Jumonville's Glen, where he prevailed over a small French force, then at Fort Necessity, where he surrendered.

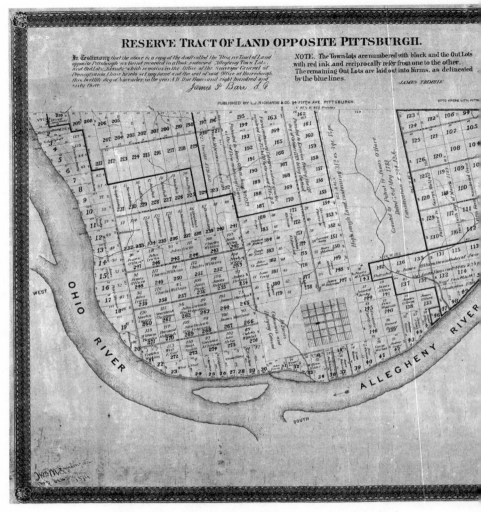

The reserve tract of land opposite Pittsburgh and the original plan for Allegheny City. Darlington Digital Library Maps Collection, Digital Research Library, University Library System, University of Pittsburgh

Now, in 1783, at the end of the Revolution, wishing to benefit the young country's veterans and anticipating further development at this confluence where the Allegheny and Monongahela rivers meet to form the Ohio, the Pennsylvania General Assembly created the three-thousand-acre Reserve Tract from the wilderness opposite Pittsburgh from a larger area called the

Depreciation Lands. The tract stretched along the north bank of the Allegheny and Ohio rivers, its northern boundary extending in a nearly straight line from the mouth of Woods Run, an Ohio River tributary near the present State Correctional Institution at Pittsburgh, to the mouth of Girty's Run, on the Allegheny River at what is now Millvale. The general assembly wanted Revolutionary War veterans to receive land in the Reserve Tract as compensation for their services.

David Redick, the commonwealth's surveyor, laid out the Reserve Tract in 1787, envisioning a rectangular town called Allegheny, with its center at the present intersection of Federal and Ohio streets. Allegheny Town would contain one hundred "in lots," measuring 60 by 240 feet, with four blocks dedicated to public use at its center. The town plan imposed streets and lot lines upon uneven terrain, abundant hardwood trees, and small bodies of water. A common area for grazing, now East and West parks, surrounded the town on all sides, with Federal and Ohio streets, but no lesser streets, cutting through this common. Federal Street was the southernmost section of the Franklin Road, which ran from Pittsburgh north to present Venango County. Beyond the common area, Redick created "out lots," many of ten acres, with the idea that landowners would combine them for farming. Each purchaser of a town lot was to receive an out lot at no additional cost. In 1788, the commonwealth auctioned both Allegheny's in lots and the out lots beyond the town.

The newly platted Allegheny Town was originally within Pitt Township, which straddled the Allegheny River and took in much of present Pittsburgh. Then, as Allegheny County's population and commerce increased, new townships formed. Allegheny Town was included in Pine Township when it was cut from Pitt Township in 1796. Part of Pine Township became Ross Township in 1809, and it contained Allegheny Town until the town became a borough.

Another important early development in the North Side's history came when James Robinson of Pittsburgh began a ferry between Pittsburgh and Allegheny in the 1780s. He moved to the north shore of the Allegheny River, at present-day Federal Street, not long before his only child, William Robinson Jr., was born, in 1785. Nineteenth-century historians regarded the birth of William Jr., reportedly the first white child born in what became Allegheny City, as a landmark event.

The Robinson family, occupying a log dwelling, reportedly withstood an Indian attack soon after settling north of the river, and the family persevered. In 1788 James Robinson purchased the land on which he lived in the newly created Reserve Tract, close to the site of today's PNC Park. In 1803, Robinson built the first brick house in the future Allegheny City, likely with the assistance of his slaves. Slavery, while increasingly rare, remained legal in Pennsylvania in the early nineteenth century; the state's 1780 Act for Gradual Emancipation had not freed Pennsylvania's slaves, but it had provided for freeing their future children.

The original Reserve Tract plan had projected Allegheny Town as the seat of Allegheny County, which the Pennsylvania General Assembly created in 1788 from parts of Washington and Westmoreland counties. Pittsburgh residents, however, objected to this plan, and in 1791 the commonwealth decided that the county's courthouse and jail would be in Pittsburgh. Interest in Allegheny Town thus diminished, in spite of the ambitions of its developers and its early settlers, and the town grew slowly. In 1810, Allegheny Town had only around 450 residents, nearly all of whom lived in modest log or frame houses.

At the beginning of the nineteenth century, most of southwestern Pennsylvania's people were Scotch-Irish, their roots in the Ulster province of Northern Ireland. Even as Allegheny Town and Pittsburgh gained in population, most new settlers in both communities were still Scotch-Irish, English and Irish immigrants moving to the town as well, but in smaller numbers. A typical property owner coming to Allegheny Town could build a small house for a few hundred dollars. Overwhelmingly Presbyterian, Allegheny Town residents began holding formal church services in or before 1811. Their first house of worship was a small Presbyterian church built on the West Commons in about 1815.

Beyond the commons, the out lots also attracted settlers, most of them farmers. John Woods, a farmer and Virginia native of Irish descent, settled in 1794 along the Ohio River tributary that became known as Woods Run. In the same vicinity the young Scotch-Irish immigrant Hugh Davis began farming about 1801; decades later Davis, having apparently prospered, would serve as Allegheny Borough burgess (mayor) and treasurer. Benjamin Herr, a farmer of Swiss descent, moved from Pittsburgh to the Allegheny riverbank about 1808, settling about two miles northeast of Federal Street. Herr's land included an island named for him, and his children remained in this vicinity well into the nineteenth century. The area also saw the arrival of nascent industry: Beelen and Denny's glass works, the first factory north of the Allegheny and Ohio rivers, began operation at Woods Run about 1800, though a scarcity of fuel soon forced production to cease.

Brunot's Island, in the Ohio River at Woods Run, was also occupied early, Dr. Felix Brunot purchasing the island about 1797 and moving his family there from Philadelphia. Brunot was a French immigrant who had served the Marquis de Lafayette during the Revolutionary War, and his family hosted the westward-bound explorers Meriwether Lewis and William Clark on the island in 1803. This visit nearly ended in tragedy when Lewis's airgun accidentally discharged, the shot grazing a woman who fell to the ground, alarming onlookers before she revived.

While it continued to slowly grow, Allegheny Town gave little hint of its future glory during the second decade of the nineteenth century. While Pittsburgh incorporated as a city in 1816, Allegheny remained a quiet village. One of the first Pittsburgh directories, published in 1815, contained a separate section for the outlying communities of Bayards Town (now the Strip District), Lawrenceville, and Birmingham (now the South Side), but Allegheny was too insignificant to mention. The most important sign of progress in Allegheny Town was probably the construction of the first bridge from Allegheny to Pittsburgh and the Western Penitentiary, both beginning in 1818.

The Allegheny Bridge stood on the site of the modern Sixth Street (now Roberto Clemente) Bridge, where James Robinson's ferry had made its first relays more than three decades earlier. Robinson had died in 1814, leaving a considerable fortune to his son and only heir, William Robinson Jr. The younger Robinson now became the first president of the Allegheny Bridge

Company, a private firm that charged tolls to cross the span. The Allegheny Bridge Company spent $35,000 of its own capital and $40,000 in state funds to construct that first bridge, completed in 1820. The covered wood bridge, supported by stone piers, had separate rights-of-way for pedestrians and vehicles. At its opening, it was the second river-crossing bridge at Pittsburgh; the first, a covered wood bridge over the Monongahela, had opened to traffic in 1818, on the site of the present Smithfield Street Bridge. William Robinson Jr. had doubtlessly invested part of his inheritance in the bridge's construction, and now he saw a quick return, not only in toll revenues but in the increased value of his extensive real estate north of the river. Ferries still competed with the Allegheny Bridge, bringing passengers to the foot of Beaver Avenue (then Ferry Lane) and to a point on the shore near today's Andy Warhol Museum.

In 1819, East Ohio Street became part of the new Pittsburgh and Butler Turnpike, or toll road. The turnpike began at Federal Street and ran northeast along the Allegheny River flood plain for several miles to Pine Creek at present Etna. It then turned north and proceeded to Butler. This road quickly became a regionally important thoroughfare, which General Lafayette used when he toured the United States and was feted on Stockton Street in Allegheny Town in 1825. In 1835, the road from Allegheny to Beaver also became a turnpike. Today's Port Authority bus routes that run along Western Avenue and through Manchester and beyond follow nearly the same route as this 1835 turnpike to Beaver, a horse-car line that began in 1859 or 1860, and Allegheny's late nineteenth-century streetcars.

Construction of the Western Penitentiary was launched when the commonwealth sliced out a ten-acre piece of the West Commons as its site in 1818. The project brought masons, stonecutters, carpenters, plasterers, and other artisans to Allegheny Town; required the construction of additional homes; and supported the town's merchants, as a small army of skilled and unskilled workmen spent the next eight years constructing a massive towered sandstone building. In 1826, an observer described the nearly completed penitentiary as "a very majestic and formidable pile." The writer continued, "The cells are each 6 feet by 8, with a large iron ring in the centre, to which the convict will be chained. . . . Here will the [criminal] expiate his offences in a manner that must convey more terror to the minds of wicked men than all the systems of punishment devised in our country."

Of course, other large construction projects were also under way in Allegheny Town. The City of Pittsburgh acquired property near the town's

The original Western Penitentiary, located in Allegheny Commons from 1826 to the 1880s.
Robert M. Palmer and Hartley M. Phelps, *Palmer's Pictorial Pittsburgh and Prominent Pittsburghers Past and
Present, 1758–1905*, 1905. Courtesy of Historic Pittsburgh Full-Text Collection, Digital Research Library,
University Library System, University of Pittsburgh

northwest corner to build its almshouse, an institution that housed the indi-
gent, in 1821–22. The two-story wood-frame building faced Ohio Lane (now
Western Avenue), its ten-acre grounds extending to present Allegheny Avenue,
North Franklin Street, and Sedgwick Street. A cemetery occupied part of the
grounds. The Presbyterian Church of the United States established a seminary
on the West Commons, south of the penitentiary, in 1825. The seminary was
founded six years after Allegheny property owners had prevented a proposed
grant of West Commons land to the Western University of Pennsylvania (now
the University of Pittsburgh), apparently fearing the loss of pastureland.

Leather-aproned artisans constituted the majority of early manufacturers
in Allegheny Town. Blacksmiths, shoemakers, boat builders, and other crafts-
men accounted for most of the town's production of goods in the first quarter
of the nineteenth century. In contrast, the Irwin "rope walk" was Allegheny
Town's first "manufactory," its workers fabricating rope by hand while walking backward in its long building. John Irwin, a Revolutionary War veteran,
and his wife, Mary, had founded the rope walk in Pittsburgh in 1794, the

business reportedly the first of its type in or beyond western Pennsylvania. After John Irwin's death, Mary Irwin and her son, John Irwin Jr., ran the business in Pittsburgh until 1813, notably making the rigging for Commodore Oliver Hazard Perry's naval fleet. In 1813, John Irwin Jr. moved the rope walk across the river to a ten-acre property bounded by what are now Brighton Road and Ridge, Galveston, and Western avenues.

By 1826, the rope walk employed fourteen workers and was one of Allegheny Town's largest employers. The directory that year reported that the facility produced "cordage of all kinds, from the smallest wrapping twine to the largest ship cables." It manufactured $15,000 worth of goods annually and had a warehouse near the Point in Pittsburgh for shipping along the rivers. Between 1835 and 1847, the rope walk expanded westward along Ridge and Western avenues toward Allegheny Avenue. It operated there until 1858, the longest-lived of several nineteenth-century rope walks in Allegheny and Pittsburgh. The Irwin family lived on its grounds in a white frame house facing what is now Brighton Road.

Iron manufacturing also became an important part of Pittsburgh's economy in the early nineteenth century. Allegheny Town's first iron mill was the Juniata Rolling Mill, built by Colonel James Anderson, Sylvanus Lothrop, and Henry Blake in 1826–27 on the western part of the present PNC Park site. By 1833, the Juniata Rolling Mill employed seventy-five men and was the third-largest iron mill of approximately thirty then operating in the Pittsburgh area. Under a succession of owners and managers, the Juniata Rolling Mill made nails, some lower-quality steel, and iron blooms—the crude masses from which wrought iron was made—until 1859.

Meanwhile, Allegheny's population continued to grow, nearly quadrupling between 1826 and 1830, at least partly thanks to Pittsburgh's growth. The 1826 Pittsburgh directory estimated the town's population at 702, reporting, "In Allegheny Town there are 85 houses, forming about 93 tenements—of which 13 are brick, and the balance, good two story frames, generally." In 1828, a Pittsburgh official noted that 61 houses had been built during the past year in the town across the river. The first official count of Allegheny's population, in the 1830 census, found 2,801 free residents, 50 of whom were "free colored persons," and 8 slaves. Pittsburgh's population in that year was 12,568.

Spurred on by this accelerating growth, the town incorporated as a borough in 1828, extending from the Allegheny River north to a short distance beyond present Carrington Street, just above the Mexican War Streets. Madison

Avenue (then East Lane) formed Allegheny's eastern boundary, and present Brighton Road (then Pasture Lane), Western Avenue (then Water Lane), and Beaver Avenue (then Ferry Lane) marked its western line. In an election held in a Federal Street tavern that occupied the twentieth-century site of the famous Boggs & Buhl department store, the voters of the new borough elected rope manufacturer John Irwin Jr. as their first burgess. Irwin defeated bridge builder William Robinson Jr. in that initial election.

Population growth and borough status warranted the founding of additional churches. Allegheny residents founded a Methodist Episcopal congregation in 1828 and constructed a church on Arch Street in 1830. Allegheny's first Episcopal congregation was organized in 1830, and in 1835, fifteen Allegheny residents who belonged to the First Baptist Church of Pittsburgh established the First Baptist Church of Allegheny. This congregation worshipped in a schoolhouse until it commissioned a church on Sandusky Street in Allegheny in 1843.

In the twentieth century, Allegheny native and historian Charles W. Dahlinger would call the 1830s "the Golden Age of Allegheny Town," and indeed, the town's population nearly quadrupled again in that decade. Pittsburgh also gained in population in the 1830s, but its respectable 68 percent growth did not match that of the town across the river. Allegheny's rapid development was a result of the growth of Allegheny's cotton industry, German immigration, residential subdivision, and Allegheny's emergence as a commuter suburb of Pittsburgh. Perhaps the most important factor in the growth of Allegheny Town, however, was the construction of the Pennsylvania Canal. The Pennsylvania legislature had established a canal commission in 1824 in response to concerns about the commonwealth's loss of commerce to New York and Ohio following construction of the Erie Canal and the Ohio Canal. The arduous process of building the canal had begun in 1826, and the Western Division, between Pittsburgh and Johnstown, had been finished in 1829, the first canal boats reaching Allegheny and Pittsburgh. By 1834, the construction of the entire canal, from Philadelphia to Pittsburgh, was complete. In Allegheny, the canal entered what is now the North Side via a right-of-way that generally followed the present railroad tracks, parallel to East Ohio Street. It continued west until it turned south in the Deutschtown area, then crossed the Allegheny River, traveling to Pittsburgh on an elevated waterway called an aqueduct. The canal then continued south, partly via a tunnel, to its western terminus on the Monongahela River.

The canal provided more efficient means of transporting manufactured

The Allegheny waterfront, including the Eagle Cotton Mill. Cotton mills were major
employers in Allegheny before the Civil War. Robert M. Palmer and Hartley M. Phelps, *Palmer's*
Pictorial Pittsburgh and Prominent Pittsburghers Past and Present, 1758–1905, 1905. Courtesy of Historic
Pittsburgh Full-Text Collection, Digital Research Library, University Library System, University of Pittsburgh

goods, raw materials, farm produce, and passengers across Pennsylvania than
travel on the state's rudimentary roads ever could. Its link with the Ohio
River also meant that goods could be easily transported to Wheeling, Cincinnati, and farther points. Although slow in comparison to later means of transportation, in the nineteenth century the canal gave an immediate economic
boost to the Pennsylvania communities through which it passed.

Both Allegheny and Pittsburgh had canal basins for loading, unloading,
and repairing canal boats. Allegheny's basin stretched between present Reedsdale and General Robinson streets, about five hundred feet west of Federal
Street. A canal spur continued west from the canal's bend in Deutschtown to
connect the canal to Allegheny's basin, the spur as much as twelve feet below
grade at Federal Street. Bridges spanned the canal there and at other crossings.
In addition to the canal trough itself, called a prism, and basins, bridges, and
the aqueduct, the canal system in and near Allegheny included a towpath, lift
locks, and waste weirs for draining extra water. The canal prism, measuring
forty feet wide at its top and twenty-eight feet at the bed, its water four feet
deep, was lined with massive slabs of cut stone that were well caulked to prevent leakage. The canal's entire right-of-way, including the eleven-foot-wide

towpath on the lower side of the prism, was at least sixty-four feet wide.

Property owners quickly lined Allegheny's canal basin with warehouses and stores and other buildings that catered to travelers, including taverns. In 1828, the Allegheny council authorized the town's first market house, a one-story wood building near the intersection of Federal and Ohio streets, a short walk from the canal. The canal fostered commerce all along its route through Allegheny, as boat operators typically stopped at any point where they might do business. Dahlinger wrote that "in summer when fruits and vegetables were brought into the town, there was a regular market for their sale nearly the entire length of the canal."

Cotton manufacturing also boomed in Allegheny in the

Industrialist and abolitionist Charles Avery founded Avery College, a school for African American teachers. Carnegie Library of Pittsburgh Pennsylvania Department, Pittsburgh Photographic Library

1830s. The ailing American cotton industry had begun to revive in 1824, when the federal government imposed tariffs on imported cotton and other goods, and between 1828 and 1836, four steam-powered cotton mills commenced operation in lower Allegheny, south of the Pennsylvania Canal. The city's first cotton mill, the Anchor, was located on General Robinson Street, west of Federal Street, in the First Ward. Other mills were in the Fourth Ward, east of Federal Street. Their location was ideal for receiving raw material from the South, via the Mississippi and Ohio rivers, and shipping on finished goods—such as yarn, ticking, sheeting, and cordage—by river or canal.

In 1836, Allegheny's three most established cotton mills, the Pittsburgh, the Hope, and the Eagle, used a combined 4,300 bales of cotton; had 13,600 spindles; and turned out $530,000 of product. Together they employed 560 workers, many of whom were women and girls. Work in these cotton mills was not hazard-free; a boiler explosion in the Eagle mill killed thirteen employees in 1833 or 1834. Pittsburgh's three mills, across the river, had considerably fewer employees and spindles and less product value than Allegheny's. Historians, however, have noted a significant commonality between the owners of Allegheny's and Pittsburgh's cotton mills: in both cases these were men who had made their fortunes in other commerce, generally lacking the involvement and experience with the industry that was common among proprietors of the area's iron works, breweries, and tanneries.

A paper mill, a tannery, foundries, a brewery, and sawmills also commenced operation in or around Allegheny in the 1830s. At least one factory, the Globe Plow Works, moved there from Pittsburgh. The plow works, the Hinds and Howard paper mill, and a wagon factory were all located in Manchester, coming into its own as a residential and industrial neighborhood just west of Allegheny. Largely undeveloped before the 1830s, save for a few homes on multiacre tracts of land, Manchester now began to undergo industrial growth and residential settlement thanks to the Beaver Road and the Ohio River, its early development oriented to these transportation routes, in the area west of what is now Route 65; what is now residential Manchester remained sparsely populated. In 1837, Manchester had an estimated five hundred residents, a market house and taverns, stores, and a school, in addition to three factories, its largest the plow works, with seventy-five employees. A contemporary observer noted that "as there is a considerable quantity of level and beautifully located land above, below, and around [Manchester], (and it is so near Pittsburgh and Allegheny,) it must increase rapidly in population, business and importance."

Both American-born residents and immigrants worked in Allegheny's burgeoning manufacturing and commercial sectors, many still of Scotch-Irish and English origin. Most of the Scotch-Irish and English residents lived in the center of town or to the south or west. German and Swiss families had begun to populate southeastern Allegheny in 1822, after the Voegtly and Rickenbach families bought 161 acres along the Allegheny River and present East Ohio Street and on Troy Hill, moving there from Pittsburgh. This area was solidly German by 1840, and Alleghenians called it Deutschtown. Recognizing the growth of Allegheny's German community, publisher Victor Scriba moved his newspaper *Freiheits Freund* (Freedom's Friend) to Allegheny from

Chambersburg, in south-central Pennsylvania, in 1837. Scriba himself lived on what is now Progress Street, in Deutschtown, and later on Troy Hill. Although Scriba would move the newspaper to Pittsburgh several years later, it remained important to Allegheny's German community into the twentieth century.

The Voegtlys, the Rickenbachs, and many of the neighborhood's new families belonged to the German Evangelical Church in Pittsburgh until 1833, when they withdrew from the congregation in a dispute over finances. Family patriarch Nicholas Voegtly Sr. then donated land for the construction of a new German Evangelical church on the north side of East Ohio Street, across from the present Sarah Heinz House. This edifice, constructed in 1833, became known as the Voegtly Church.

The congregation quickly established its first graveyard, north and east of the church. Although the immigrants may have been a young group, a

Voegtly Church, built on East Ohio Street in Deutschtown in 1833. Courtesy of Pittsburgh History & Landmarks Foundation

Stockton Avenue and Monument Hill. Robert M. Palmer and Hartley M. Phelps, *Palmer's Pictorial Pittsburgh and Prominent Pittsburghers Past and Present, 1758–1905*, 1905. Courtesy of Historic Pittsburgh Full-Text Collection, Digital Research Library, University Library System, University of Pittsburgh

cemetery was essential: a study of the first Voegtly Cemetery, published a century and a half later, noted that among the immigrants "pathological conditions included trauma, infection, extreme arthritis, and tuberculosis. Dental health was generally poor. . . . Mortality rates were high and life expectancy was generally low, especially among infants and children." The first Voegtly Cemetery eventually contained hundreds of burials and was full by 1861, when the congregation began to bury their dead in a second cemetery, on Troy Hill. Despite its size, the congregation's original cemetery was forgotten in the twentieth century and became a parking lot, church members under the mistaken impression that all of the burials had been reinterred on Troy Hill. Then, in the 1980s, construction work for the East Street Valley Expressway led to the discovery of intact burials in the first Voegtly Cemetery. The Pennsylvania Department of Transportation had the remains transferred to the Troy Hill cemetery, and analysis of these remains and artifacts marked a milestone in the interpretation of Pittsburgh's German-immigrant culture in the mid-nineteenth century.

Not all of the German newcomers, of course, belonged to the Voegtly Church; some were among Allegheny's early Roman Catholics. The borough

Orphan Asylum
of Pittsburgh
and Allegheny.
Constructed in 1837–
1838, this building
remains a landmark
in its neighborhood.
Pittsburgh Steelers/Karl
Roser

had no Catholic church of its own, the nearest mass held in Pittsburgh, but
Allegheny did have a brief Catholic presence in the form of a convent and
girls' school that the Order of St. Clare established just east of the head of
Federal Street in 1828. The institution remained there only seven years, but its
presence gave that neighborhood the lasting name of Nunnery Hill.

Allegheny also had a small African American population. Skilled workers—a cooper, a riverman, a shoemaker, a barber, and a coachman—and unskilled laborers headed most of Allegheny's African American families, most
of whom lived east or north of the commons. Few or none owned their own
homes.

Land subdivision and speculative development abetted Allegheny's growth in the 1830s. With canal construction, owners of some of the borough's "out lots" hired surveyors to subdivide their properties. Among the first of these subdivisions was a ten-acre tract just east of Federal Street, laid out into streets, lots, and a canal wharf in about 1830. Over the following decade this neighborhood continued to develop, with houses, at least one church, and small industrial shops. The Mechanics Retreat plan, two blocks of Jacksonia and Carrington streets just west of Federal, extended Allegheny's settled area northward in 1832. This plan offered small, undeveloped lots to working-men and their families, less than a mile's walk from Allegheny's factories. Its main roads were originally called Jackson and Carroll streets, which appear to have been named for President Andrew Jackson and for Charles Carroll of Maryland, the longest-lived signer of the Declaration of Independence, who died in 1832. In Deutschtown, landowners created plans of lots along present Pressley Street and around the intersection of Madison Avenue and East Ohio Street. East Ohio Street in Deutschtown was lined with small commercial buildings and dwellings by 1839, and freestanding and attached houses went up along the streets just to the north. Meanwhile, two sizable subdivisions in growing Manchester helped cast that neighborhood's early identity as a river-oriented blue-collar village.

Closer to Allegheny's center, bridge developer William Robinson Jr. sub-divided land west of Federal Street, near the bustling canal basin. Robinson was probably the most active builder on Federal within three blocks of the river: by the mid-1830s, he had commissioned Robinson's Row, several at-tached stores and dwellings on Federal near Lacock Street, and Colonnade Row, five attached brick Greek Revival rental houses at the southwest corner of Federal and General Robinson streets. Colonnade Row's façade featured Classical columns and elaborate iron ornamentation, its houses three stories high, twenty-two feet wide, and about eighty feet deep. Robinson rented the Colonnade Row houses to prominent Pittsburghers, his tenants including the young banker and iron manufacturer Thomas M. Howe, who later created Woodland Road in Pittsburgh's East End, and Letitia Holmes, who commis-sioned the landmark Holmes Hall mansion on Brighton Road in Allegheny West in the late 1860s. Robinson himself still lived in the family home at the foot of Federal Street, where he maintained a well-tended garden extending down the bank of the Allegheny River.

Two of Allegheny's and Pittsburgh's most prominent early architects fig-ured in the construction of spacious rental rows in the same neighborhood.

James Kerr lived in Jackson's Row, a group of three-story party-wall brick rental houses on Robinson and Isabella Streets, structures that he may have also designed. John Chislett, born in England in 1800, came to Pittsburgh in the early 1830s, eventually moving to Allegheny's Federal Street. Chislett owned and probably built a row of houses on Lacock Street, renting one to the commission merchant G. H. Taylor.

Allegheny's most exclusive residential area in the 1820s and 1830s may have been the lots facing the South Common, on what is now the southern perimeter of Allegheny Center Mall. Residents called this area the Second Bank because of its elevation above lower Federal Street. Lafayette visited the Second Bank home of Thomas Barlow in 1825. The industrialist and abolitionist Charles Avery and the prominent merchant Harvey Childs were early Second Bank residents. Later in the century, Allegheny's government named the Second Bank Stockton Avenue.

Charles Brewer's mansion, built in 1830 on what is now Western Avenue. Library of Congress Prints and Photographs Division (HABS PA, 2-PITBU, 7–1), Washington, D.C.

In early 1840, just before Allegheny became a city, George W. McClelland offered for rent other exclusive dwellings: nine just completed brick rental houses in central Allegheny. McClelland had arranged these homes in three groups at the corner of the town's central diamond and Sandusky Street, calling the groups Washington, Madison, and Jefferson. J. M. Davis, a Presbyterian minister, and David Elliot, a Western Theological Seminary professor, were among McClelland's first tenants. He planned to build seven more brick houses later in 1840.

Brick houses such as McClelland's were emblematic of the city's growth in population and prestige. Indeed, as Allegheny continued to expand, builders in the center of town typically chose brick rather than the wood-frame construction that had been common. While on the outskirts of town frame construction remained the norm, brick was more costly and connoted greater affluence. The gradual replacement of frame buildings with larger brick structures demonstrated the community's maturation.

At the same time, Allegheny's ties to Pittsburgh were growing increasingly stronger. The Hand Street (now Ninth Street) Bridge and the Mechanics (now Sixteenth Street) Bridge were both built in the late 1830s, the Mechanics Bridge notably enabling Deutschtown residents to walk to the iron mills and other factories in Pittsburgh's Strip District.

Seeing that Allegheny had overrun its boundaries, borough officials took in additional territory on Allegheny's tenth anniversary as a borough, April 14, 1838. The town's western boundary moved to Sedgwick and Fulton streets in present Manchester, and its northern edge shifted to a continuation of Columbus Avenue, then Island Lane. Its eastern boundary became Saw Mill Run in Deutschtown. The borough's expansion came four years after it had erected its first town hall, a two-story brick building, including a fire company, with a low gabled roof, arched window and door openings, and a large domed cupola that contained a bell.

Among Allegheny's many new residents in the 1830s was William B. Foster, whose young son Stephen later became a beloved American composer. The Foster family, moving to Allegheny from Lawrenceville in the early 1830s, initially paid $125 per year to rent a small home near the riverbank, on or about the present site of the Equitable Gas Company headquarters. The family moved in a short time to a three-story brick dwelling in the neighborhood around Federal and Robinson streets. Young Foster attended one of the borough's early private schools, the Allegheny Academy, and accounts of his childhood include tales of his putting on plays with other children in his neighborhood in the 1830s. His older brother Morrison was superintendent of the Hope Cotton Mill in Allegheny in the 1840s, and his father served as Allegheny burgess (mayor) in the same decade.

Also on lower Federal Street, as noted earlier, was prominent Pittsburgh architect John Chislett, who donated his design of the Orphan Asylum of Pittsburgh and Allegheny, on present-day North Taylor Avenue in the Mexican War Streets, a few years after he moved to Allegheny from Pittsburgh. This building (constructed in 1837–38) remains a landmark in its neighborhood and is probably the most significant structure remaining from Allegheny's borough era. Its Greek Revival features are similar to those of the 1836 Burke Building that Chislett designed on Fourth Avenue, Downtown. The Bank of Pittsburgh and the 1835–41 Allegheny County Courthouse were also among the architect's important early work. Chislett also dealt in stone on lower Federal Street and may have supplied façade and foundation materials for the orphan asylum and other buildings that he designed. Also a landscape architect, Chislett is further remembered for his design and superintendency of Allegheny Cemetery in Lawrenceville between the 1840s and the 1860s. He probably also designed the landscaping in the open land that originally surrounded the orphan asylum. The asylum property was taken over in the 1860s by the Allegheny Widows Home, which commissioned the construction of the well-preserved red-brick rowhouses that still stand along Sherman and North Taylor avenues.

As noted earlier, construction of new bridges increasingly strengthened the ties between Allegheny and Pittsburgh, and beginning about 1830, Allegheny and its immediate environs attracted wealthy residents who commuted to their businesses in Pittsburgh. Charles Brewer, a Downtown dry-goods merchant, built a three-story Greek Revival mansion on Water Lane (now Western Avenue) west of Allegheny Avenue in 1830. William Robinson Jr. became another of Allegheny's commuters around 1836, when he became president of the new Exchange Bank of Pittsburgh. Another Pittsburgh merchant, Samuel Church, built a brick mansion on a four-acre parcel at the southwest corner of Western and Allegheny avenues in the early 1830s. Church, however, experienced financial troubles soon after the house's completion, and he lost the property at a sheriff's sale on New Year's Day in 1841.

The neighborhood of Manchester also experienced growth. James Anderson, whose business interests included the Juniata Rolling Mill and

The late 1830s Hogg-Brunot double house, on Stockton Avenue at the corner of the East Commons, thought to have been an Underground Railroad stop. Library of Congress Prints and Photographs Division (HABS PA, 2-PITBU, 19–1), Washington, D.C.

later the Exchange Bank, commissioned a brick mansion on a twenty-acre tract there in 1830. His former home survives as the Anderson Manor senior citizen home on Liverpool Street. When it was first built, Anderson's house faced south, toward Pennsylvania Avenue, then part of the road to Beaver. The late nineteenth-century subdivision of the house's grounds and the construction of new dwellings closer to Pennsylvania Avenue hid the original façade from public view. The Classical Revival and Colonial Revival features on its present façade, facing Liverpool Street, including the two-story porch, were part of a 1906 remodeling and expansion by the Women's Christian Association of Pittsburgh.

By the end of Allegheny's borough era, a few of the town's prominent families opted to commission and live in spacious party-wall houses. As noted earlier, prominent architect James Kerr lived in such a house in Jackson's Row. In 1839, Pittsburgh merchant James E. Breading and Dr. Joseph Trevor had a three-story brick double house constructed on the Second Bank, at the corner of the East Common. The two houses (later called the Hogg-Brunot double house) measured about 25 feet wide by 110 feet deep, and each had fourteen rooms, three sets of stairways, and considerable plaster ornamentation. One or both contained a large coal vault that historians have surmised was an Underground Railroad hiding place. The Historic American Buildings Survey recorded the details of these houses in 1963, not long before construction of the Allegheny Center Mall project caused their demolition.

Indeed, few of these early houses remain: the former Anderson mansion in Manchester is the sole known survivor of the North Side's grand dwellings of the 1830s and one of only a small number of North Side buildings known to predate Allegheny becoming a city in 1840. A simple clapboard dwelling on Pressley Street at Moravian Way in Deutschtown is another survivor of the borough era. Some pre-1840 buildings may remain on eastern Jacksonia and Carrington streets, in the old Mechanics Retreat plan; in Deutschtown, along and north of East Ohio Street; and in scattered locations in the upland neighborhoods. Unfortunately, demand for larger buildings, urban renewal, and neglect over the last century and a half have removed most of the old borough's remnants.

CHAPTER 2

Allegheny's Early Boom
The 1840s to the Civil War

O N APRIL 13, 1840, Allegheny Borough became Allegheny City. Census takers that year, walking the new city's streets and alleys, found 10,089 residents among the roughly two square miles of mills, businesses, and homes.

To commemorate Allegheny's wilderness origins, the city government created a seal depicting James Robinson's humble log cabin of the 1780s. Robinson's son, the bridge builder William Robinson Jr., still occupied the family homestead at the foot of Federal Street, along with his wife, Mary, with whom he had ten children. Now Allegheny City's voters elected him their first mayor, in 1840. Allegheny government, along with a mayor, had a select council and a common council, each with at least two members from each ward and its own president. As in Pittsburgh, most council members were businessmen; a few were doctors or lawyers or skilled tradesmen. William Robinson Jr., after his term as the city's first mayor, would go on to represent the First Ward on Allegheny's select council, serving as its president between 1849 and 1856.

Between 1840 and 1867, the years considered here, Allegheny City comprised four wards. The north-south and east-west lines that marked the ward boundaries ran along Federal Street, Ohio Street, and Western Avenue, meeting at the center of the original town plan. The First Ward, where William Robinson Jr. spent his entire life, lay west of Federal Street and south of present West Ohio Street and Western Avenue. Allegheny City's northwest quadrant was the Second Ward, west of Federal and north of West Ohio and Western. The Third Ward lay immediately east of the Second Ward, and the Fourth Ward constituted the southeastern section of the city. The First and Fourth wards contained most of the city's people, industry, and commerce in 1840 and for some years afterward.

Demographically, the city's four wards demonstrated clear characters and significant diversity. The First and Second wards attracted mostly Scotch-Irish, Irish, and English families. Irish immigration in particular increased markedly at midcentury, the result of the devastating blight that attacked Ireland's potato crops between 1845 and 1851, causing upward of one-quarter of the country's population to emigrate or die. Irish immigrants soon headed more households in the First and Second wards than any other immigrant group.

Many of these new Irish families attended St. Peter's Roman Catholic Church, founded in 1848. Allegheny's Roman Catholic German Americans founded St. Mary's Church, also in 1848. St. Peter's and St. Mary's were both located on Anderson Street in the Fourth Ward

▲ The Allegheny City seal, which depicted James Robinson's log cabin of the 1780s. Carnegie Library of Pittsburgh Pennsylvania Department, Pittsburgh Photographic Library

▼ Allegheny City in 1851. Library of Congress Geography and Map Division (G3823.A4G46 1851 .S5), Washington, D.C.

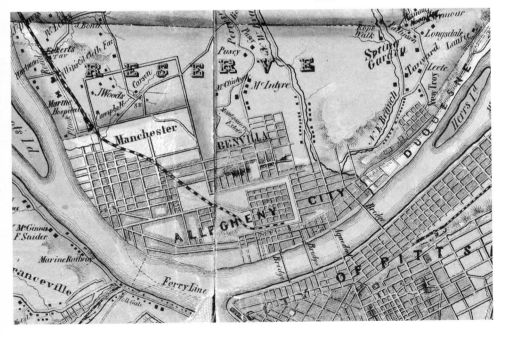

The former St. Mary's Church, now Pittsburgh's Grand Hall at the Priory. Pittsburgh Steelers/Karl Roser

for a short time at midcentury, and St. Peter's would remain until after the Civil War. St. Mary's congregation built a large red-brick church on Lockhart Street (then Liberty Street) in Deutschtown in 1853–54.

Significantly, the new church building was constructed without windows to thwart possible attacks by members of the Know-Nothing Party—members of a sometimes violent nativist movement of the 1840s and 1850s that opposed immigration by Roman Catholics and others. At midcentury, such nativist sentiment swelled in northeastern and midwestern cities where Irish and German immigrants had settled and in California, a destination for both Irish and Chinese, marked by riots in Philadelphia, St. Louis, and other US cities. The fear of Know-Nothing violence was peaking nationwide around the time that St. Mary's was being built, and Allegheny's immigrants might have been particularly fearful because of the recent ascendance of Joe Barker as mayor of the bustling city across the river: Pittsburgh voters had just elected the anti-Catholic demagogue while he was imprisoned for one of his many inflammatory speeches.

In spite of the similar bonds imposed on many of the residents of Allegheny City's two western wards by their recent immigration, they differed in other ways. Some were well-to-do; others labored in the city's cotton mills or small factories, in the canal warehouses, or on the riverfront. Those of modest means included the family of Will and Margaret Morrison Carnegie, who in 1848 arrived in the First Ward from Dunfermline, Scotland, with their sons, thirteen-year-old Andrew and Thomas, age five.

The Carnegies rented a two-room apartment in a frame house on a dirt alley near Rebecca (now Reedsdale) Street. The house, which the Carnegies later owned, stood just northeast of where Heinz Field stands today. Will Carnegie and young Andrew worked long hours in the Blackstock, Bell & Company cotton mill, a few blocks from their home. Neither lasted long at the mill, however, and in 1849 young Andrew launched his famous ascent in American industry with a new job in a Pittsburgh telegraph office.

As a teenager, Carnegie supplemented his brief formal education by borrowing books from Colonel James Anderson's home library in Manchester. In response to the avid patronage of Carnegie and other "young working boys," Anderson added to his collection and moved it to a building on Federal Street, near the center of Allegheny. The collection, by then called the Mechanics and Apprentices Library, is widely believed to have been western Pennsylvania's first public library. It remained open until about 1862.

Carnegie never forgot the role that Colonel Anderson's library played in his youth. Under its benevolent influence, beginning in 1883, in his hometown of Dunfermline, he would fund the construction of thousands of public libraries around the world. In 1904, Carnegie would honor Anderson with a monument in front of the Allegheny City Carnegie Library at Federal and Ohio streets. That library, which opened in 1890, was the first public library that Carnegie funded in the United States. (The Carnegie Library that opened in Braddock in 1889 was originally owned by Carnegie's steel company.)

Back in the 1840s, however, before his fame and philanthropy, Andrew Carnegie would have walked past Woodlawn, the Logan mansion, on Allegheny Avenue at present Lincoln Avenue, on his way to borrow books at Colonel Anderson's home. John T. Logan, a partner in a Pittsburgh hardware company, had purchased the bank-owned former Samuel Church house for ten thousand dollars in 1843. Logan, whose family later attended the North Presbyterian Church at North Lincoln and Galveston avenues, dealt in hardware in Downtown Pittsburgh for many years before he cofounded the Logan-Gregg Hardware Company in 1867. His business activities also included Allegheny City's Penn Cotton Mill, a short-lived flour mill, and positions with the Allegheny Valley Railroad and the Monongahela Navigation Company. He

Woodlawn, on Allegheny Avenue at present-day North Lincoln Avenue.
Carnegie Library of Pittsburgh Pennsylvania Department, Pittsburgh Photographic Library

Heiress Mary Schenley owned land in Deutschtown and leased lots to the people who owned the buildings on them. Carnegie Library of Pittsburgh Pennsylvania Department, Pittsburgh Photographic Library

was a trustee of the Western Theological Seminary and the House of Refuge.

Perhaps to mark his considerable status within the community, Logan had the newly purchased brick dwelling enlarged and remodeled before he and his wife, Henrietta, moved in, the addition of a pedimented front gable and side wings and massive two-story front columns transforming it into an example of the fashionable Greek Revival style. The house's interior contained "high ceiled parlors with . . . intricate centerpieces and mouldings, furnished with pier glasses and mahogany furniture." The Logan family named the property Woodlawn, because its grassy front lawn contained groves of mature oak trees. The house faced Western Avenue before North Lincoln Avenue was extended west of Allegheny Avenue in the late nineteenth century.

Woodlawn would be demolished in the mid-twentieth century. By that point, the city government had widened Allegheny and Ridge avenues, taking strips of the Logan property. Later, North Lincoln Avenue's extension left the house with a shallow front yard and separated it from Western Avenue and its storied oak groves. In 1931, the Logan heirs donated the mansion to the Presbytery of Pittsburgh, which used it as the Logan Neighborhood House, which provided community services. An automobile dealership purchased the Logan house from the Presbytery in 1949, and it was demolished around that time, but it is well documented by a Logan family member's recollections, published by the Historical Society of Western Pennsylvania, and by other sources. The property had a circular carriage drive that extended from Western Avenue. To the west of the mansion stood a frame barn in which the Logan family kept carriages, horses, and chickens. Between the rear of the house and Ridge Avenue were gardens in which vegetables, fruits, and flowers grew. The Logan children and their friends—offspring of the neighborhood's manufacturers, merchants, professionals, and less prosperous residents—played on the grounds. Growing up in a simpler time, the Logan sons and their friends took skiffs out on the Allegheny and Ohio rivers, at times roaming far from home.

To the east of the East Common, the Third and Fourth wards continued to attract German immigrants who wished to live in a predominantly German community. East Ohio Street, on the border of the two Deutschtown wards, was eventually lined with buildings containing storefronts and shop owners' living quarters. The streets north of East Ohio developed with a mixture of large and small houses, corner stores, and artisans' businesses, including blacksmith shops and wagon works.

East Ohio Street and the nearby part of Deutschtown developed unlike most other sections of Allegheny, thanks to the heiress Mary Schenley. Schenley, for whom the park in Pittsburgh's East End was later named, had inherited much of the land in the area bounded by present-day Avery Street, Cedar Avenue, East North Avenue, and East Street. She lived in London and leased lots to the people who owned the buildings on them: they thus paid her rent on the land beneath their buildings. This form of ownership also occurred in parts of the industrial neighborhood north of Allegheny West and in Downtown Pittsburgh and the Strip District, but it was generally uncommon in Allegheny County. Along the two principal streets of Schenley's Deutschtown holdings, Cedar and East Ohio, her land ownership may have discouraged investment during the pre–Civil War period: most of the houses and commercial buildings that lessees constructed there at midcentury were wood frame instead of the more expensive and prestigious brick.

Allegheny, Pittsburgh, and some outlying towns were growing rapidly, and the need for better roads was becoming increasingly clear. In the 1840s and 1850s, private companies, perceiving this need, converted a number of highways to plank roads—dirt roads covered by oak planks placed lengthwise, then crosswise, their wooden surfaces usually twelve to thirteen feet wide—and charged tolls for their use. The city's first plank road was the

The Marshall house, most likely Ridge Avenue's first mansion, was built in the late 1840s. Courtesy of Pittsburgh History & Landmarks Foundation

Allegheny and Perrysville Plank Road, which ran along what is now Perrysville Avenue beginning in 1849. The Allegheny and New Brighton Plank Road (now Brighton Road) was built in about 1855. The roads' planked surfaces, however, tended to deteriorate quickly, becoming impassable as wagon wheels sank deep in mud. Allegheny and other municipalities eventually took over the maintenance of these roads, replacing the planks with macadam or other materials.

Allegheny's growth was also marked by the development of a recognizable commercial district in the streets that made up Allegheny's central Diamond. An 1841 city directory listed five grocers, three taverns, four physicians, two auction houses, two cordwainers (leather workers), two milliners, two confectioners, a shoe store, a tailor, a barber, a cowbell manufacturer, a gun manufacturer, a wagon shop, a saddler, an attorney, a bookstore, and a foundry on the Diamond. The city's first bank, the Allegheny Savings Fund Company, opened in 1845 on Federal Street, just below the Diamond.

That lower section of Federal, close to the new bank, contained even more retail and service businesses: ten grocers; five taverns; and an assortment of shops that catered to canal merchants, farmers who came from nearby townships to sell their produce, and the city's own burgeoning population. East Ohio Street (then the Butler Road), between the East Common and the foot of Troy Hill, was also a significant commercial street by 1841, with grocers, taverns, and small retail shops. Perhaps because of its proximity to the Pennsylvania Canal, with its passengers in need of head coverings, three bonnet makers worked on East Ohio Street.

Allegheny's expansion also spilled across municipal lines into adjoining areas that the city would annex later in the nineteenth century. Manchester, just west of the city, grew steadily for several years before it was incorporated as a borough in 1843. During the period between 1840 and the Civil War, Manchester remained a river-oriented, working-class community. Notably, in the 1840s, German immigrants began to settle in Manchester in significant numbers: by the 1850 census, families with one or both heads of German birth accounted for 19 percent of the borough's 325 families.

German immigrants and others also settled east of the city, in the narrow strip of land below Troy Hill, along the Pennsylvania Canal. This neighborhood, with its handful of tanneries, breweries, sawmills, and other small manufacturers, became Duquesne borough in 1849. There, small frame houses stood cheek-by-jowl with small factories along River Avenue (then Bank Lane), their lots backing up to the canal towpath. The Allegheny River brought lumber from northwestern Pennsylvania's forests to Duquesne's sawmills, and stacks of lumber marked the banks of the river's back channel, by Herr's Island, a part of Duquesne also shared by residents and industry. During this period, when lumber was Duquesne's primary industry, the borough's officials included a measurer of boards. Along East Ohio Street, at the foot of Troy Hill, determined builders cut houses and breweries into the hillside, banked and protected with hand-laid stone retaining walls. Around the same time, the borough created the aptly named Ravine Street (now Rialto Street), a narrow 28-percent-grade road running straight up to Lowrie Street, on top of Troy Hill. Rialto Street is now one of Pittsburgh's steepest streets, and bicyclists know it as one of the city's "Dirty Dozen" most challenging climbs.

German immigrants also moved into Reserve Township, including areas that Allegheny later annexed—Troy Hill, Spring Hill, and the Spring Garden and East Street valleys. A few streets, like Troy Hill Road and Itin Street, allowed access to these hilltop communities, whose topography and distance from industry ensured that land there was relatively inexpensive. Adam Reineman, a former Chambersburg resident, like his friend Victor Scriba, bought considerable land on Troy Hill and Spring Hill at midcentury. He and his heirs spent the next several decades subdividing his holdings and selling lots to other German families.

In spite of all this road building and rapid development, a few Duquesne residents continued to farm: Duquesne Borough Council minutes note that in 1850, a Herr family member requested that a bridge be built across the canal to connect the sections of his farm that the canal had separated. Farming, however, was being phased out in the area, replaced by more typical urban industries. In the middle of the nineteenth century, German immigrants founded several small breweries in Duquesne borough and eastern Deutschtown. Their proprietors lived on the breweries' premises with their families and some of their employees, the better to oversee their small enterprises, the largest of which employed only six workers in 1860. These breweries were banked into hillsides, connected to natural or artificial caves where brewers stored beer in those days before refrigeration and pasteurization. Pittsburghers of Scotch-Irish and English descent had brewed beer since the late eighteenth century, producing ales, in the tradition of the British Isles. Deutschtown and Duquesne borough's new German brewers introduced another beer style, the lager, to the region. Lagers, which now comprise virtually all mainstream American beer brands, use different yeast strains than ales and require more fermentation time. Conrad Eberhardt, George Ober, and John N. Straub owned a trio of these early German breweries along Vinial Street, at the foot of Troy Hill, in the 1840s. Eberhardt's and Ober's heirs later became partners in a brewery that bore their family names, while Peter P. Straub, who apprenticed at Eberhardt & Ober, later founded the Straub brewery in St. Mary's, Pennsylvania. Today the Penn Brewery occupies the Eberhardt & Ober complex, continuing the German tradition of brewing lagers.

Other new industries flourished as well. In Duquesne borough, eastern Deutschtown, and Spring Garden, German immigrants and others established ten or more tanneries and numerous associated businesses such as slaughterhouses, soap factories, and leatherworking shops. Many of the slaughterhouses were along Sawmill Run, which came to be called Butchers Run. The neighborhood's leatherworkers and their associates shaped the raw product from nearby tanneries into shoes, saddles, carriages, trunks, and other goods.

Less production-oriented development was also taking place. Two miles down the Ohio River from Allegheny, the federal government selected a site for the US Marine Hospital, for riverboat workers, largely because of Pittsburgh and Allegheny's role in river commerce. The government commissioned construction of the hospital in about 1845 and completed it in 1851. This facility was particularly important during the Civil War. Also in the Woods Run area, which would later be part of Allegheny City but at the time was in McClure Township, was a reform school called the House of Refuge, which opened around 1850. A later writer explained that the House of Refuge was "for the reformation and moral and religious education and training of vicious, incorrigible, and depraved children, or youth of both sexes." The hospital and reform school were both demolished for industrial expansion in the late nineteenth century.

Woods Run also held farmland and a few suburban estates then; manufacturing, including the Pittsburgh Forge & Iron Company's plant, came to the neighborhood about a decade later. Some Woods Run manufacturers built rows of small tenement houses for employees and their families, close to their works. This practice was not common in Allegheny and Pittsburgh, where established neighborhoods provided enough housing, and indeed, these mid-nineteenth-century tenement houses cannot have been pleasant, standing close enough to the mills that residents could see, hear, and smell ironmaking.

Up in the city's northwest quadrant, the Second Ward remained Allegheny's least populated section. When Allegheny became a city, bridge builder William Robinson Jr. owned an undeveloped field there that extended about six hundred feet north from the West Common and one thousand feet east from Pasture Lane (Brighton Road). In 1847, Robinson subdivided this land into a street grid and building lots, calling his plan the Buena Vista Extension of Allegheny. Although Robinson, contrary to legend, did not serve in the Mexican War (1846–48), holding the title of general through an appointment in the Pennsylvania militia, he named the streets in his new development for battles and generals of that war. Home construction in what thus became known as the Mexican War Streets generally proceeded west from Palo Alto Street, which adjoined already developed city blocks along Sherman and Arch streets. Robinson initially sold 20-by-110-foot lots along Palo Alto, Resaca, Monterey, and Buena Vista streets for three hundred dollars. By the Civil War, Palo Alto and Resaca streets were lined with modest but well-built houses. Monterey and Buena Vista streets remained largely undeveloped until after the war.

Most of those who purchased Robinson's lots and built the neighborhood's early houses were skilled workers such as blacksmiths, stair builders, cabinetmakers, carpenters, machinists, shoemakers, and paving contractors. Many were self-employed. The early houses they built in the Mexican War Streets, some of frame construction before the Civil War, displayed understated interpretations of the Greek Revival style, if only in their façades, with elements like wide front-door transoms and classical door surrounds that were loosely derived from Greek temples. Toward the end of the 1850s, homebuilders here and in other Allegheny neighborhoods also began to incorporate Italianate features, adopting a style that was new to the Pittsburgh area but had been used on the East Coast for about a decade: arched window openings, brackets, and ornate window hoods.

Wealthier buyers bought the few larger lots that faced the West Common, along present West North Avenue, and commissioned more substantial homes. Such prominent families, together with their peers building in central Allegheny City, strengthened the community's role as a Pittsburgh suburb. Other wealthy homeowners began to populate the slopes north of the central city, Fineview and Perry Hilltop, the latter reached via the Perrysville Plank Road (now Perrysville Avenue). In Allegheny West, wealthy families also began to build houses along Ridge Avenue, an east-west route named for the topographic feature along which it ran, in the late 1840s. Back in 1830, and perhaps for some years after, farmland had survived on Ridge Avenue. By the 1850s, this pleasant unpaved country lane was lined by a few sizeable dwellings, manufacturers' and merchants' mansions that were among the larger and more ornate houses in Allegheny and Pittsburgh. Sixty years later, Ridge Avenue would be one of the wealthiest streets in America, with iron and steel millionaires' mansions lining a three-block section east of Allegheny Avenue.

Archibald M. and Mary Marshall commissioned what was likely Ridge

The original Allegheny Observatory, built in 1860; its clock regulated times for forty-two railroads. Allegheny Observatory Records, 1850–1967, UA.5.1, University of Pittsburgh Archives

Avenue's first mansion soon after purchasing a two-acre tract of land at the southwest corner of the West Common for $4,400 in 1847. Their center-entry brick dwelling was built in the Greek Revival style, the most popular architectural style in the Pittsburgh area between about 1830 and the late 1850s. Two-story wood columns that supported a low-gabled porch roof contributed to the house's stately appearance. Although Ridge Avenue's early twentieth-century mansions made the Marshall house look modest in comparison, it certainly stood out in its day.

Archibald Marshall had been born in Ireland about 1815 and grown up in Butler County, Pennsylvania. He owned a grocery and dry-goods store on the Allegheny Diamond by 1839, when the *Pittsburgh Gazette* noted that he offered for sale a patent medicine, Hygeian Vegetable Universal Medicines. At this point, Archibald and Mary Marshall shared their Ridge Avenue mansion with Mary's brother Thompson Bell, president of the Western Savings Bank and founder of Thompson Bell & Company, a private Pittsburgh bank. During the Civil War, Marshall sold his store and began to manufacture rope, twine, and oakum as part of the firm of Marshall, Fulton & Bollman. He joined the venture for which he was best known, Marshall, Kennedys & Company, about 1870. Marshall, Kennedys & Company operated the Pittsburgh City Flour Mills at Fifteenth Street and Liberty Avenue in the Strip District, later expanding to a complex of five-story red-brick buildings at Lacock and Hope streets (now the Riverside Center for Innovation). Success allowed the Marshalls to employ a coachman and as many as four live-in female servants and to build a substantial rear addition onto their house by 1882.

The Marshalls and their heirs and other descendants would occupy the house for about ninety years. Their granddaughter Mary Bell Fitzhugh and her husband, attorney Carroll Fitzhugh, lived in the Marshall House between the late 1890s and the 1930s. Carroll Fitzhugh was also an amateur playwright and actor who served as president of the Pittsburgh Stage and Play Society. In the early twentieth century, the Fitzhughs were responsible for the construction of yet another rear addition to the house and a brick garage. They sold the house in 1940, for $5,000.

The US Army used the Marshall House at a dormitory during World War II, and in 1953 it was purchased by a cement masons' union, which still owned it when fire struck the second story in 1960. It survived long enough to appear in James Van Trump and Arthur Ziegler's 1967 book *Landmark Architecture of Allegheny County, Pennsylvania*, which noted that the house, although deteriorated, was "the only porticoed Greek Revival house still standing in Pittsburgh." It was soon demolished.

Back in the mid-nineteenth century, however, when the Marshall mansion had only recently been built, Allegheny West's residential development to the south was hastened when the old Irwin rope walk found itself put to new uses. In 1858, the Irwin family ended ropemaking and subdivided the rope-walk tract into large residential lots. The Irwin lots, extending from Ridge Avenue to Western Avenue in the First Ward, created a right-of-way roughly bisecting the plan, called Central Street (renamed Lincoln Avenue soon after the 1865 assassination of the president). A few of the lots that the Irwins sold on Western already contained substantial brick houses, which the family seems to have built as rentals. The neighborhood's increasing popularity also encouraged a bit of speculative home construction. George Allen, a bricklaying contractor based in downtown Pittsburgh, constructed an Italianate center-entry house at 940 Western Avenue in 1860, holding a lease on the property from Elizabeth F. Denny, who owned the land through inheritance. In early 1861, Allen sold the lease to Jane Moor Lee, the wife of bookkeeper William A. Lee, the Allegheny Valley Railroad's freight agent. The Lees owned and lived at 940 Western Avenue until 1870, owning the property outright beginning in 1867.

Concurrent with all this growth, the city's first public transportation, the Pittsburgh, Allegheny & Manchester Passenger Railway, began operation in 1859 or 1860. The railway started at Penn Avenue and Sixth Street in Pittsburgh, crossed the Allegheny River at Federal Street, and split into two routes along Western Avenue and Reedsdale Street on the way to Manchester, horses pulling passenger cars that ran on tracks set into the streets. The horsecar line encouraged Allegheny's further growth as a suburb, enabling middle-class families headed by men who worked in Downtown Pittsburgh to move to Allegheny West and Manchester.

It should be noted that although nineteenth-century Allegheny is often viewed as a city of immigrants from the British Isles and Germany, African American families also played an important role in the city's development: the 1850 census recorded black Alleghenians working on riverboats and in the city as carpenters, barbers, painters, grocers, blacksmiths, coachmen, and laborers. More than half of Allegheny's 122 black families lived in the Third Ward, and 33 of the city's black families had managed to acquire real estate despite daunting economic and social barriers. Of these home-owning families, 16 lived in the Third Ward and 3 lived in the Fourth Ward, all on Avery Street. Allegheny's black population supported three churches at midcentury: the First Wesley Church, the Third Bethel Church, and a Baptist congregation.

Allegheny and Pittsburgh's black residents had arrived via varying paths. Although the area never attracted a black population comparable in size to those of Philadelphia and Chicago, its location along the Monongahela River and its proximity to the Mason-Dixon Line made it a destination for some who had fled slavery and a stopping point for others. Some black Alleghenians had been freed by their owners, while others had been born free, in eastern Pennsylvania or in the South. Census records from 1850 indicate that most black Alleghenians and Pittsburghers had been born in Virginia. Those African Americans who made homes in the area certainly encountered prejudice, but white Pittsburgh also evidenced some degree of respect for their participation in religious life and in abolition and temperance societies.

Among those white Allegheny residents determined to help make a place for African Americans in the city's civic life was Charles Avery, the cotton manufacturer and abolitionist for whom Avery Street was named. He founded and endowed Avery College, a school for African American teachers that is thought to have been an Underground Railroad station. The school building, demolished in the twentieth century to make way for highway construction, stood at Avery and Nash streets in Deutschtown. Despite Charles Avery's efforts, Allegheny's public schools remained segregated until 1880, twenty-two years after his death. Pittsburgh public schools had ended racial segregation in 1874.

Allegheny, like other US cities of the mid-nineteenth century, was also marked by labor unrest. Cotton mills were still the city's largest industry

Allegheny's City Hall of 1863, designed by Colomb Gengembre; demolished in 1938 for Buhl Planetarium construction. Carnegie Library of Pittsburgh Pennsylvania Department, Pittsburgh Photographic Library

in the 1840s, seven mills employed fifteen hundred workers by the end of the decade. These workers began their shifts at 5 A.M. and worked into the evening. While some men held skilled positions and were paid enough that they could own modest homes, mill owners paid uniformly low wages to women and children workers, who performed repetitive, unskilled tasks. As area workplaces grew steadily larger, workers' strikes became more common. Allegheny's female cotton mill workers struck in 1843, averting a wage cut; they struck again in 1845, in a failed attempt to reduce work hours. In 1848 the Pennsylvania legislature passed a weakly worded law that limited factory work to ten-hour days, and in response, owners closed the cotton mills on July 1, 1848.

Then, on July 31, the Penn Cotton Mill became the site of unprecedented area labor unrest. While other mills remained closed, the Penn, whose employees could no longer afford to remain at home, reopened on the owners' terms. Unemployed female cotton mill workers and sympathizers subsequently invaded the large brick building, which occupied the present Alcoa office site, at the foot of Federal Street. The crowd damaged the mill's machinery, smashed its windows, and beat a mill owner, police officers, and the Allegheny County sheriff. The rioters' actions amazed Allegheny and Pittsburgh residents, who had assumed women to be incapable of violence. In the wake of the riot, political parties, newspapers, and clergy weighed in on its causes and consequences. Some opined in favor of the workers. The *Pittsburgh Morning Post* noted, "Under the ten hour system [the cotton manufacturers] would have a profit of 35 per cent. If this be correct, and we do not doubt it, might not the cotton lords get along under the [new ten-hour-day] law. They might be compelled to reduce their individual expenses some, but they could live!" Others took the side of the owners, the *Pittsburgh Gazette* reporting that Democratic candidates for state assembly "appeared rather disposed to earn notoriety by quasi approval even of violent measures" and suggesting that these candidates were only pandering to the workers to win their votes.

After some other, lesser disputes between mill owners and workers and the conviction of thirteen rioters, the mills returned to full-time operation in 1849. The riot and its aftermath, however, had an impact: it had publicized the hours and working conditions suffered by children and compelled the local legal system to take women more seriously.

Six cotton factories still operated in Allegheny when the Civil War began, in 1861. The war increased demand for cotton goods, but it disrupted the supply of raw cotton that came to Allegheny and Pittsburgh via the Missis-sippi and Ohio rivers. Much local cotton production thus shifted to New England and other areas. Allegheny's cotton industry, although considerably diminished, remained alive after the war but declined over the next few de-cades, ending when the Penn Mill and a small newer mill on Reedsdale Street closed in the early 1890s.

Allegheny, like other nineteenth-century US cities, was also marked by the new American railroad network, which would dramatically change both urban areas and the countryside. The local rail transformation began in 1848, when William Robinson Jr. and other capitalists incorporated the Ohio & Pennsylvania Railroad, the first railroad in the Pittsburgh area. It was designed to run between Allegheny City and Crestline, Ohio, north of Columbus. The Ohio & Pennsylvania, with Robinson as its president, began operating the easternmost part of its line in 1851, railroad officials of necessity shipping the first locomotive to Allegheny from Philadelphia via the Pennsylvania Canal. A possibly apocryphal story relates that young Andrew Carnegie watched workmen unload this first locomotive in Allegheny. The railroad had two Allegheny stations: its Inner Depot at Federal Street at the South Common and its Outer Depot in Manchester. Its route headed northwest from the Federal Street depot through the West Common. The tracks were at ground level, rather than below grade as they are today, a wooden fence separating them from the rest of the common ground. In 1856, the Ohio & Pennsylvania merged with the Pittsburgh, Fort Wayne & Chicago Railroad. In 1857, the railroad constructed a bridge across the Allegheny River, extending its line to Pittsburgh: Allegheny was no longer the line's eastern end. The Pennsylvania Railroad, which reached across the state to Downtown Pittsburgh by 1854, now firmly linked Allegheny to the East Coast.

The Pennsylvania Railroad, the Baltimore and Ohio Railroad, and other lines doomed the Pennsylvania Canal. The railroad transported goods and passengers far more quickly and ran in winter cold, while the canal froze over. The canal lost business steadily in the 1850s and early 1860s. It ceased opera-tion between Pittsburgh and Johnstown in 1864, though some of its eastern sections remained active until the end of the century. The Western Pennsyl-vania Railroad purchased the canal's Western Division right-of-way and built its line along the former canal route, between Federal Street and a point near Freeport, in Armstrong County.

By 1860, the federal population census counted 28,702 Allegheny residents. Allegheny was the twenty-ninth-largest city in the United States, just ahead of Syracuse, New York, and Hartford, Connecticut. Manchester and Duquesne boroughs held plants where one hundred or more men produced iron nails and cast-iron goods, and manufacturing continued at Woods Run in McClure Township. Allegheny itself contained a handful of foundries and machine shops, but the growth of the iron and steel industry, aided by the new railroads, would largely mark the next stage of area's history, after the Civil War (1861–65). On war's eve, cotton was still king in Allegheny, with more than fourteen hundred workers employed in the city's mills.

CHAPTER 3

Conflict and Newfound Prosperity
Allegheny in the Civil War

O N TUESDAY, November 6, 1860, voters streamed to Allegheny's polls. They knew that the imminent threat of Southern secession and war placed the country's future at risk and thus overwhelmingly turned out for Abraham Lincoln, the Republican candidate for president. In the First Ward, for example, 562 voters cast ballots for Lincoln, 98 for Northern Democrat Stephen Douglas, and 85 for John Bell of the Constitutional Union party. These voters' efforts, however, proved fruitless: they could do nothing to stem the tide of war, which would sweep through the country only five months later. While the Civil War's armed conflicts took place far from Allegheny and Pittsburgh, the war nevertheless had a profound effect upon Allegheny and nearby communities. The war altered the city's economy and manufacturing concerns, its families prominent and obscure, and even its topography.

Before the newly elected president made it to office, however—and before the first shots of the war were fired at Fort Sumter—Pittsburgh was the site of what one local historian called "the first overt act of the war" when citizens of Pittsburgh and Allegheny grew anxious over Secretary of War John B. Floyd's directive to ship heavy weapons from the US Arsenal in Lawrenceville to Southern forts in December 1860. The proposal alarmed local businessman William Robinson Jr., who ran an emergency meeting in response on Christmas Day, attended by prominent Pittsburgh and Allegheny citizens. Their telegram to outgoing president James Buchanan, a native Pennsylvanian, convinced the president to forbid the weapons shipment, and Secretary Floyd resigned on December 29 to join the Confederacy. He would serve as a Confederate general until he died in 1863.

Perhaps in response to the clear support he enjoyed among the area's citizenry, Abraham Lincoln visited Allegheny and Pittsburgh as president-elect in February 1861, during a multicity tour that was taking him to his inauguration in the nation's capital. The *Pittsburgh Gazette* reported that on February 15 thousands of citizens gathered at the depot and lined up along Federal Street, to the south, for a glimpse of Lincoln, adding, "The [Sixth Street] bridge was also lined, notwithstanding a strong east wind [that] rendered it a very uncomfortable place for crinoline." The upper windows of Federal Street's shops and homes provided an exceptional vantage point for a fortunate few. They waited for nearly three hours as railroad workers cleared an unrelated accident near Rochester, Beaver County, and the special train carrying "Honest Abe" and his party finally rolled into Allegheny's Pittsburgh, Fort Wayne & Chicago Railroad depot on Federal Street at 8 P.M.

Allegheny mayor Simon Drum of Parkhurst Street escorted President-elect Lincoln from his railcar in a heavy downpour. Lincoln politely acknowledged the crowd's demand with some brief remarks, noting the unpleasant weather and the lateness of the hour and encouraging citizens to attend his scheduled speech in Pittsburgh the following morning. Mayor Drum, along with Pittsburgh mayor George Wilson, both cities' municipal councils, and local military groups, then escorted Lincoln to Pittsburgh's famous Monongahela House hotel, on the Monongahela Riverfront, at Smithfield Street. The next morning, Lincoln gave a widely reported speech on economic affairs and the possibility of secession and war from the Monongahela House balcony. During this inaugural trip, Lincoln's speeches were usually vague attempts to pacify the South, but at Pittsburgh his tone was more decisive. After he condemned the Southern states' discontent as a "manufactured crisis" invented by "designing politicians," he left for Cleveland from the Federal Street depot, with another large crowd to see him off.

The crowds that marked Lincoln's arrival and departures also drew skilled pickpockets, who slipped into the crowds around the Federal Street depot to prey upon Pittsburghers, Alleghenians, and residents of outlying villages who had come to see the president-elect and perhaps shop. The most successful took a wallet containing $490 in cash and a $500 check—enormous sums for the time—from William Ward of Pittsburgh. Some of the pickpockets disposed of the now-emptied wallets by placing them in the pockets of unsuspecting residents. Pittsburgh newspapers surmised that the pickpockets were following Lincoln on his tour, taking advantage of the president-elect's popularity.

As wartime president, of course, Abraham Lincoln needed more concrete demonstrations of this popularity, calling for seventy-five thousand volunteers in April 1861. In Allegheny County, manufacturer and former congressman Thomas M. Howe of Stockton Avenue chaired recruitment efforts. Civic leaders quickly set up recruiting stations in Pittsburgh and Allegheny's business districts, Allegheny containing at least one station, on lower Federal Street.

Banker Thomas M. Howe's son-in-law, James H. Childs, was one of the first Alleghenians to heed Lincoln's call. Childs, a partner in the Hope Cotton Mill who lived with his family on Cedar Avenue, near Lockhart Street, enlisted as a first lieutenant in Company K of the First Pennsylvania Volunteers, one of the three-month companies that

Thomas M. Howe, a manufacturer and former congressman and a resident of Stockton Avenue, chaired Allegheny County recruitment efforts for the Civil War. *History of Allegheny County, Pennsylvania*, pt. 1, 1889

served at the beginning of the war. When his initial term ended, Childs reenlisted as a lieutenant colonel, and then a colonel, in the Fourth Pennsylvania Cavalry. Colonel Childs would fight in engagements at Gaines Mill, Glendale, and Mechanicsville, Virginia, part of the Seven Days Battle in mid-1862. He died in a cornfield in the Battle of Antietam in Sharpsburg, Maryland, on September 17, 1862, when a cannonball knocked him from his horse and passed through his body. Childs, only twenty-eight years old, remained conscious long enough to ask an assistant to convey messages of love to his wife, Mary H. Howe Childs, and their three children.

Allegheny mayor Simon Drum, who had escorted Lincoln on his inaugural visit, also heeded the call for support, resigning in 1862 to enlist in the 123rd Pennsylvania Volunteers, a nine-month regiment that drew nearly all of its members from Allegheny County. Drum directed the activities of about one hundred soldiers as captain of Company H. Reverend John Barr Clark, of Allegheny's Second United Presbyterian Church, served as colonel of the 123rd, recruiting men from his pulpit before going off to war. The 123rd Regiment would fight at the battles of Fredericksburg, December 12 to 15, 1862, and Chancellorsville, May 1 to 5, 1863, both demoralizing losses for the Union Army.

At Fredericksburg, the 123rd's first battle, the regiment suffered no casualties when it bravely crossed the Rappahannock River in a rain of Confederate shells. On the battlefield, however, 20 of the regiment's men perished, and 115 were wounded. Private John R. Munden of the 123rd Regiment's Company C, a blacksmith who lived on Fleming Street, and Private George Walter of Company F, a laborer from Spring Garden Avenue, both died on Fredericksburg's battlefield. His fellow soldiers buried Private Alexander Dallas of Company E, an oil refiner who lived on Pressley Street, where he fell; his family later reinterred him in Union Dale Cemetery. Captain Daniel Boisol, a Federal Street dentist who served in Company G, passed away in a Washington, DC, hospital on December 28 from bullet wounds suffered in the battle.

In 1863, after the brutal loss at Fredericksburg, the 123rd took part in General Ambrose Burnsides's ill-fated Mud March, in which Burnsides had Union forces struggle for two days to travel upstream along the Rappahannock River in heavy rain and deep mud, intending to have some Union troops approach Confederate general Robert E. Lee's side while others massed from his rear. The Mud March's failure resulted in President Lincoln's replacement of Burnsides with Joseph Hooker, and the 123rd idled near Fredericksburg from January 24 to April 27, in an orderly village of tents and log huts called Camp Humphreys. Civil War soldiers spent most of their time in such camps, bored and knowing little of the war's progress.

Also in 1863, Simon Drum mustered out of the 123rd and returned to Allegheny, where he would participate in the city's political and business life until his death in the late 1890s. Allegheny voters would elect him to the common council in 1865, make him mayor in 1868, and return him to the common council again in the early 1890s. In his business life, Drum opened a hardware store on East Ohio Street in 1864; owned a planing mill; worked as a building contractor; and represented the Ben Franklin Insurance Company, founding Simon Drum's Insurance Agency on the Diamond in 1890. Henry M. Pratt, the son of a Federal Street hat dealer, was another local who would largely escape the war's ravages. He was about seventeen when he left his family's home on Arch Street to enlist as a private under Simon Drum in Company H. After he returned safely from the war, Henry M. Pratt installed and repaired plumbing and gas lines in Allegheny buildings for many years.

Of course, not every Alleghenian who participated in the war was so lucky. Indeed, 14 percent—about one in seven—of the Allegheny County men who fought in the Civil War died during their service. Robert Washington Bard, a hardware store clerk, lived with his parents in a substantial rowhouse on Anderson Street, just north of Robinson Street, before he went to war. After a brief stint with the Pittsburgh Rifles in 1862, Bard enlisted in Company H and was soon promoted from sergeant to first sergeant. Bard died at Camp Humphreys on February 11, 1863, two months short of his twenty-sixth birthday. Bard was among the many Union soldiers who perished from disease, rather than in battle. Of the 123rd Regiment's seventy-one deaths, only forty-one occurred in combat. Some soldiers died in camp, like Bard; others passed away in the Confederacy's notorious prisons, such as Libby and Andersonville. One soldier, Colonel Andrew McKain, a carpenter and butcher of Company B, was on his way home at war's end, going to Benton Alley, in Allegheny's Mexican War Streets, when he stepped in front of a train in Harrisburg. The rest of the 123rd Regiment continued on without McKain to Allegheny, where enthusiastic crowds awaited their arrival.

Well before the regiment's return to Allegheny, however, local leaders and Union Army strategists, observing the war's progress, worried that Confederate forces might attack Allegheny and Pittsburgh because of their position as a rail- and river-transportation hub and the presence of two facilities that produced ordnance, the Fort Pitt Foundry in the lower Strip District and the Allegheny Arsenal in Lawrenceville. The foundry, whose employees included men from Deutschtown and Duquesne borough who walked across the Mechanics Street Bridge, made the majority of the Union Army's cannons, in 1864 producing the largest cannon ever made: twenty feet long, with a twenty-inch opening, and able to send a half-ton ball five miles. The arsenal, farther away, probably employed no Alleghenians. Both facilities, however, were important to the greater Pittsburgh area because of the volume of ordnance they manufactured, their contribution to the booming war economy, and—more ominously—the extent to which they now made Pittsburgh and Allegheny a potential Confederate target.

Indeed, Confederate forces were now massed in West Virginia, Maryland, and even Ohio, reportedly planning to invade north of the Mason-Dixon Line. Paying particular attention to western Pennsylvania and adjoining counties in Ohio and West Virginia, the War Department thus created the Union Army's Department of the Monongahela, which quickly established its headquarters in Pittsburgh, directing the building of thirty-seven earthen fortifications around Pittsburgh and Allegheny over just three weeks in June and July 1863, four of them in Allegheny. Fort Black, which local Civil War historian Arthur B. Fox called "the only true fort" among these, was on a hill in Greenfield; others occupied vantage points in Millvale, Stanton Heights, Mount Washington, Morningside, the Hill District, East Liberty, the West End, and Oakland.

To build the forts so quickly, a citizens' committee called for employers in and around Pittsburgh and Allegheny to suspend business and assign workers to their construction. As local newspapers alarmed the public with daily reports of Confederate forces moving closer, large and small business owners stepped forward in response. On June 22, 1863, nineteen area cooper-shop owners met in the Gerst brewery hall at Suisman Street and Madison Avenue in Deutschtown. When Charles Shepley offered twenty men from his cooperage on East Street, the group selected him as its captain. Gregg, Alexander & Company's oil-barrel works on Darrah Street at River Avenue offered fifteen men, and Frederick Helm reported that his shop at 620 East Ohio Street could spare six. John Rentz of Carpenter Way expected seven of his coopers to work, and George Eberhardt of Tripoli Street near East Street offered two. The coopers, with a captain, first lieutenant, and second lieutenant, adopted both a military structure and military inspiration: the *Daily Gazette* reported that "the Allegheny coopers would meet at Gerst's hall, and march to the lower end of the Hand [now the Ninth] street bridge, meet the Pittsburgh coopers at Robert Bole's shop, and proceed thence to the Pennsylvania Railroad depot, preceded by a band of music." Other area industries, of course, stepped forward as well. McIntyre & McNaugher, Allegheny street pavers, well equipped for fort construction, assigned seventeen workers to the fort-building effort. The W & H Walker soap and candle factory of Tripoli Street in Deutschtown and the Maffett & Old blacksmith shop of Rebecca Street sent seven and seventeen men, respectively. Architects Barr & Moser of Allegheny delayed their design of landmark area buildings to lend three workers to the effort.

Allegheny's black citizens also played a large role in the rapid construction of the forts. Five prominent African American residents—H. B. Williamson of Federal Street and E. R. Parker of Cedar Avenue, both cuppers and leechers; Samuel Neal, an Avery College teacher who lived on Sandusky Street; restaurant owner Moses Howard of White Oak Way; and barber Robert J. Davis of River Avenue—helped to organize a gathering of the city's black men in the Diamond on June 29. Approximately 160 black Alleghenians, along with 60 white men, built Fort Kirkwood in Millvale, overlooking the Allegheny River and guarding the city's eastern approach.

All told, the local force responsible for the construction of Pittsburgh and Allegheny's forts—its coopers, the black residents who built Kirkwood, and countless other groups—totaled more than ten thousand civilians. In a further display of local patriotism, business owners contributed equipment and teams of horses to the construction effort. Contemporary newspaper accounts indicate that nearly all businesses complied with the call to suspend business for the construction push, and those who continued to operate risked public embarrassment. Some tavernkeepers, however, quietly remained open, with their back doors unlocked. The *Pittsburgh Gazette* reported on July 2 that in the Fourth Ward a Chestnut Street tavernkeeper named Falhauber was more vociferous in his refusal to close; according to the newspaper, Falhauber "treated the Committee very indecently, used low and profane language, and ordered them out of the house." In the Mexican War Streets, residents visited Allegheny mayor Alexander C. Alexander to complain that Peter Metz and his employees were still at work at Metz's carpentry shop on Day Way, behind his house at 1239 Resaca Place. Metz, according to the *Gazette,* "has been appealed to by his neighbors, but can neither be coaxed nor shamed into a proper sense of his duty. . . . The bold defiance of public opinion exhibited by Metz, is deserving of the severest censure, and if trouble comes upon him he will have but himself to blame. He certainly cannot ask the protection of a community which he refuses to aid in defending, and he cannot hope for the countenance or patronage of a people whose sentiments he has defied and outraged."

In spite of these few dissenters, the thirty-seven forts were well and rapidly built. Most were circular, and all were intended to include cannons and other weaponry. In Allegheny, Fort McKee, built by some 621 workers, occupied hillside land around Sunday and Colfax streets in the California-Kirkbride neighborhood. The army intended Fort McKee to guard the Pittsburgh, Fort Wayne & Chicago Railroad yard that then occupied the present site of Pittsburgh's main post office on California Avenue. Five hundred ninety men, 224 of them unidentified, built Fort Brunot, a redoubt that occupied a site on Marshall Avenue where the Pressley Ridge School now stands. Henry Anshutz of Lockhart Street directed thirteen employees of his Pittsburgh stove

Col. James H. Childs (standing) with other officers of the Fourth Pennsylvania Cavalry in August 1862. Library of Congress Prints and Photographs Division (LC-B817-7464), Washington, D.C. Alexander Gardner, photographer

factory to help build Fort Brunot, while the Patterson mill on Beaver Avenue in Manchester sent sixteen. Many residents called Brunot Fort McKeever, for the family on whose farm it stood. Fort Fulton, a circular structure about 240 feet in diameter, commissioned to guard against attack from the north along the East Street valley, stood on or adjoining the site of the Northview Heights public housing community. Fulton, still partly visible according to a 1991 study, was also called Fort Childs, for Captain James H. Childs of Allegheny. An unnamed fortification at or near the intersection of Perrysville and Marshall avenues and Marshall Road, its site just north of the city line, called Haslett's Hill by local residents, was constructed by employees of the Pittsburgh, Fort Wayne & Chicago Railroad. All this local effort, however, was expended to little end. By the time fort construction ended in July, the Confederate threat to Pittsburgh had diminished considerably. Volunteers manned some of the fortifications, but only briefly. The War Department scrapped its plan to install cannons at area forts and later abandoned the sites altogether, either during the war or soon afterward.

The conflict was going poorly for the Union in early 1863. The US Army, however, still did not permit blacks to serve, with the exception of Massachusetts's Fifty-fourth Regiment, whose white officers commanded black soldiers. Black men who were determined to help the Northern cause, then, had few options open to them: they could enlist with the Massachusetts Fifty-fourth, as a few Pennsylvanians did, or they could travel to Louisiana to join that state's Native Guards, an all-black military unit whose men were drawn primarily from the New Orleans area. Samuel J. Wilkinson of Allegheny, whose parents had brought him to Allegheny borough within a few years of his birth in Chambersburg, Pennsylvania, in about 1835, chose the second of these options, enlisting in the Second Regiment of the Native Guards. Unlike the Massachusetts regiment and the later-formed US Colored Troops, the Native Guards included black officers up to the level of major. Approximately twenty-nine, including Wilkinson, held the rank of captain.

By the time Wilkinson enlisted, however, General Nathaniel P. Banks had begun to purge black officers from the Native Guards and appoint white officers in their place. The force quickly lost its black officers: sixteen left in a mass resignation on February 19, 1863, while others continued to resign throughout the years, many citing racial prejudice. Wilkinson retained his position until July 20, 1863, when he and Captain Samuel W. Ringgold resigned rather than have their performance evaluated by a board composed of men of lesser rank. By early spring of 1864, all but three of the Native Guards' black officers had resigned. Wilkinson remained with the Native Guards' successors, the Corps d'Afrique and the US Colored Troops, apparently as a private. He would muster out of the army in New Orleans in 1865, returning to Allegheny. Back home, Wilkinson, who had supported his young family as a gravedigger and laborer before the war, worked as a paperhanger, railroad porter, bank watchman, fish salesman, and elevator operator. He owned his home on Howard Street, in the East Street valley, and joined numerous fraternal lodges. He died on August 30, 1904, in an elevator accident at work in Downtown Pittsburgh. The *Pittsburgh Press* reported a few days later, in its "Notes for the Afro-Americans" section, that Wilkinson had "hundreds of friends all over the country" and "took an active part in every movement affecting the welfare of his race."

Wilkinson, of course, was not the only local African American to serve the Union during the Civil War. Over the two years after the War Department created what came to be known as the US Colored Troops, on May 22, 1863, Pennsylvania contributed about 8,600 of the 179,000 black soldiers whose service helped win the war. Lafayette Massey was one of these soldiers. Born in the tobacco country of Amherst, Virginia, about 1831, he appears to have arrived in Allegheny in the 1850s. By 1858, he worked as a whitewasher, living along the Pennsylvania Canal in Deutschtown. On March 3, 1864, Massey went to Philadelphia to enlist in Company G, Twenty-fifth Regiment US Colored Troops. The Twenty-fifth spent much of its time on garrison duty, learning infantry and heavy artillery use at Fort Barrancas, Florida. A number of its members contracted scurvy as a result of poor access to food. Massey would muster out in Philadelphia on December 6, 1865, returning to Allegheny, where he worked as a paperhanger before becoming a wagon driver, or expressman, in the early 1870s. He and his wife, Elizabeth, who named one of their children Avery, apparently in honor of the Allegheny abolitionist, leased property from Mary Schenley at the southwest corner of Cedar Avenue and Virgin Way by about 1872. They eventually owned five small houses on this lot, living in one and renting the others. Lafayette Massey applied for a veteran's pension in 1889 and retired about three years later. He lived on Cedar Avenue until about 1901.

Not all of the soldiers who made a mark on the region were Allegheny citizens. The city's position along transportation routes ensured that countless Union soldiers passed through, many camping on the West Common, near

An Italianate double house on Palo Alto Street, Mexican War Streets, built during the Civil War. Pittsburgh Steelers/Karl Roser

the Western Penitentiary, and the East Common. These camps were temporary and unnamed, unlike several camps across the river in Pittsburgh, and the soldiers who stayed in them occasionally disturbed the peace, compelling the Allegheny City government to hire additional police officers. Thousands of captured Confederate troops also passed through Allegheny on their way to prison camps via the Pittsburgh, Fort Wayne & Chicago Railroad. They did not disembark in Allegheny, instead transferring to the Pennsylvania Railroad in Downtown Pittsburgh. In June 1863, Confederate prisoner Thomas S. Dannals of the Twelfth Louisiana Regiment caused a brief stir when he jumped from an eastbound train in Allegheny. Military officials quickly arrested Dannals, a Beaver County native who told them that he wanted to swear allegiance to the Union. Dannals was sent on to the prison camp, later returning to the county where he was born.

Some Confederate soldiers stayed in Allegheny for several months in 1863 and 1864, after General Hunt Morgan led a Confederate excursion across the Ohio River into Indiana and then eastward in June 1863. Morgan's forces lost Ohio's only Civil War battle on July 19, and Union forces captured Morgan himself on July 26. The army sent more than one hundred of Morgan's men to Allegheny's Western Penitentiary, most of them members of a handful of Kentucky cavalry regiments. The Confederates were treated well at the aging stone prison, perhaps because nearly all were officers. Prison staff permitted the men to leave the prison to enjoy its grounds and attend church services, and they received fresh food, clean clothing, and medical attention. They were transferred from Western Penitentiary to the prison camp in Point Lookout, Maryland, in March 1864.

While some Alleghenians gossiped about the recently departed Confederate soldiers, others made plans to raise funds for the North in the shadow of the penitentiary. In June 1864, civic leaders held the Pittsburgh Sanitary Fair for the Relief of Sick and Wounded Soldiers in hastily erected wooden buildings on the Diamond and the West Common. Some of Allegheny's most prominent citizens—including Thomas M. Howe, attorney William Bakewell, and glass manufacturer Ormsby Phillips—and their Pittsburgh counterparts exhorted the county's citizens to donate "anything that could be eaten, worn sold or was curious to look at." Years later, a veterans' group published a poem that described the fair's offerings:

> Here are lots of substantials—bread, butter and cheese
> And bright airy trifles the fancy to please
> Here are carts, wagons, harrows, ploughs, mattocks, and hoes
> Shoes, notions, boots, stockings, and all sorts of clothes
> For the ladies are ribbons, pins, cotton, and lace
> Bright mirrors where each may behold her sweet face.

The Sanitary Fair raised $361,516 to feed Union soldiers who stopped in Allegheny and Pittsburgh and to provide medical care for wounded soldiers. Fair organizers contributed more than half of the funds raised to the Western Pennsylvania Hospital on Polish Hill, which the War Department had converted to Allegheny County's first veterans' hospital in 1861. The donation enabled the hospital to treat thousands of western Pennsylvania soldiers free of charge for years after the war. The War Department also placed wounded soldiers in part of the Marine Hospital at Woods Run for a brief time in 1862.

In spite of the sacrifices made by so many of the area's residents, the Civil War also brought economic growth, the War Department pumping considerable money into the local economy between 1861 and 1865 as demand for iron, steel, leather, and other manufactured goods increased. The Fort Pitt Foundry and the Allegheny Arsenal were still the largest area manufacturers of war goods, but several Allegheny businesses also contracted to supply the government. At least four Allegheny leather workers supplied saddles to the Union Army. Henry Seitz, Thomas Maritz, and Arthur Clendining, all on or near Federal Street, and Henry Grobe, whose shop was near East Ohio and Chestnut, made artillery harnesses for the Allegheny Arsenal. Area leather workers bought their materials from local tanneries, nearly all in or near eastern Allegheny City. The Phelps, Parke & Company wagon works at Beaver Avenue and Liverpool Street in Manchester borough produced fifty-two wagons for the army on short notice in July 1861; around the same time Frederick Eshelman's wagon shop, nearby on Beaver Avenue, made five hundred wagons for the army. In addition, of course, Pittsburgh's iron and steel production soared, and although comparatively little iron- and steelmaking took place in Allegheny, industrial prosperity drove both cities' wartime economy. Along with area manufacturers, central Allegheny's businesses increased their sales during the war. The troops who camped on the commons and the travelers who used the Pittsburgh, Fort Wayne & Chicago depot patronized the city's hotels and saloons, its wholesale and retail groceries, its barbershops, tailors, pharmacists, and tobacco stores.

Employment surged with the new demand. Historians have noted that even as Lincoln's calls for enlistment removed men from the workforce, northwestern Pennsylvania's new oil industry competed for those skilled and unskilled workers who were not in the military. Thousands of men left Pennsylvania farms and cities to drill, transport, and refine oil in boomtowns like Oil City, Pithole, and Titusville during the Civil War. Many of these places grew from muddy shantytowns to permanent settlements, attracting additional migrants who established retail and service businesses. The Allegheny and Pittsburgh area became an early refining center, thanks to the cities' river and rail connections to the oil fields. Several refineries that would be considered tiny by today's standards operated on Herr's Island and nearby, on River Avenue. The 1863 Pittsburgh directory listed dozens of Allegheny City and Duquesne borough men working locally in the oil industry, as refinery owners and managers, brokers, merchants, office staff, refiners, and oil-barrel makers. Some, like refinery owner Henry Holdship and merchants R. D. Cochran and Hugh McKelvy, would remain in the oil business for many years.

The war and resulting industrial prosperity concomitantly inflated real estate values, with prices for buildings and undeveloped parcels roughly doubling between 1860 and 1865 in Allegheny and Pittsburgh. Established neighborhoods grew in density, with property owners commissioning houses on streets such as North Lincoln Avenue in Allegheny West, North Taylor Avenue in the Mexican War Streets, and Avery Street in Deutschtown. Rapid inflation in the costs of building materials and land also led to an increase in the construction of party-wall houses, which share side walls. John McDonald,

Western Theological Seminary on Ridge Avenue. J. C. Bragdon, *Views of Pittsburg*, 1903. Courtesy of Historic Pittsburgh Full-Text Collection, Digital Research Library, University Library System, University of Pittsburgh

an Irish immigrant who worked as a carpenter and building contractor, constructed a brick double house at 1221–23 Palo Alto Street in about 1862, where he would live with his family for the rest of the 1860s. McDonald's houses share a wall at their second stories and attics and a narrow street level breezeway with an arched opening, allowing access to backyards without sacrificing upper-story living space. Many attached houses were built without such breezeways.

McIntosh Row, which still stands on Western Avenue near Brighton Road, was probably the first of nearly a dozen rental rows built in Allegheny West in the last four decades of the century. Before the war, Federal Street shoe merchant Laughlan McIntosh had bought an undeveloped lot at the northwest corner of Western Avenue and Brighton Road, running 220 feet back to Rope Way, for $4,500 on New Year's Day 1860. Now, during the war, in 1864–65, McIntosh built four attached three-story brick houses in a simple version of the Italianate style on Western Avenue. He and his family moved into one and rented the other three dwellings to tenants. Pleased with his investment, in 1869 McIntosh decided to build another row of four houses. These houses were substantially larger than the earlier homes, and McIntosh built one with a storeroom that he leased to a druggist. McIntosh would die in 1891, but his daughter Lucretia Mott Martin would own property on Western Avenue into the twentieth century.

The construction of churches also boomed with the changes the Civil War brought to the area. Fifteen Allegheny City residents established the North Presbyterian Church in 1863, breaking from an older church whose members supported the Confederacy, their new church's name referencing its founders' belief in the Union. Although the North Presbyterian Church later became known for its membership's wealth and prominence, its founders were primarily middle-class and working-class Alleghenians. While oil refiner Jacob Forsyth lived on Western Avenue in Allegheny West, most of the congregation's charter members lived on the Mexican War Streets or in the neighborhood just east of Federal Street, including Federal Street druggist Henry Schwartz, Dr. Thomas F. Dale, several carpenters, a bricklayer, a traveling salesman, and two bookkeepers. The congregation initially met in the Western Theological Seminary chapel on Ridge Avenue, but in about 1868 it moved to a new building, at the southeast corner of North Lincoln and Galveston avenues. The original North Presbyterian Church building was one of a handful of structures that are documented as having featured

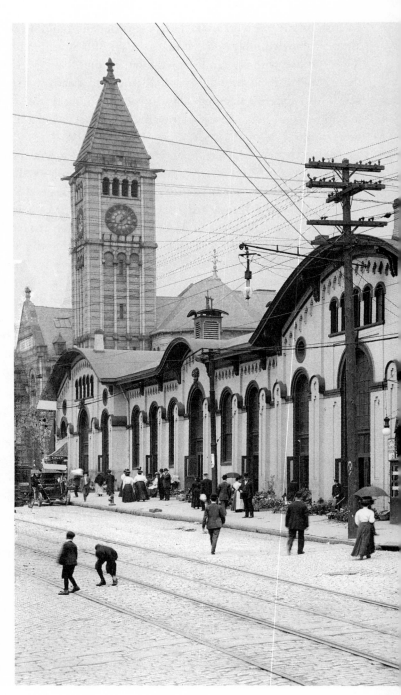

The Market
House, one
of the city's
most iconic
structures, was
commissioned
by the Allegheny
government and
built during the
Civil War.
Library of
Congress Prints
and Photographs
Division (LC-D4-
36463), Washington,
D.C.

stained-glass windows by William Nelson of Woods Run, an Irish immigrant who was Pittsburgh's first stained-glass manufacturer. A new church building replaced the original edifice in the 1890s, but it was demolished in the 1960s.

One of the city's most iconic structures was also built during the war, when the Allegheny government commissioned the Market House, replacing an earlier, smaller structure. The Market House occupied a city block at the southwest corner of Federal and Ohio streets. Built in 1863 for about $33,000, it featured brick corbels, round-arched window openings, and paired brackets that displayed both Romanesque Revival and Italianate style influences. Alleghenians flocked to the crowded building from every neighborhood to buy fresh vegetables, fruits, meats, eggs, dairy products, flowers, and other goods, the building's immediate success quickly paying for its construction. The apparently forward-thinking city government prohibited smoking tobacco and walking dogs on the property and ordered that it occasionally remain open overnight. It would serve North Siders well for more than a century before it was demolished in the 1960s for the construction of Allegheny Center.

The prosperity brought by the war did not disappear with the end of the conflict in 1865. Indeed, the return of peace allowed Allegheny City to build further on its recent development. Allegheny now stood ready to begin its period of greatest growth.

CHAPTER 4

The Boom Continues
The Civil War to 1877

AFTER THE CIVIL WAR, industry and transportation networks in Allegheny and Pittsburgh continued to expand, and the cities' economies became ever more intertwined. Indeed, the robust postwar economy of 1865–73 brought Allegheny new industry, new residents at every socioeconomic level, and new homes, shaping the city's neighborhoods and making this the North Side's period of fastest growth. Some of the new Alleghenians came from rural communities around western Pennsylvania, a population shift that was playing out in many parts of America. The city's new residents, of course, also came from Europe and from Pittsburgh.

Industry in Allegheny, as elsewhere in the country, was undergoing significant change. Cotton manufacturing, although in decline, was still Allegheny's largest industry when the war ended. In the mid-1860s, however, iron and steel production had already begun to accelerate along the Ohio River: demand for goods quickly grew, and manufacturers built plants on large flat riverfront properties with railroad access. Cotton was still important at the turn of the decade: three of the city's five largest workplaces were Kennedy, Childs & Company, the Eagle Cotton Mill, and the Anchor Cotton Mill, which together employed 808 workers in 1870. The 1870 manufacturing census, however, revealed the shape of the future: by that point, Allegheny's iron mills and associated factories together employed more workers than all the city's cotton mills.

Among all these new iron mills was Lindsay & McCutcheon's, in lower Manchester, which began operation in 1863 at the present site of the West End Bridge and employed 160 workers in 1870. The Pittsburgh Locomotive and Car Works began operation on a small scale in 1865, on Beaver Avenue in northern Manchester; it expanded in 1867 and in 1870 was Allegheny's largest workplace, with 375 employees. Nearby, at Woods Run, the Pittsburgh Forge & Iron Company, established in 1864, employed 159 residents in 1870. The Harbaugh & Mathias rail mill, which opened at Woods Run in 1865, had 232 employees in 1870.

Allegheny's four largest iron and steel works, although relatively new, were comparable in size to most of Pittsburgh's plants. Schoenberger & Company's iron mill, the largest in Pittsburgh's Strip District, and Andrew Carnegie's Union Mills, in Lawrenceville, each employed 400 workers. The only significantly larger local mill was Jones & Laughlin's enormous American Iron Works on the South Side, with 1,800 men and 100 children working there. The South Side was also home to dozens of plants that produced glass, perhaps Pittsburgh's only significant product that did not also become a lasting part of the North Side manufacturing scene.

In 1870, Allegheny was also home to fifteen foundries and machine- and engine-building shops, which together had 390 workers. The largest of these was the Joseph Graff & Company foundry in the Fourth Ward, where 100 individuals made axes, shovels, and hinges. In northern Manchester, along the Pittsburgh & Western Railway, former Allegheny mayor Lewis Peterson's new Rosedale Foundry, which operated well into the twentieth century, began to turn out railroad and mill components. Most of Allegheny's foundries were in the First and Fourth wards, adjacent to rail lines and river shipping.

The Allegheny River also made Allegheny an ideal site for processing hard and soft woods from the thick forests of northwestern Pennsylvania. In 1870, about forty wood-processing establishments operated in the city, and about half of the woodworking factories and shops were located in Deutschtown. Among the largest were planing mills, which produced dimensional lumber, window sashes, doors, and clapboards, and cooperages, which made barrels for sale to beer brewers, oil refineries, nail mills, and other manufacturers. Manchester was home to several coffin manufacturers: the Keystone Coffin Company; Hamilton, Lemon, Arnold & Company; and Wilson, Brown & Company. Allegheny also housed box factories, cabinet makers, wood turners, two barge yards, and a match factory that employed one woman and three children.

By 1870 the city also contained five quarries or stone yards that together employed 267 men, although nineteenth-century Allegheny is not remembered as a center of building-material production. The western slope of Spring Hill, overlooking the East Street Valley, yielded stone that workers

A view of the East Street Valley in 1874. Carnegie Museum of Art Collection of Photographs, 1894–1958 (85.4.97), Carnegie Museum of Art

extracted for construction and other uses, as well as abundant clay for Allegheny's brickyards. Not all masonry materials processed in Allegheny were of local origin: on Anderson Street at the Western Pennsylvania Railroad, for example, twenty men employed at the Beggs and Lindsay marble and granite works took stone that arrived by rail and fashioned elaborate mantels that graced Pittsburgh's 1872 city hall and some of Allegheny's and Pittsburgh's finest mansions.

Older industries also continued to thrive. In Deutschtown and the Spring Garden Valley, and along present-day East Ohio Street, German immigrants and their descendants brewed beer and tanned leather in ever-greater quantities, small-scale production still characterizing both industries. The city's ten breweries employed 40 men, and its thirteen tanneries employed 137. Tanning was a particularly key piece of Allegheny's economy, far more important than it was in Pittsburgh. Allegheny's tanneries and interdependent businesses—slaughterhouses, soap and candle factories, a glue and fertilizer works, harness and saddle factories, bellows makers, and countless shoemakers—dominated the Spring Garden Valley's culture. Such businesses also discharged fetid wastes into Saw Mill Run, which residents subsequently renamed Butchers Run.

All the industrial expansion just beyond Allegheny's borders helped convince city leaders to annex neighborhoods to its northwest and northeast in the late 1860s and early 1870s. Manchester became the city's Fifth and Sixth wards, and part of Reserve Township became the Seventh Ward (Spring Hill and part of Spring Garden) in 1867. The city annexed a piece of McClure Township, containing Perry Hilltop, the same year. Most of Duquesne borough became the Eighth Ward (part of Spring Garden, along with Troy Hill, East Ohio Street, and Herr's Island) in 1868. Allegheny annexed another bit of McClure Township in 1870 and the remainder in 1873. By that year, the city had most of its 1907 land area, although sections of the East Street Valley, Spring Hill, and Spring Garden neighborhoods were still in Reserve Township.

As its borders moved outward, the city lost a tangible link to its past when William Robinson Jr. died on February 25, 1868, at age eighty-two. His obituary in the *Pittsburgh Daily Gazette* stated, "He is gone. One of the old landmarks is removed. A link that connected the present with the past has been broken and cannot be replaced." Robinson's funeral was at his home.

Robinson died owning considerable property in Allegheny. His house and

Allegheny City converting the Commons to East and West Parks between 1868 and 1876.
Carnegie Library of Pittsburgh Pennsylvania Department, Pittsburgh Photographic Library

grounds at the foot of Federal Street still stood, improbably, amid commercial blocks, factories, and other older dwellings. Robinson's children inherited his commercial and residential properties on and adjacent to Federal Street, along with undeveloped out lots in Manchester. These properties were among the larger holdings that developers subdivided for middle-class and wealthy families who made their homes in Allegheny after the war. Members of the Denny family subdivided land in Manchester and Allegheny West around the same time.

As the city's population continued to increase in density, the Allegheny government took the first steps toward converting the Commons to East Park and West Park in 1867. The city appointed a park commission, which contracted with the New York landscape-architecture firm of Mitchell & Grant to design the two parks. Charles Davis, who became Allegheny's city engineer about 1868, supervised park construction, leveling terrain; creating lakes, winding drives, and footpaths; constructing fountains and iron bridges and fences; and building a stone wall along the railroad tracks that cut through West Park. The city also landscaped the area that had long been called Hogback Hill, in the southernmost part of West Park; it became known as Monument Hill after the Allegheny County Soldiers Monument was placed there in about 1870. The city officially completed construction of East and West parks in 1876. Alleghenians were thus granted an amenity that their neighbors across the river lacked: Pittsburgh's only park was the considerably smaller Iron City Park in Lawrenceville. Now, in Allegheny, the city blocks facing the two beautiful new parks, along Irwin, North, and Cedar avenues, eventually became some of the most desirable residential real estate on either side of the river. In spite of all the upscale development, however, the parks remained firmly rooted in the varied life of the city. The railroad tracks gave the parks an urban feel—as did the hulking Western Penitentiary, which still stood at the northwest corner of Sherman Avenue and West Ohio Street. The penitentiary presented a physical and spiritual counterpoint to St. Peter's Roman Catholic Church, built in the Gothic Revival style on the opposite corner between 1871 and 1874.

St. Peter's congregation had hired respected Pittsburgh architect Andrew Peebles to design their new building. Peebles, who designed buildings in the area between 1871 and 1896, was also the only Pittsburgh architect invited to compete to design the Allegheny County Courthouse and Jail. Other prominent buildings recorded as Peebles's work include the First Lutheran Church in Downtown Pittsburgh; Dungeness, a mansion on Cumberland Island, Georgia, that served as a winter home for the Pittsburgh industrialist Thomas Carnegie, brother of Andrew; and offices and a warehouse for Jacob Painter's Pittsburgh Iron Works on First Avenue in Downtown Pittsburgh. Although Peebles designed several important area buildings and was obviously held in professional esteem, comparatively little is known of his work because he practiced during an era from which scant documentation of architects' commissions survives.

Meanwhile, further from the city's center, Allegheny West in 1865 remained a sparsely developed neighborhood populated by well-to-do, middle-class, and working-class families. The community's largest homes—mansions, in the smaller scale of their day—lined Ridge Avenue and Brighton Road (then Irwin Avenue), with a few substantial dwellings also facing Lincoln Avenue. Western

St. Peter's Roman Catholic Church, at the corner of Arch and West Ohio streets.
Pittsburgh Steelers/Karl Roser

Avenue contained a mix of prosperous and working-class families' homes, as well as the Pioneer Paint Works factory at the corner of Galveston Street and one or two storefronts. Undeveloped lots lined Beech Avenue and the Allegheny West section of West North Avenue. During the heady settlement boom of the postwar years, however, affluent citizens commissioned some of Allegheny's largest houses on Ridge Avenue and Brighton Road, with a few on Lincoln Avenue as well, setting the stage for the emergence of the city's "Millionaires Row" along parts of Ridge Avenue, Brighton Road, and West North Avenue later in the century. Most of these were no more than about twenty-five feet wide, a span of one room and a side hallway, and three to five rooms

Italianate party-wall houses on Ridge Avenue near Allegheny Avenue, built about 1872. Courtesy of Pittsburgh History & Landmarks Foundation

deep. A few were wider, with centered entrances, like the Holmes mansion on Brighton Road and the McKnight residence on Lincoln Avenue. Brighton Road also saw the construction of large, fashionable homes by B. F. Jones, of Jones & Laughlin; Pennsylvania Railroad manager J. N. McCullough; and dry goods retailer William Semple. Among Ridge Avenue's best-known residents were glass manufacturer Ormsby Phillips; iron merchant W. Graff; and William McKelvy, partner in an Allegheny paint factory.

The Holmes mansion, at 719 Brighton Road, built between 1869 and 1871, was commissioned by Letitia Caldwell Holmes, the wealthy widow of James Holmes, who had owned a meat-packing business near the Monongahela waterfront in Downtown Pittsburgh. Letitia Holmes's new house was designed in the Italianate style, shown in its round-arched window hoods and front-door surround, the brackets beneath its box gutter, and the arched pediment above its front entry. The use of limestone for the entire façade was unusual and particularly expensive, as the house was constructed several years before the quarrying industry adopted machinery that made the extraction and transportation of architectural stone easier and less expensive.

Until the early twentieth century, Letitia Holmes shared the mansion with a number of family members, including her brother William Caldwell, president of the Monongahela Insurance Company, and her daughter Letitia C. Holmes. In 1886, the mansion hosted a wedding when Letitia C. Holmes married George P. Hamilton, a Ridge Avenue attorney. The *Pittsburgh Commercial Gazette* ran a lengthy article on the event, describing the house in effusive terms: "Every room in the house was transformed into a perfect bower of roses, and the decorations reflected great credit upon the artistic taste of the florist, who proclaimed himself in his work throughout." The Hamiltons continued to live with Letitia Holmes until they died around the turn of the twentieth century. Letitia Holmes then raised their daughter, Elizabeth Hamilton, who eloped at age twenty-two, in 1909, stealing away with thirty-one-year-old Percy E. Donner, a stockbroker, capitalist, and former US Steel plant manager. In September 1910, the *New York Times* reported some details of this marriage: "It was announced to-night that Miss Elizabeth Caldwell Hamilton and Percy E. Donner were married last November. The bride is an orphan, and the announcement was made by Mrs. Letitia Holmes, her grandmother. It was not until last night that she or any relatives of the bride were told of the marriage. Mr. Donner is one of the best known horsemen, clubmen, and business men of Pittsburg." The Donners also lived with Letitia Holmes, although their life together was far from peaceful. Percy Donner was suspended from the New York Stock Exchange for a year in 1915 for doing business with "bucket shops," businesses that dealt in commodity and stock futures. Then, around 1922, Donner was declared weak-minded in proceedings in the Allegheny County Court of Common Pleas. Elizabeth Donner, who had inherited 719 Brighton Road upon her grandmother's death, finally sold the mansion for $31,000 in 1923.

As noted earlier, of course, the Holmes mansion was not the only grand house in Allegheny West. Between 1870 and the 1930s, three generations of the Jones and Laughlin families, of iron and steel fame, built and occupied six of the area's most spectacular houses, helping to define and maintain the neighborhood's socioeconomic position. Three of their houses still stand, representing the family's second generation; the earliest one built, the B. F. Jones house on Brighton, and the last two, home to two of Jones's grandchildren, are all gone.

James Laughlin and B. F. Jones of Jones & Laughlin, one of the greatest iron and steel manufacturers in the world by the late nineteenth century. *Left: History of Allegheny County, Pennsylvania*, pt. 1, 1889w; *right:* Carnegie Library of Pittsburgh Pennsylvania Department, Pittsburgh Photographic Library

Benjamin Franklin Jones, a native of Claysville, Washington County, had been a partner in the iron-manufacturing firm of Jones, Lauth & Company since 1851. James Laughlin joined the firm in 1854, and in 1857 it became Jones & Laughlin. Over the next few decades, Jones & Laughlin became one of the greatest manufacturers of iron and steel in the world, even though it did not begin steel production until 1886. By the late nineteenth century the company employed five thousand men, mostly at its American Iron Works on the South Side and its Eliza Furnaces across the Monongahela River, in lower Oakland and Hazelwood. It continued its growth into the early twentieth century, when it created the company town of Aliquippa and expanded its Pittsburgh works. Jones & Laughlin eventually manufactured hundreds of millions of tons of steel per year and employed twenty thousand workers or even more. B. F. Jones was key to the firm's stunning success, an innovator in industrial practices that included ownership of raw-material sources such as iron-ore mines and coal mines, extending the company's holdings as

The B. F. Jones mansion on Brighton Road. Carnegie Library of Pittsburgh Pennsylvania Department, Pittsburgh Photographic Library

far as the Lake Superior region. Jones, a strong advocate for tariffs to protect American manufacturers, enjoyed a prominence that stretched beyond his company role, serving both as chair of the Republican National Committee and as president of the American Iron and Steel Association. He and his wife, Mary McMasters Jones, were also active in the social life of Allegheny and Pittsburgh. "The Joneses live elegantly on Irwin Avenue," the *Social Mirror* reported in 1888, "and go into society and entertain on a handsome scale."

The Jones home, on Brighton Road, reflected and furthered the family's industrial, political, and social prominence. B. F. and Mary McMasters Jones had their mansard-roofed Second Empire–style brick house built in 1870. Although later generations of their family and other industrialists commissioned even larger dwellings in Allegheny West, as noted above, this first Jones mansion was likely the neighborhood's largest when it was built, with the possible exception of the Holmes mansion. It had a sizeable cupola that extended from the center of the roof of the dwelling's front block; a two-story

Russell H. Boggs and Henry Buhl cofounded the department store Boggs & Buhl, a local institution that had five hundred employees by the early 1890s. *Left:* Robert M. Palmer and Hartley M. Phelps, *Palmer's Pictorial Pittsburgh and Prominent Pittsburghers Past and Present, 1758–1905*, 1905. Courtesy of Historic Pittsburgh Full-Text Collection, Digital Research Library, University Library System, University of Pittsburgh; *right:* Courtesy of the Buhl Foundation

brick carriage house, its footprint nearly as large as the mansion's, stood at the rear of the property. The mansion itself was home to both the Jones family and a host of servants who tended to the family's needs. As many as eleven servants lived in the house or the carriage house, which was probably the home of the family's coachmen (or later chauffeurs). The Jones servants generally enjoyed longevity in their positions, several members of the household staff working for the family for a decade or longer. Alice W. Ingram served as lady's maid to B. F. Jones's daughter Mary Jones Laughlin and possibly other family members for at least twenty years.

B. F. Jones died in 1903, at age seventy-eight, but the Jones mansion remained a lively place over the first decade of the new century. Mary McMasters Jones, her daughter Mary Jones Laughlin, and the two Laughlin daughters all lived in the house, along with the usual retinue of household staff. The Laughlin daughters left home when they married, and Mary McMasters

Jones died in 1911. But Mary Jones Laughlin remained in the mansion until her death in 1931, sharing the dwelling with no family members but attended by servants and chauffeurs. The mansion then sat empty for several years. A school, a photography studio, and a moving company used the mansion between the late 1930s and the late 1950s, and it was demolished about 1960.

Around the corner from the Jones mansion, on North Lincoln Avenue, the post–Civil War period also saw the construction of homes that might have seemed diminutive compared to the Holmes and Jones mansions but were substantial by other standards. At 844 North Lincoln Avenue, Hugh and Catherine Knox erected a brick Italianate house of nearly four thousand square feet between 1866 and 1867. Hugh Knox, a commission merchant in Downtown Pittsburgh who facilitated the sale of the farm products that arrived in Pittsburgh to retail merchants, maintained his office on Liberty Avenue, in Downtown Pittsburgh's bustling wholesale district. His new house's round-arched window openings are typical of the Italianate houses built in Allegheny City in the 1860s and early 1870s; later examples of the style more often used segmental-arched window openings. Despite Pittsburgh's robust economy after the Civil War's end, the Knoxes experienced financial difficulties soon after building their new home; Knox went through bankruptcy in 1869, and the family sold the house for $17,500 in 1871.

In the next block, William Forsythe, the owner of a Lawrenceville oil refinery, and his wife, Emma, built a substantial brick house in 1868. Located at 940 North Lincoln, the Forsythe home is also in the Italianate style, with a centered front entrance. From 1871 to 1887, the house was owned by the family of Joseph McKnight, a partner in a South Side rolling mill. The McKnights, who for part of that time lived a few blocks away, rented the house to Fred Gerdes, co-owner of the National White Lead Works paint factory in Millvale. In 1880, the Gerdes family employed two servants and a governess who all lived in their home, as well as a driver who probably resided in a carriage house at the rear of the property.

Western Avenue, just above North Lincoln, was also being developed, with new attached and freestanding brick dwellings springing up on narrow city lots. Some of these homes were large, indicating that the Nevin paint factory's presence did not deter wealthy families from living in the area. Joshua Rhodes, a Pittsburgh manufacturer and capitalist, lived with his family at 939 Western Avenue between about 1870 and 1909. Rhodes, an immigrant from England who owned a grocery and cracker factory before opening a brewery on Fort Duquesne Boulevard, in Downtown Pittsburgh, parlayed the capital he had amassed through the brewery and earlier ventures to rent and then purchase a pipe mill on Herr's Island in 1876–77, calling his new business the Pennsylvania Tube Company. He moved the plant to a better site along Second Avenue near the present Birmingham Bridge in the 1880s. Rhodes's company was merged into the National Tube Company in 1900 and soon became part of the US Steel Corporation. Success enabled Rhodes to invest in a host of ventures during the last quarter of the nineteenth century. He helped found the Pittsburgh & Lake Erie Railroad and was its first president. He invested in street railways that served Allegheny City and the East End and was president of the Colonial Trust Company, vice-president of Allegheny National Bank, and a director of various manufacturing firms and financial institutions.

Their increasing wealth also allowed Joshua and Eliza Rhodes to buy the lots on either side of 939 Western Avenue, demolishing the small buildings already standing and enlarging their original rowhouse into a mansion. They added multistory windowed bays to the west side of the house and a front facing two-story bay by 1890. The front porch, with cut stone supports, dates to around 1890, and by 1893 a greenhouse extended from the rear of the house's front section. The family commissioned a two-story bathroom addition in 1895 and a one-story library addition on the east elevation in 1901. A second story was added to the library addition in 1913. Eventually the Rhodes mansion, with its grounds and support buildings, occupied six city lots. Behind the mansion, the family built a group of brick service buildings: a two-story stable in the 1880s, a one-story carriage house between 1890 and 1893, and a one-story laundry building in 1901. Records from the 1910 census show that the family employed a parlor maid, a chambermaid, a cook, a waitress, and a chauffeur, all of whom lived at 939 Western, performing daily tasks and assisting with the elaborate social events the family hosted. Anecdotal accounts indicate that Eliza Rhodes and her daughters had a live-in seamstress. The family's female servants lived in modest quarters in the mansion's rear wing, and its coachmen (or chauffeur) stayed in one or more of the alley buildings.

Allegheny West's Beech Avenue had existed, at least on paper, by 1852, created by Elizabeth F. Denny, although it remained undeveloped into the 1860s. The street's earliest houses, brick, with eight or more rooms, went up about 1866. Although Denny eventually divided her land along both sides of Beech Avenue into twenty-foot-wide building lots, most of the street's houses are wider, with side porches and walkways into backyards, occupying parcels that combined lots in Denny's plan. About one-third of the houses on Beech Avenue were built during the street's initial burst of development, which lasted from 1866 to 1873, ending with the Panic of 1873.

Lot owners who commissioned houses for themselves were responsible for most of this initial construction. Indeed, all of Beech Avenue's houses that were built before the early 1880s were constructed in the Italianate style or the related Second Empire style. The façade of one dwelling, 942 Beech, shows the fading influence of the Greek Revival style in its band of short attic windows, while a short distance away, the highly ornamented façade at 948–50 Beech, constructed in 1880–81, hints at the architectural diversity that would come in the next decade.

Although most of these early houses were commissioned by lot owners, one exception can be seen at 824–30 Beech, the speculative development of the Manchester contracting firm Frazier Brothers, which built the Second Empire–style row around 1871. Frazier Brothers then sold the houses—clearly intended for families of means, each with ten or more rooms and front and rear staircases—to wealthy English immigrant grocer William Sedden in 1872, for $11,000 each. Sedden in turn rented the houses to tenants, the row's earliest residents including Henry Phipps, whose namesake son was famously a business partner of Andrew Carnegie; Joseph Klee, a clothing manufacturer who later had five houses built at 927–35 Beech Avenue; and Lewis Irwin, an oil manufacturer and a member of the family that had operated Allegheny City's famed rope walk.

The Gibson-Sweitzer house at 842 Beech Avenue is one of the North Side's largest and most elaborate rowhouses, its façade's stone door surround and window hoods dating to a time before the development of quarrying machinery made the extraction and carving of architectural stone easier and less costly. Attorney Robert M. Gibson and his wife, Eliza, commissioned the house in 1873 or 1874, after the area's initial burst of development. Robert M. Gibson, a Washington County native, had come to Pittsburgh in 1868. Like most attorneys of his time, he had not attended law school but instead "read law," serving an apprenticeship with an experienced attorney. In 1884, another attorney who, like Gibson, had "read law," Jacob Bowman Sweitzer, bought the house for $15,500. Sweitzer, who had served with distinction in the Civil War and been honored for his bravery at Gettysburg, had a successful private practice and also served as US attorney for western Pennsylvania.

Like Beech Avenue, the area that is now residential Manchester—east of Chateau Street and north of Western Avenue—was largely undeveloped in 1865. Most Manchester residents lived in modest houses near the Ohio River, in an area that was cleared for urban renewal in the mid-twentieth century. Colonel James Anderson's mansion occupied a multiacre estate until about 1866, and a few other houses also dotted the neighborhood. During the next several years, however, families and developers commissioned hundreds of the houses that still stand in Manchester. Manchester's largest postwar houses rose along parts of Pennsylvania Avenue and West North Avenue (then Fayette Street), while substantial but less grand dwellings went up on these streets and on parts of Sheffield, Liverpool, and Chateau streets.

As in Allegheny West, some of the new affluent residents of the neighborhood were clearly willing to live adjacent to industry. For example, both the Graff, Hugus & Company stove foundry and a lumberyard operated at Pennsylvania Avenue and Sheffield Street, while the Standard White Lead Works made paint at Pennsylvania Avenue and Bidwell Street. Some more modest homes went up in northern Manchester, on Columbus, Adams, and Nixon streets in Allegheny's Sixth Ward, close to the Pittsburgh Locomotive and Car Works and the Pittsburgh, Fort Wayne & Chicago railyard.

German immigrants established at least two churches in the Sixth Ward: the First United Evangelical Protestant Church of Manchester in 1865 and St. Joseph Roman Catholic Church in 1866.

Jewish families had started to move to Allegheny City from Downtown Pittsburgh toward the late 1850s, and many more now followed during the city's postwar housing boom. Most were German immigrant business owners and members of Rodef Shalom synagogue, then on Eighth Street, Downtown. Many ran dry goods stores, owned small clothing factories or distilleries, or traded in livestock. Asher Guckenheimer, for example, had moved to Allegheny in 1859, living on East North Avenue, across from the East Common. In the 1860s his half brothers and business partners, Isaac, Emanuel, and Samuel Wertheimer, moved to Manchester and Allegheny West. Guckenheimer and the Wertheimers were partners in Asher Guckenheimer & Brothers, which owned a distillery in Freeport, Armstrong County. The four brothers were among Allegheny's most prominent Jewish residents for decades. Emanuel Wertheimer served on Allegheny City's common and select councils and as a Pennsylvania legislator. He was also a leader of Rodef Shalom and the Concordia Club.

Daniel and Solomon Stein, partners in Stein Brothers, a wholesale clothing and cloth firm at Fourth Avenue and Wood Street, also moved to Allegheny in the late 1860s. The two brothers first lived in adjoining houses on Western Avenue, before Daniel and his family moved to 850 Beech Avenue and Solomon moved to 919 Galveston Avenue. In 1874, Daniel and Amelia Stein's youngest child, the writer Gertrude Stein, was born at 850 Beech Avenue. Although the family left the Pittsburgh area permanently a few months later, Gertrude Stein's association with Beech Avenue remains an integral part of Allegheny lore.

Like the Guckenheimers, the Wertheimers, and the Steins, most of Allegheny City's Jewish families settled in Allegheny West or Manchester, while a smaller number lived above their stores on lower Federal Street. The few who made their homes on the eastern side of the city included the German immigrants Abraham and Julia Katz and their daughter Augusta, who would later marry department store owner Jacob Kaufmann. After Abraham, a laborer and peddler, died in the late 1860s, Julia and Augusta Katz lived above a tiny confectionery that Julia ran at 402 East Ohio Street. Several blocks away, Benjamin Hirsch, who had just emigrated from Alsace-Lorraine, opened a notions store at 1020 Spring Garden Avenue. Hirsch was illiterate, but he later prospered as a rag dealer and real estate investor on Foreland Street in Deutschtown.

Across Allegheny, waves of migration were changing the shape of the city. Middle-class migration after the Civil War, for example, transformed the Mexican War Streets. The 1865 Pittsburgh directory lists 197 employed men living on these streets—Palo Alto, Resaca, Monterey, Buena Vista, and North Taylor. Most were blue-collar workers, mostly skilled and many self-employed, including carpenters, cabinetmakers, stair builders, machinists, and several blacksmiths, molders, and shoemakers. The streets were also home at the time to merchants and professionals—a doctor and two ministers, as well as residents with white-collar positions, such as a bookkeeper, clerk, and salesman. The area's demographics, however, began to shift in the booming postwar economy, as newcomers to the Mexican War Streets constructed houses on the many available lots and purchased small older houses for enlargement or for demolition and new construction. These new homes were considerably grander than those that had been built for the neighborhood's original residents. Some blocks—particularly Palo Alto Street, Resaca Place, and the 1200 block of Monterey Street—clearly illustrate this transition, larger houses from the late 1860s to the early 1890s standing among modest earlier dwellings. North of the Mexican War Streets and the city's center, other new Allegheny residents were also shaping the city, including the small number of middle-class families who built houses on tracts of land in the Perry Hilltop and Fine-view neighborhoods. At the time, many of these hilltop streets had not yet been laid out, and some of the early families who occupied the larger estates gave their names to present-day streets like McClintock, Osgood, Drum, and Wilson.

Many of these new middle-class and wealthy residents of Allegheny West, Manchester, and the Mexican War Streets had moved from older neighborhoods on both sides of the river, such as the lower Federal Street area, Downtown Pittsburgh, and the lower Hill District. These old neighborhoods were now becoming increasingly devoted to commercial and industrial uses, and families of more modest means replaced those who had relocated. In the meantime, the three middle-class neighborhoods continued to shift in shape and density during the postwar boom, with homeowners commissioning most of the detached dwellings and investors building most of the rows of party-wall houses.

George, John, and William Frazier, doing business as Frazier Brothers, may have been Allegheny's most prolific speculative homebuilders during this boom. Frazier Brothers had established themselves well before the boom, opening a planing mill near the Ohio River in Manchester in 1850. By 1865, if not earlier, the firm had already begun to purchase undeveloped land and construct rows of party-wall brick houses. Frazier Brothers' row of ten brick houses at 1515–33 Bidwell Street in Manchester was built around 1865. This particular development was originally called Frazier's Row, its houses numbered 1 through 10. Among its earliest residents were Romulus B. Cool, a druggist in the Allegheny Market House; the chair makers Abraham and Fielding Small; and J. H. Welty, a Federal Street carpet dealer. Frazier Brothers continued to build party-wall houses over the coming years: 824–30 Beech Avenue, 1130–34 Sheffield Street, and certainly other homes that were not attributed to the firm. Frazier Brothers oversaw every aspect of production, using lumber processed by its own planing mill. George Frazier in fact lived part of the time near the company's lumber operations in Jefferson County, Pennsylvania. This level of control over production might explain why the firm prospered despite a $25,000 fire that destroyed its Allegheny City planing mill in 1869, the three brothers building and living in some of the grandest houses in Manchester and Allegheny West.

Other property owners also commissioned rows of attached houses, ensuring that the many affluent families opting to live in rented homes in the nineteenth and early twentieth centuries enjoyed a range of options. Mortgage lenders required down payments of as much as one-third of purchase price, and loan terms were often for no more than several years, so it was not unusual for even the wealthy to rent.

The boom years between the Civil War's end and the Panic of 1873 also brought the rapid growth of Allegheny's heavily German eastern neighborhoods. In Deutschtown, Avery, Lockhart, and Pressley streets emerged as a genteel enclave housing some of the neighborhood's elites, as well as skilled blue-collar workers and a few laborers. This area's streetscape, featuring mostly brick and some frame dwellings, without setbacks, averaging twenty feet wide, eventually came to resemble parts of Manchester and the Mexican War Streets.

The rest of Deutschtown, along with adjoining Troy Hill, Spring Hill, and the Spring Garden and East Street valleys, also continued to develop, featuring mostly detached brick and wood-frame buildings, some three stories high, others only one-and-a-half-story cottages of three or four rooms. Most of the neighborhood's workingmen held blue-collar jobs, and indeed, in much of Deutschtown and the two valleys, housing competed for space with tanneries, breweries, woodworking shops, blacksmith shops, and taverns. Some more affluent families lived in Deutschtown as well, including the owners of these breweries, tanneries, and other small businesses. These business owners, however, typically shared their homes with one or more of their employees.

Deutschtown's heavily German population made the neighborhood a logical destination for new residents from Bohemia, in what is now the western part of the Czech Republic. Allegheny's Bohemians clustered in the neighborhood around Chestnut Street, on and below East Ohio Street. The Bohemian Exchange, a saloon, opened at 850 East Ohio Street around 1871. Also in 1871, these recent immigrants, who were mostly Roman Catholic, founded St. Wenceslaus Church, Pennsylvania's only Bohemian Roman Catholic parish. The parish eventually bought a former Protestant church on Progress Street, a block east of Chestnut Street, and established a school there. Later in the nineteenth century, the Bohemian community spread northward to the western end of Troy Hill and the adjacent part of Spring Garden and Deutschtown. Some of the minority of Bohemians who were not Roman Catholic founded the First Bohemian Presbyterian Church on Troy Hill. The

Bohemian National Hall on Vinial Street and the Bohemian Catholic Hall on North Canal Street also became centers of the community.

Most of Allegheny's black residents still made their homes in the crowded Third Ward, although at least a few black families lived in nearly every neighborhood. Even the Third Ward, however, contained no predominantly black section, the neighborhood's black families living side-by-side with German neighbors. As in Pittsburgh and other cities, black men often worked as laborers, drivers, or cooks. The Third Ward also housed sixteen black barbers in 1870, as well as clergymen, schoolteachers, a music teacher, two retail fish dealers, and two partners in a Pittsburgh restaurant. A few dozen of Allegheny's black families owned their homes in 1870, nearly all of modest value. Laborer Zachias Blair and his wife, Sidney, both from Virginia, had settled in the upper Mexican War Streets. They owned, purchasing a tiny wood-frame dwelling on Monterey Street above Jacksonia, valued at $1,600. Charles W. Harris, a railroad porter, and his wife, Eliza, owned a small frame house at 209 Hemlock Street, worth $1,000. Families like the Blairs and the Harrises, while of modest means, enjoyed greater status and stability than their peers who rented their homes.

In the late 1860s, three black families, Virginia natives, also commissioned the construction of adjoining brick houses in Manchester, then an overwhelmingly white neighborhood. Although their story is atypical of the circumstances of most black families in nineteenth-century Allegheny and Pittsburgh, it does help to illustrate what capital and good fortune made possible. Paul J. Caperton and George Stevenson were partners in a restaurant at Sixth Street and Penn Avenue in Downtown Pittsburgh, and Joseph McGruder worked in a lumberyard. On July 16, 1867, the three men purchased undeveloped lots on Page Street, paying $450 each, the seller, J. P. Fleming, financing each transaction. By 1869, they had built party-wall Italianate houses. McGruder had financed the construction of his home with a $1,200 mortgage, while Caperton and Stevenson had financed their homes with $1,500 mortgages. James Brady, the Pittsburgh banker who made the construction loans, sold the three mortgages to the Dollar Savings Bank of Pittsburgh, which held the loans until Caperton, Stevenson, and McGruder satisfied them in the 1870s. Page Street's three black families survived the economic depression of the 1870s and remained on the street into the 1890s. Caperton and Stevenson closed their Pittsburgh restaurant during the downturn, finding work as janitors, but Caperton, at least, rebounded, as a caterer and owner of a restaurant on Beaver Avenue in Manchester in the 1880s and 1890s.

As Allegheny's population grew, so of course did its commercial space. East Ohio Street was the main commercial street in the eastern part of the city, retail stores and other small businesses stretching along both sides of East Ohio for several blocks between the East Common and Chestnut Street. Many of these buildings were of frame construction, some with rambling rear additions. While Mary Schenley's ownership of the ground beneath the buildings that stood to the west of Madison Avenue appears to have deterred investment in commercial buildings, the commercial district nevertheless thrived. By 1873, the East Ohio Street business district contained three banks, sixteen saloons, ten shoe stores, eleven groceries, five bakeries, and four drug stores, among other businesses. Meanwhile, Beaver Avenue became western Allegheny City's main commercial street. In the early 1870s it was less densely developed than East Ohio Street, but it was still home to banks and numerous retail shops, an Odd Fellows hall, three or more wagon factories, and a streetcar barn. Streetcars ran along both Beaver Avenue and East Ohio Street, encouraging the nascent business districts.

Allegheny's central Diamond, however, together with Federal Street between the Diamond and the Allegheny River, remained the city's most important business district. One area anchor got its start in 1869, when R. H. Boggs and Henry Buhl opened a dry goods store in a narrow storefront on Federal Street, a half-block south of the Diamond. The two young men achieved modest success in the store's earliest years, Boggs living in a small rowhouse on Allegheny Avenue above Pennsylvania Avenue, Buhl in an Anderson Street boardinghouse. By the early 1890s, Boggs & Buhl was a four-story department store with five hundred employees. The store's popularity rivaled that of Kaufmann's and Joseph Horne's in Downtown Pittsburgh.

The commercial developments, of course, were not uninterrupted. Allegheny's rapid postwar development hit a wall with the Panic of 1873, which caused a nationwide economic depression. The September failure of the New York banking firm Jay Cooke & Company launched a period of three years or more that saw a string of bank and other business failures and home foreclosures, locally and nationally. About half of the Pittsburgh area's banks failed, including the Allegheny Savings Bank, the Franklin Savings Bank of Allegheny, and the People's Savings Bank of Allegheny, all on Federal Street,

O'Hara Street (now Spring Garden Avenue between Madison Avenue and Chestnut Street) after the Butchers Run Flood of 1874. Carnegie Museum of Art Collection of Photographs, 1894–1958 (83.6.3), Carnegie Museum of Art

and the Manchester Savings Bank on Beaver Avenue. As the United States experienced deflation, property values in Allegheny and Pittsburgh dropped by one-quarter or more. As in any economic downturn, those who had taken on considerable debt in more prosperous times were now hit hard. Families from all walks of life lost their homes, and in 1875 the Allegheny Directors of the Poor reported that the number of residents applying for assistance had increased from the previous year.

Then, as Alleghenians struggled with economic hardship, disaster struck. On Sunday, July 26, 1874, Deutschtown's Butchers Run flooded after prolonged heavy rains. Residents and business owners near the Allegheny River tributary had felt safe despite the downpour, because a sewer that measured eight feet in diameter typically sufficed to drain the stream in heavy rain. This time, however, the floodwaters gathered on upper Madison Avenue, two miles from the Allegheny River, pulling away the roadbed and the top of the sewer, creating a trench said to be twenty feet deep. Carrying away frame dwellings, their occupants, and the debris from a glue factory, the stream quickened and then divided at the V-shaped intersection where East Street branched from Madison, below the southwest tip of Spring Hill. Growing wider, the waters eventually came together again, the flood following the run east to Chestnut Street, reaching a depth of twenty feet. On Chestnut Street, the *New York Times* reported, "the width of the sweep of water was probably two hundred feet, and buildings of frame and brick fell before it as if made of sand." The *Times* described the flood's aftermath: "The scene in the devastated district of Allegheny is one which beggars description. For hundreds of yards Madison avenue is lined with the wrecks of dwellings, furniture, bedding, dead animals, timbers, stones, &c. . . . The victims were stripped almost entirely of clothing by the water and floating timbers; some having one shoe on, some the shirt-band about the neck, and others being without a shred." All told, the flood took about 150 lives; many who survived lost all of their possessions. Although the Woods Run section of Allegheny City, Becks Run on the South Side, and other areas flooded that day, Deutschtown's loss was by far the greatest.

Over time, the local and national economy improved. Still, in 1877, millions of American workers remained unemployed. The Pennsylvania and Baltimore and Ohio railroads, continuing to feel the downturn's effects, cut employee wages and reduced manpower on their trains. In response, railroad workers rioted in Baltimore and other eastern cities, destroying railroad property. Unrest quickly spread to Pittsburgh, where railroad workers and sympathizers burned the Pennsylvania Railroad's roundhouse, depot, other buildings, and rail cars in the Strip District. National Guardsmen killed about forty rioters in Pittsburgh, which witnessed the worst violence of any city that suffered railroad riots. One of the strike leaders was Robert A. Ammon of Columbus Avenue in Manchester, who founded the National Trainmen's Union in June 1877. Ammon, a brakeman, the son of a Pittsburgh justice of the peace and insurance broker, has been portrayed in both heroic terms and as an unprincipled scoundrel. Charged with theft in several cases in the nineteenth and early twentieth centuries, Ammon eventually served a prison sentence for his part in a New York City fraud scheme.

Like Ammon's character, the strikes themselves have been variously interpreted. In the short run, the violence marked an unsettling counterpoint in the lingering economic depression. Its more lasting significance was as a milestone marking a shift in American labor relations. Locally, while the riots devastated the Pennsylvania Railroad's Pittsburgh facilities, Allegheny went physically unscathed. At the railyard in Manchester, strikers protected railroad property from damage. In an 1878 account, Allan Pinkerton, founder of the famous detective agency, noted "the exceptional good behavior of the striking trainmen in Allegheny City." He attributed the Allegheny strikers' caution to their regard for James D. Layng, the Pennsylvania Railroad's general manager. Whatever the reason for the moderation of the local riots, Allegheny, in their wake, continued to recover from the 1870s depression, setting the stage for what would be its heyday.

CHAPTER 5

The Heyday of the Middle Class

1877–1890

I N LATE 1874, fifty-seven of the city's men and women gathered to organize a new financial institution that would provide mortgages and small
business loans to its members. Most were workers of modest means, including a shoemaker, carpenters, a barber, and entrepreneurs such as a photographer, a saloonkeeper, and a jeweler. Largely of German origin or descent,
the organizers made their homes in eastern Allegheny City. They called their
new corporation the North Side Building and Loan Association.

Over the next dozen years, similarly titled businesses sprang up all over
Allegheny: the North Side Hotel on Federal Street, the North Side Elevator and Feed Mills at West North Avenue and Brighton Road, and Lacock
Street's North Side Printing Company. At Woods Run, A. F. Schwerd dubbed
his famous wood-column factory the North Side Planing Mill. Indeed, by
1880, Pittsburgh newspapers often used the "North Side" moniker as a nickname for Allegheny. Decades before Pittsburgh officially swallowed Allegheny
City, the two cities' economies and social scenes were clearly and inextricably
intertwined.

The reach of Allegheny businesses, of course, stretched well beyond this
urban neighbor across the river. In 1875, Francis Torrance and James W. Ar-
rott founded the Standard Manufacturing Company to make bathtubs and
associated fixtures. This new company, a predecessor of today's American
Standard, originally operated on River Avenue in the present vicinity of the
H. J. Heinz plant; later in the century it opened a second factory on Preble
Avenue near Woods Run. The Standard Manufacturing Company thrived
partly because it developed a mechanical casting process that replaced earlier
manual piecework; by the early twentieth century, it employed more than one
thousand workers at its Allegheny City plants and thousands more at facilities
outside Pittsburgh.

George Westinghouse moved his air-brake factory from Liberty Avenue, in Pittsburgh's Strip District, to larger quarters in Allegheny City in 1881. The new Westinghouse buildings occupied over one and a half acres on the north side of General Robinson Street, adjacent to the present site of PNC Park. Its manufacture of air brakes for locomotives at the site where the Anchor Cotton Mill had long stood, reliant on the city's rivers and the Pennsylvania Canal to transport its materials and products, symbolized the country's industrial transformation. The success of the Westinghouse Air Brake Company enabled its move to an even larger plant in Wilmerding in 1890, but it kept ownership of the General Robinson Street plant, leasing it to Westinghouse affiliates well into the twentieth century.

In the late 1880s, two little-known food processors with origins in Sharpsburg relocated to Progress Street, near the north end of the Sixteenth Street Bridge. Lutz Brothers (later Lutz & Schramm) established a plant two blocks west of the bridge in 1887; two years later, the H. J. Heinz Company built what was originally called the Keystone Pickle Factory three blocks east of

George Westinghouse moved his air brake manufacturing operations to Allegheny City in 1881. Carnegie Library of Pittsburgh Pennsylvania Department, Pittsburgh Photographic Library

H. J. Heinz, owner of the famous food-processing complex in eastern Allegheny City. Frank C. Harper, *Pittsburgh of Today: Its Resources and People*, vol. 2, 1931

the bridge. These two plants made largely the same foods: pickles, preserves, mustard, horseradish, vinegars, and sauces. Lutz Brothers became Lutz & Schramm around the same time it moved to a larger plant on River Avenue, at the beginning of the twentieth century. Distributing its products in the northeastern and midwestern United States, it remained at its River Avenue site until 1959. Heinz, of course, meanwhile became one of the world's largest food manufacturers.

Heavy industry too continued to be attracted to Allegheny's riverfront and adjoining blocks, with its railroad access and generally flat parcels. The McKinney Manufacturing Company, which claimed to be the world's largest hinge manufacturer, moved in 1876 from Cincinnati to the foot of Juniata Street in Manchester. In Manchester's northwest corner, the Pittsburgh Locomotive Works eventually employed nearly one thousand men at its eleven-acre complex and manufactured as many as three hundred locomotives per year for customers like the Pennsylvania, Baltimore and Ohio, and Union Pacific railroads. Along the Pittsburgh, Fort Wayne & Chicago Railroad

Lutz & Schramm, a food-processing company that competed with H. J. Heinz.
Robert M. Palmer and Hartley M. Phelps, *Palmer's Pictorial Pittsburgh and Prominent Pittsburghers Past and Present, 1758–1905*, 1905. Courtesy of Historic Pittsburgh Full-Text Collection, Digital Research Library, University Library System, University of Pittsburgh

Carnegie Library and Music Hall and Ober Park Fountain, circa 1905. Library of Congress Prints and Photographs Division (LC-D4-18652), Washington, D.C.

corridor, just north of Allegheny West, the Pittsburgh Tool Company began making machinists' tools and associated goods about 1893.

As Allegheny's industry expanded, property values increased steadily in its middle-class and wealthy neighborhoods—Allegheny West, the Mexican War Streets, Manchester, and a small part of Deutschtown near East Park. At the same time, the growth of industry and commerce on both sides of the river encouraged population growth. Middle-class and wealthy families were leaving Downtown Pittsburgh and the oldest sections of Allegheny, and the middle class was largely unable or unwilling to move to sparsely settled areas with little public transportation, like upper Allegheny City and Pittsburgh's East End. Thus, the prices that prospective homeowners paid for undeveloped lots in Allegheny's middle-class neighborhoods continued to rise. In Manchester's southern half, then Allegheny's Fifth Ward, lot buyers typically paid around 50 cents per square foot in the late 1870s and early 1880s. Lot prices surpassed

$1 per square foot by 1887, when Deutschtown druggist Frederick H. Werle bought an undeveloped lot on Allegheny Avenue for $3,800. While Allegheny West had fewer undeveloped lots than Manchester, it also experienced rising values. By 1880, Beech Avenue lot buyers were paying $1 or more per square foot, and by the decade's end, the few remaining vacant lots on Beech were selling for nearly $1.50 per square foot. Lot prices in the Mexican War Streets are more difficult to track, simply because by the 1880s most prospective homebuilders there were buying small houses to demolish or enlarge. The limited data available, however, indicates that lot prices in the Mexican War Streets were comparable to those in Manchester. Meanwhile, in Pittsburgh neighborhoods like East Liberty, central Shadyside, and Lawrenceville, undeveloped lots were selling for around 50 cents per square foot in the late 1880s.

Western Allegheny City's housing market was strong enough that many buyers paid high prices to erect large single-family homes adjacent to the city's heavy industry—its numerous plants, foundries, machine shops, tanneries, and other manufacturers. While all this industry helped tether Allegheny's industrial economy to Pittsburgh's, it also ensured that Allegheny's physical environment resembled its neighbor's: smokestacks belched soot; the sounds of trains and streetcars were nearly ubiquitous. At the time, of course, such tangible marks of industry were seen as a sign of prosperity, and most families—even those who lived comfortably—could see, hear, or smell industry near their homes. The three-story brick house that Frederick H. Werle commissioned on his undeveloped lot on Allegheny Avenue in 1887, for example, was one block west of the Pittsburgh, Fort Wayne & Chicago Railroad. The Standard White Lead Works paint factory stood across an alley from the rear of Werle's house and other large Allegheny Avenue homes, and across Bidwell Street from Sheffield Street's largest houses. A sawmill operated in the exclusive 1300 block of Liverpool Street in the 1880s, and many of Allegheny West's largest houses were near the Nevin paint factory at Western and Galveston avenues, the industrial sites above West North Avenue, and a foundry on Beech Avenue.

Gradually, this pattern shifted. Some Alleghenians chose to escape the city's increasing density, moving to Perry Hilltop or Fineview or even as far as Brighton Heights or Observatory Hill, seeking more land or more affordable housing. Perry Hilltop and Fineview, within just a mile of the Diamond, were fairly practical alternatives for middle-class and upper-class families; the small lots on Perry Hilltop's side streets also provided home sites for families

The warden's residence at the Western Penitentiary was the site of a society wedding in 1887. *Art Work of Pittsburg*, pt. 7, 1893. Courtesy of Historic Pittsburgh Full-Text Collection, Digital Research Library, University Library System, University of Pittsburgh

headed by clerks and skilled blue-collar workers. As the city continued to expand outward, its oldest sections, around and south of the Diamond, became less desirable. As more and more commercial and smaller manufacturing enterprises, such as foundries, opened, middle-class families increasingly began to choose homes in quieter communities. Robinson's Portico Row still stood on lower Federal Street, but its units became rooming houses around 1880, instead of single-family homes.

As the population's desires and means shifted, so too did the city's architecture. Particularly in rowhouse neighborhoods, Allegheny's new middle-class homes illustrated the demand for larger dwellings. Between the late 1870s and 1890, the dormers of side-gabled houses grew wider to create more useable living space on third stories. Builders also increasingly used mansard roofs, rather than side-gabled roofs, to create more third-floor living area. Constructing houses with mansard roofs, rather than side-gabled roofs, substituted bedrooms for attic space. It also enabled builders to opt for a three-story rear ell, rather than a two-story rear ell, allowing space for an additional one or two rooms on the third floor. The houses' rear ells, typically around two-thirds the width of their front sections, also grew wider to provide more living space. As a result, in the mid-1880s builders began to place houses' back doors on the ells' rear elevations, rather than on the ell sides, where they had been.

Of course, not all middle- and upper-class Allegheny families seeking more space built new homes. Some commissioned significant additions to houses that were ten, twenty, or thirty years old. Indeed, the 1880s saw a spate of mansard-roof additions to houses that had side-gabled front blocks, replacing little-used and poorly lit attics with full third stories containing two or three bedrooms. Some buyers purchased modest dwellings set back from the street and then commissioned spacious front additions that used the small original houses as rear ells.

As house forms evolved in the 1870s and 1880s, so too did domestic architectural styles. Beginning in the late 1850s, Allegheny County's builders had used the Italianate style more frequently than any other architectural idiom. This style still enjoyed considerable popularity by the 1870s, although many local builders had defaulted to an Italianate template that showed little innovation. The late 1870s brought the use of arched, sometimes incised, smooth limestone Italianate lintels above window and door openings, made possible by innovations in the quarrying industry. Allegheny's new mansard roofs expressed the Second Empire style; thus, while the city's flat-fronted Second Empire rowhouses were otherwise identical to the city's typical Italianates, the larger freestanding mansarded dwellings clearly expressed a diverging style.

In 1881, a retired Irish immigrant grocer began a building campaign that would give his adopted neighborhood of Manchester its most iconic architecture—and inspire the creation of the Pittsburgh History & Landmarks Foundation more than eighty years later. Eccles Robinson had inherited a six-acre tract bisected by Liverpool Street and bounded by Pennsylvania Avenue, Manhattan Street, North Franklin Street, and Fulton Street from his father, Samuel Robinson, a nephew of William Robinson Jr. The Manchester neighborhood had grown up around the Robinson property, which in the early 1870s still contained only the old Robinson house facing Pennsylvania Avenue. By the early 1880s, Eccles Robinson was seventy-two years old and in declining health. He had never married, and he had a reputation as an eccentric. He lived in the family home with his widowed sister, Annie Abbott. He hired Manchester contractor Henry Landgraf to build a series of identical, stunning, three-story red-brick Second Empire houses with stone trim and elaborate front porches along the entire length of the north side of Liverpool Street's 1300 block. Construction proceeded from west to east, and the block was complete when workmen finished the four houses closest to Fulton Street in 1884 or early 1885. Robinson rented the houses to prosperous tenants. Among the early residents of Robinson's houses were the families of Daniel Wightman, the superintendent of the Pittsburgh Locomotive Works; Allegheny County clerk of courts David K. McGonnigle; livestock dealer Joseph Trauerman; and varnish manufacturer B. J. Thallheimer. Robinson's grand new homes were not only beautiful but a fashionable and popular address, as tenant longevity proves. While Robinson himself died in 1889, some of the tenants of Robinson's row remained in their homes far longer than was typical for middle-class tenants, even into the twentieth century. Attorney Albert Barnes Smith's family, for example, lived on Liverpool Street for about twenty years, and malt manufacturer Jacques Weil lived next door for about eighteen years. The related Strassburger and Joseph families, partners in a Federal Street tailor shop, occupied Liverpool Street continuously between approximately 1882 and 1907.

While Eccles Robinson commissioned the rowhouses on the north side of Liverpool's 1300 block, he sold most of the lots on its south side to several purchasers. The Hamilton family owned the five houses at the southeast corner of Liverpool and Manhattan, living in one home and renting the other four to tenants. Wholesale grocer Gustave Langenheim hired a neighborhood teenager, the budding architect Frederick Osterling, to design a freestanding three-story mansion at 1315 Liverpool Street in 1883. Langenheim paid an estimated $17,500 to build the mansion and $2,500 more for its carriage house. Osterling's $600 fee was more than the annual income of some of Allegheny City's unskilled and semiskilled workers at the time. Eccles Robinson also sold adjacent lots in the 1300 blocks of Pennsylvania Avenue and North Franklin Street to families who would erect dwellings that were substantial, if not quite as grand as those on Liverpool. The contractor Henry Landgraf himself was one of the lot buyers; he constructed a house on North Franklin that he and his family owned and occupied for decades. Another Robinson family member commissioned the last five houses that rose on the 1300 block of Liverpool, in 1895, a Richardsonian Romanesque rental row at the corner of Fulton Street.

Also in the early 1880s, Pittsburgh-area builders began to adopt the Queen Anne style, a few years after it had become popular on the East Coast. Among Allegheny's early Queen Anne–style houses are a mansion that Charles Bartberger designed for tannery owner William Flaccus on Cedar Avenue in Deutschtown (1883) and a double house by an unknown architect on Sheffield Street in Manchester (1882–83). Bartberger also drew up plans for a picturesque Queen Anne house on Liverpool Street for another tannery owner, Charles Stifel, in 1885. In the late nineteenth century, many of Allegheny and Pittsburgh's best houses, of whatever style, featured stone mantels carved by Alexander Beggs & Son in its plant on Anderson Street in Allegheny. One partner in the firm, William D. Beggs, and his wife, Emma, had a substantial house built on Beech Avenue in 1887. This house displays the Queen Anne style in its offset, steep, elaborately ornamented front gable, its diagonal northwest corner, its front-porch trim, and its use of stained glass, while its round-arched second-floor windows, outlined with molded brick, indicate the secondary influence of the Richardsonian Romanesque style.

Near the end of the 1880s, more affluent Allegheny property owners began to commission houses and other buildings in the Richardsonian Romanesque style. Nationally famous architect Henry Hobson Richardson of Boston had died in 1886, but many architects and members of the public regarded the Allegheny County Courthouse on Grant Street in Pittsburgh as his greatest work. The style that Richardson had developed, dependent on expensive building materials and custom stone carving, was best suited to significant public buildings and larger dwellings. In 1889, the new Carnegie Library on Allegheny's central Diamond also rose in the Richardsonian Romanesque style. Architects, however, now incorporated the style in their design of the substantial new houses on Brighton Road and West North Avenue, Beech Avenue, and several other streets in Allegheny West, Manchester, the Mexican War Streets, and Deutschtown.

The distinctive rough-cut stone façade of the house at 848 Beech Avenue shows a somewhat unusual interpretation of the Richardsonian Romanesque, its first story's arched opening nearly as wide as the house itself, underscored by a powerful stone balustrade. John Leitch, general bookkeeper of the Tradesmen's National Bank, and his wife, Ida Diffenbacher Leitch, built this imposing home in 1889, when John was only twenty-nine years old and Ida just twenty-three. Ida was the only daughter of publisher Jacob Diffenbacher, who had commissioned the large Romanesque house at 843 Beech, built in the early 1890s. Less than a decade after she moved into her beautiful new home, Ida Leitch died of pneumonia, in 1897. Her heartbroken husband moved out of the house after her death and lost the property at a sheriff's sale in 1898. Her publisher father Jacob Diffenbacher died in 1898 at Dixmont, the Western Pennsylvania Hospital for the Insane; his obituary attributed his insanity to his daughter's death.

Another notable example of the Richardsonian Romanesque style stands at 913 Brighton Road, in Allegheny West, facing West Park. Jacob and Augusta Kaufmann bought this twenty-year-old Italianate house for the considerable sum of $30,000 in 1890; they then had the house enlarged, adding a new full third story, and remodeled with Richardsonian Romanesque influences. Jacob Kaufmann was one of four German immigrant brothers who were partners in the Pittsburgh department store that bore their name. He and Augusta Kaufmann had moved from Penn Avenue in Downtown Pittsburgh to Sheffield Street in Manchester about 1883; Jacob's brothers Isaac, Morris, and Henry Kaufmann and their families had all moved from Downtown Pittsburgh to substantial houses on Sheffield and Bidwell streets in Manchester within a few years. The Kaufmann families moved often within Manchester in the 1880s, occupying several large dwellings that still stand in that neighborhood.

In 1888–89, another area landmark arose when Harmar D. Denny of Ridge Avenue built Denny Row, nine red-brick party-wall houses of ten rooms each, on West North Avenue, at the height of Allegheny West's popularity among upper-middle-class families. The row was eclectic in design, with varied façades and architectural features that exhibited a mixture of styles: Richardsonian Romanesque round-arched windows and arched corbels, bricks arranged as quoins in the Colonial Revival style, windows and front-porch gables drawn from the Queen Anne style. The design of prestigious rental rows with varied rather than repetitive façades was popular in midwestern and northeastern cities in the 1880s and 1890s, and indeed, Denny Row's first tenants included some of the Pittsburgh area's most prominent families, who rented the houses for $60 a month in 1896. George A. Howe, a steel mill owner and a member of the family that developed and originally occupied Woodland Road in

Squirrel Hill, moved with his family from Shadyside to West North Avenue. The mill owner James I. Bennett and George P. Black, a partner in the Phoenix Roll Works in Lawrenceville, both took houses in the row. James O'Hara Denny, Harmar D. Denny's partner in managing the Denny estate, moved with his family from fashionable Penn Avenue in Downtown Pittsburgh to West North, where they remained for two years, employing a butler, Richard Brown, and female servants. The South Side glass manufacturer Christian Ihmsen McKee, the pants manufacturer Solomon Kaufman, and the attorney James Bakewell also lived in Denny Row in the 1890s.

All the elite families that were moving to the area soon began to organize themselves through various cultural institutions. Some of Allegheny and Pittsburgh's most prominent Jewish residents, for example, founded the Concordia Club, a social and literary organization, in 1874. The 1884 charter that formalized the club specified that it was to be located in Allegheny City, and most of the members identified in its charter were Alleghenians, some the owners of businesses in Downtown Pittsburgh. The club's president, Jacob Eiseman, was an agent with an office at Seventh Avenue and Smithfield Street; he lived on Sherman Avenue, near Allegheny's Diamond. Treasurer Morris Kingsbacher, a jewelry wholesaler, and director Myer Joseph, a clothier, lived in large houses on Manchester's Liverpool Street. Another charter member and part of the club's house committee, Ludwig Kaufman, was a traveling salesman who rented a large rowhouse on North Franklin Street. The members convened for purposes beyond merely social ones. Notably, in late 1885, nineteen American rabbis gathered at the Concordia Club to craft guidelines for Reform Judaism, resulting in a document known as the Pittsburgh Platform. The club, which became an Allegheny institution, was initially housed in a large attached dwelling on Stockton Avenue near Sandusky Street, which it had purchased and converted to its clubhouse. In 1892, the club replaced its original clubhouse with a larger Richardsonian Romanesque building on the same site, designed by Frederick Osterling the same year that he prepared plans for Henry Clay Frick's mansion in Pittsburgh's Point Breeze section.

Many of Allegheny's most prominent families were organized in a less tangible way in the 1880s when Mrs. M. W. Brown Haven of Allegheny began to publish the *Pittsburgh and Allegheny Blue Book,* a directory of elite families that listed residents of Pittsburgh, Allegheny, and suburbs such as Sewickley and Edgewood. Such directories were intended primarily for society women, who may have needed to know that Mrs. R. H. Boggs of West North Avenue received guests on Mondays; that Mrs. R. S. Robb accepted callers in her North Taylor Avenue home on Tuesdays; and that attorney Josiah Cohen and his wife, Carrie, were living with Mrs. Cohen's father, retired rabbi Louis Naumberg, on Sheffield Street.

The *Blue Book* was soon joined by other publications aimed at the wealthy classes. A book called *The Social Mirror* called attention to the elite of the two cities, discussing the personalities, looks, and wealth of hundreds of Allegheny and Pittsburgh women. About 1880, the *Bulletin,* a weekly magazine for and about the two cities' social elite, began publication, subsequently reporting for decades on hundreds of area social events—dances, dinners, weddings, children's parties, church bazaars. In late 1887, for example, the *Bulletin* described a party that the McKee family had given at their Ridge Avenue home: "Mr. and Mrs. H. Sellers McKee . . . were assisted in receiving by a number of well known young ladies. Plants, palms and exquisite roses were placed in attractive profusion in rooms and hallways" and the dining room. After dinner, the Toerge orchestra played, and younger guests danced until a late hour. Brothers George and Fred Toerge of Pittsburgh led the Toerge orchestra, which performed in some of the two cities' finest homes, including that of Andrew Carnegie, and was a predecessor of the Pittsburgh Symphony Orchestra. Like the McKees' party, most of the Allegheny society events that the *Bulletin* covered took place in Allegheny West or adjacent neighborhoods, although one 1887 wedding was a notable exception: "The residence of Warden E. S. Wright, at the Riverside Penitentiary [at Woods Run in Allegheny], was redolent with flowers, Thursday evening, on the occasion of the marriage of his eldest daughter, Miss Frances Wright, to Mr. Benjamin G. Follansbee. The ceremony was performed at 8:30 by Rev. John L. Milligan, long time chaplain of the institution. . . . Music was provided by the Gernert and Guenther orchestra."

Some cultural attractions catered to both the city's elite and its middle-class populace. One of Allegheny's more unusual attractions, the Cyclorama of the Battle of Gettysburg, opened at Brighton Road and Beech Avenue in 1887. The three-story cyclorama building contained a painting of the pivotal Civil War battle that covered its interior wall, with accompanying wax mannequins and other realistic features. General Jacob Bowman Sweitzer of Beech Avenue participated in the exhibit's grand opening, describing the battle to guests who had paid fifty cents a head. After the Gettysburg exhibit

The Cyclorama Building housed one of Allegheny's more unusual attractions, a painting of the Battle of Gettysburg that covered its interior wall, with accompanying wax mannequins and other realistic features. *Pittsburgh Illustrated*, pt. 9, 1889. Courtesy of Historic Pittsburgh Full-Text Collection, Digital Research Library, University Library System, University of Pittsburgh

was removed in 1888, the Cyclorama Building housed dances, political rallies, boxing matches, and religious services. An attached two-story section of the building contained an ice cream parlor and a catering business.

The city was also growing as an intellectual and cultural center. In the early 1880s, the Western University of Pennsylvania (now the University of Pittsburgh) moved from Downtown Pittsburgh to two former Presbyterian seminary buildings on West North Avenue in Allegheny. Needing more room, the university moved in 1890 to a tract of about ten acres on the east side of Perrysville Avenue, at Observatory Avenue. The school's new three-story Romanesque buildings dwarfed the original Allegheny Observatory, also on the property. Nearby lived John Brashear, the famous Pittsburgh astronomer, and his wife, Phoebe, who had moved to Allegheny City from their modest home on Pittsburgh's South Side Slopes in about 1886, bringing along their daughter and son-in-law, Effie and James McDowell. The industrialist and philanthropist William Thaw financed the Brashears' move to a three-story frame Second Empire home that still stands on Perrysville Avenue on Perry Hilltop.

The new Western University of Pennsylvania on Perry Hilltop, circa 1890, with the original Allegheny Observatory in the background. Carnegie Library of Pittsburgh Pennsylvania Department, Pittsburgh Photographic Library

Brashear, who would earn international recognition as an astronomer and a manufacturer of scientific instruments, erected a frame shop for making lenses and telescopes next to his new house, with Thaw's assistance. It was soon replaced by a three-story brick shop. Brashear taught astronomy at the nearby university and served as its chancellor as well. The growing university would leave Perry Hilltop for Oakland in 1908.

The university's buildings were not the only significant public structures that went up in Allegheny between 1877 and 1890. Henry Hobson Richardson (of the imposing Richardsonian Romanesque style), the most highly esteemed nineteenth-century American architect, made his mark in Allegheny City when he designed Emmanuel Episcopal Church at the corner of Allegheny and West North avenues (1885–86). Biographer Margaret Henderson Floyd called Emmanuel Episcopal "one of Richardson's most memorable designs," although the building's comparatively unornamented form earned it the nickname "the bake oven church." Emmanuel Episcopal's chief

Emmanuel Episcopal Church, 957 West North Avenue. Pittsburgh Steelers/Karl Roser

architectural hallmarks are its inward-sloping walls and its brickwork, a stark contrast with Richardson's elaborate and contemporaneous Allegheny County Courthouse and Jail. It was the last church Richardson designed.

Another notable church building went up across town, on Troy Hill, when Father Suitbert Mollinger of Most Holy Name of Jesus Roman Catholic parish commissioned the construction of a remarkable addition to his parish's complex of buildings. St. Anthony's Chapel, which went up on Harpster Street in 1880, serves as a museum displaying the priest's collection of thousands of saints' images and relics, including bones. Mollinger, who was wealthy, was determined to share his collection of relics—one of the largest in the United States—and he paid for the chapel's construction with his own funds. St. Anthony's chapel continues to attract visitors seeking peace and healing.

While Charles Taze Russell's 1879 founding of the Jehovah's Witnesses in Allegheny City did not leave behind an enduring edifice, it certainly had a lasting effect in the United States and beyond. Russell and his father, Joseph

John Brashear, an internationally recognized astronomer.
Carnegie Library of Pittsburgh Pennsylvania Department, Pittsburgh Photographic Library

L. Russell, had moved to Allegheny City from Pittsburgh in 1877–78, first living at 1004 Cedar Avenue. Together they owned J. L. Russell & Son, a men's shirt business with stores on Federal Street near General Robinson Street and on Fifth Avenue in Downtown Pittsburgh. Charles Taze Russell used the business's storefronts when he founded Bible Students, the original name of the Jehovah's Witnesses, in 1879, with locations at each shirt store. The Jehovah's Witnesses maintained its headquarters in a four-story building that the church owned on Arch Street, near Allegheny's center, from 1889 until 1909, when its headquarters moved to Brooklyn.

Another public institution in Allegheny was the Western State Penitentiary. By the end of the Civil War, western Pennsylvania's population growth had made the penitentiary building that stood in Allegheny's West Park obsolete, and in 1876, officials broke ground for a larger penitentiary along the

Ohio River, at Woods Run. Troy Hill architect Edward M. Butz designed the new prison, as well as (probably) the warden's residence that now stands vacant on its grounds. After the new stone edifice's 1882 completion, some prominent Alleghenians urged city officials to preserve the old prison because of its historical and architectural significance. Nevertheless, the prison was demolished, and the city landscaped its former grounds and built a bandstand; Phipps Conservatory rose on the northern part of its site in the 1890s. Just a few blocks southeast of the old stone prison, Allegheny General Hospital opened its doors on Stockton Avenue, halfway between Federal Street and East Park, in 1886, having been chartered by some of Allegheny's most prominent residents—including Dr. R. B. Mowry, railroad owner William McCreery, wholesale druggist George A. Kelly, and steel manufacturer James Park Jr. The hospital reportedly treated 369 patients in 1886.

Even as western and central Allegheny City strengthened its economic and social links to Pittsburgh, the city's heavily German eastern neighborhoods remained a community apart. Deutschtown absorbed more immigrants, primarily Germans, along with some Bohemians and Czechs. With little room remaining in Deutschtown, established families and some newcomers moved

The Teutonia Männerchor singing society's hall, constructed in 1888 on Phineas Street in Deutschtown. Pittsburgh Steelers/Karl Roser

The Western
State Penitentiary
at Woods Run,
built 1876–1882.
Carnegie Museum
of Art Collection of
Photographs, 1894–1958
(85.4.15), Carnegie
Museum of Art

to Spring Hill, Troy Hill, and the Spring Garden and East Street valleys. Together, all these neighborhoods, especially Deutschtown, formed a vibrant community of a few square miles: residents spoke German; gathered in beer halls and singing societies to drink the lagers their neighbors brewed; and inhaled the scents of beer being brewed, livestock being slaughtered, leather being tanned, and soap and fertilizer being produced. Eastern Allegheny City's German landmarks included the Teutonia Männerchor, a singing society whose 1888 social hall still stands on Phineas Street. At the Teutonia Männerchor and similar clubs, members socialized and held singing competitions with German choirs from all over the northeastern and midwestern United States. George Ott designed the Teutonia Männerchor's new hall in 1888, and the brewer Eberhardt & Ober hired architect Joseph Stillburg to design the brewery buildings at Vinial Street and Troy Hill Road in the early 1880s.

While blue-collar work dominated Allegheny's eastern neighborhoods, those who owned the German community's eastern Allegheny businesses

lived there as well. Adam Reineman, for example, was a real estate investor and bank president who by 1870 had accumulated more wealth than William Thaw, B. F. Jones, Henry Laughlin, or William B. Scaife. Reineman lived in half of a three-story double brick house on Lowrie Street, Troy Hill, constructed in the mid- to late 1870s. A clock tower, later removed, topped the Reineman dwelling. Around the corner, brewery partner John Ober moved into a stick-style house at the top of Troy Hill Road in the 1880s; the Ober family's two-story brick stable, on Lowrie Street, was ornamented by a carved stone horse head. Nearby, also on Troy Hill, Ober's brewing partner William Eberhardt commissioned a Second Empire brick mansion in 1886 that still stands on Harpster Street. Eberhardt's property, of about one acre, was called Washington Park. John Ober's brother, brewery superintendent Charles F. Ober, lived on unassuming Peralta and Constance streets in Deutschtown before he commissioned a large three-story brick house built nearby, on Avery Street, in 1891. Alfred A. Lappe of the M. Lappe & Sons tannery lived

The former Eberhardt and Ober Brewery at Vinial Street and Troy Hill Road is now the home of Penn Brewery. Pittsburgh Steelers/Karl Roser

on Lowrie Street, and William Wettach, owner of a tannery on Spring Garden Avenue, resided in a three-story Second Empire dwelling that survives on Phineas Street. Wettach's wife, Sara, was one of the granddaughters of Nicholas Voegtly, one of Allegheny's most prominent residents earlier in the century.

Even in the heart of Deutschtown, however, not everyone was German. Samuel and Jane Lytle Clark and their children had come to America from County Derry, Ireland, settling on East Ohio Street about 1875. Samuel Clark opened a grocery, and the family lived on the premises. In the early 1880s, the Clarks' teenage son, David, began to make candy in the building. Later in the 1880s, D. L. Clark incorporated and moved to McKeesport, but he returned to the North Side in the twentieth century to expand his candy company and make the nationally famous Clark Bar.

Horsecar lines carried Allegheny residents between their homes and the Diamond and Downtown Pittsburgh. In 1880, the Pittsburgh, Allegheny & Manchester ran from Downtown Pittsburgh to Manchester, with one branch that extended east through Deutschtown and climbed Troy Hill. The Pittsburgh, Allegheny & Pleasant Valley line went north through the Charles Street neighborhood. The city gained further routes in the first half of the 1880s: the Union Passenger Railway built a line from Downtown to Preble Avenue in Manchester, the Transverse Passenger Railway ran between Lawrenceville and Chestnut Street in Deutschtown, and the People's Park Passenger Railroad ran up East Street.

In 1883–84, the four horsecar lines then serving Allegheny City (excluding the unbuilt People's Park) had a combined eighteen miles of track; owned 853 horses and mules; and carried 8,565,345 passengers. In 1888, however, electric streetcars began to replace horsecar lines in Allegheny, with the construction of the Observatory Hill Passenger Railway. In 1890, the Federal Street & Pleasant Valley Passenger Railway reorganized as an electric streetcar network, acquiring the Observatory Hill and People's Park lines; electricity from overhead wires replaced horses on the Pittsburgh, Allegheny & Manchester line in 1891.

The Monongahela Incline, Pittsburgh's first funicular railway, had begun operation between the South Side and Mount Washington in 1870. Private companies went on to build several more inclines in Pittsburgh during the following decade and a half, but none in Allegheny. Several attempts to build inclines in Allegheny in the first half of the 1880s faltered. The considerable capital investment necessary to construct a successful funicular—for real estate, engineering fees, the construction of tracks and station houses full of machinery, and the purchase and installation of the wooden incline cars that glided up and down the hillsides—evidently presented too high a hill to climb. None of Allegheny's early projected inclines were ever built.

In a six-week period over the summer of 1886, however, three Allegheny incline companies incorporated that were later able to carry out their plans, at least to some extent. The Ridgewood Incline Railway Company, whose incline ran between North Charles Street and Ridgewood Street on Perry Hilltop, was the first to incorporate. Its organizers held a public meeting in June 1886, inviting Alleghenians to purchase stock to help finance the new venture. Federal Street real-estate broker Alexander Leggate, who lived on McClintock Avenue on Perry Hilltop, was the company's chairman and ran the public meeting. When the Ridgewood Incline Railway Company was chartered on July 10 of that year, its forty-six members had contributed a total of $6,000. This investment group was dominated by Alleghenians, particularly those who lived in or near the neighborhoods the Ridgewood Incline was to serve. Alexander Leggate put in $375; funeral director Hudson Samson of North Avenue gave $500; and Frederick Andriessen, a liquor dealer and a neighbor of Leggate, invested $250. John G. Hastings, a Poplar Street carpenter, B. H. Culbertson, a clerk who lived on McClintock Avenue, and John Morton, who had no occupation and lived on Perrysville Avenue, each chipped in the $25 minimum. The Ridgewood Incline began operation in time to be listed in the 1887 Pittsburgh directory, but it ran for only one or two years, and by 1890, fire had damaged its structure. Although the Ridgewood Incline might have been Allegheny's first operating incline, it was also the city's shortest-lived.

Meanwhile, on Allegheny's east side, the Troy Hill Incline Plane Company and the Nunnery Hill Inclined Plane Company incorporated in July and August 1886. The Troy Hill Incline Plane Company's charter stated that the company intended to construct an incline that would carry "freight and

The Adam Reineman double house, built in the 1870s on Lowrie Street, Troy Hill, with its original clock tower, later removed. Courtesy of Mildred McGlothlin

passengers from a point or points on Spring Garden Street up and over Troy Hill to a point or points on the West Penn Railroad [near East Ohio Street] between [Rialto] Street and [Pindam] Street." The Troy Hill Incline's southeast section, which ran parallel to and west of Rialto Street, was 370 feet long and earned $8,247 in 1892. It operated until about 1898; today its upper station survives as part of a bank branch. Construction of the Nunnery Hill line likely overlapped with construction of Allegheny's other two inclines, although Nunnery Hill, notably, was the first incline in the Pittsburgh area with a curved track. The 1,100-foot Nunnery Hill line started at the northeast corner of Federal and Henderson streets, in a two-story red-brick building that survives as a dwelling. The incline, which earned $2,375 in 1892, ran east along Henderson Street for a few hundred feet, then curved northeast, running just west of a quarry that is now a ball field and ending on the east side of Fineview's Meadville Street, at or near the present site of a war memorial.

Samuel P. Langley, noted astronomer and the first director of the Allegheny Observatory.
Library of Congress Prints and Photographs Division (LC-H261-9495-A), Washington, D.C.

Pittsburgh civil engineer Samuel Diescher, who is probably best known for his work on the Monongahela Incline, designed many of Pittsburgh's inclines and possibly all four of Allegheny's, including Nunnery Hill's pioneering curve.

Allegheny's last incline was the Clifton Avenue Incline Plane Company, cofounded by Allegheny businessman William McCreery, who had made his fortune building railroads and working as an entrepreneur and contractor. By the mid-1880s, McCreery, who was president of the Pleasant Valley Passenger Railway horsecar line, had lived on Allegheny's Clifton Avenue for nearly twenty years. His estate, with its rambling frame house, looked down from Perry Hilltop's western cliff to the North Charles Street neighborhood. In late 1887, McCreery and his family left Clifton Avenue to move to 940 North Lincoln Avenue in Allegheny West, and McCreery launched the Clifton Avenue Incline Plane Company, which ran from Strauss Street, where it connected with the Pleasant Valley line, to the old McCreery property on the Clifton Avenue hilltop. McCreery now developed his former estate by commissioning rows of three-story brick party-wall rental houses. It seemed like a perfect business scheme: his new incline made the rowhouses more accessible, justifying higher rents, and his tenants in turn paid to ride his incline. However advantageously placed, the Clifton Avenue Incline did not last much longer than the Troy Hill and Nunnery Hill lines. Although a 1925 plat map depicts the Clifton Avenue Incline, the funicular had apparently ceased operation long before that year.

In spite of his incline's failure, McCreery's 1887 move from Clifton Avenue to North Lincoln was still a precursor of the city's future, as wealthy families continued to cluster in and near Allegheny West during the later decades of the nineteenth century. The following chapter illustrates that Allegheny City's fabled Millionaires' Row was still taking shape.

CHAPTER 6

The City of Millionaires
Allegheny's Elite, 1890–1910

A N INCREASING NUMBER of wealthy families lived in Allegheny City in the closing decades of the nineteenth century, particularly in the small neighborhood that has come to be called Allegheny West. The concentration of wealth was unprecedented in western Pennsylvania, and made it one of the wealthiest communities in America. Its legacy endures more than a century later in bricks and mortar and in neighborhood lore. Back in 1870, as Pittsburgh and Allegheny's economy boomed, Pittsburgh's East End contained the region's most significant grouping of wealthy individuals, with twenty residents with assets of at least $500,000 (about $8.5 million in 2010) making their homes in Pittsburgh, most in Shadyside, Squirrel Hill, Oakland, or East Liberty. Glass manufacturer Alexander Chambers, the only millionaire in either Pittsburgh or Allegheny, lived on Fifth Avenue in Shadyside. Across the river, Allegheny City, whose population was 62 percent the size of Pittsburgh's in 1870, was home to only four men with $500,000 or more in assets. Its wealthiest citizens were the Troy Hill land baron Adam Reineman and Archibald McFarland, a lumber dealer who lived on Ridge Avenue, with assets of $750,000 each. David DeHaven, a stove manufacturer worth $730,000, and iron mill owner Jacob Painter, worth $660,000, made their homes on Sherman Avenue near West Ohio Street and North Canal Street near Chestnut Street, respectively. Wealth in Allegheny City, to the extent that it was present, was more evenly distributed across the neighborhoods in 1870 than at the end of the century

In 1892, as national media attention to wealth increased, the *New York Tribune's American Millionaires* found a whopping forty-four millionaires living in Allegheny ($1 million in 1892 would be equal to about $24 million in 2010). Pittsburgh, whose population was more than twice Allegheny's 105,000, was home to thirty-five. Allegheny's wealth was also becoming more concentrated than it had been in the city's early days: thirty-six of the city's forty-four millionaires lived in Allegheny West or on adjoining blocks in Manchester. Five made their homes in the city's core, within a few blocks of the intersection of Federal and Ohio streets. Three lived in mansions that occupied the present site of Allegheny General Hospital, and one resided in Fineview.

Until 1910, as the region's core industries continued to boom, its wealthy population kept pace, with about three dozen of the area's richest families commissioning, occupying, and sometimes enlarging grand homes in Allegheny West. Brighton Road's ten millionaires in 1892 included iron and steel manufacturers B. F. Jones and Henry Phipps Jr.; iron mill owners Jacob Painter and James McCutcheon; department store partner Jacob Kaufmann; and Harry Darlington, who had made his fortune in brewing and other pursuits. Ten more millionaires lived on Western Avenue, including iron pipe mill owner A. M. Byers, soon to erect a mansion that still stands on Ridge Avenue; iron manufacturer William H. Singer; distiller Asher Guckenheimer; brewer and tube manufacturer Joshua Rhodes; and members of the Hostetter family of stomach bitters fame. Dr. David and Kate Irwin Rankin had the stone-fronted Richardsonian Romanesque mansion at 914 Western Avenue built in 1893, providing both a home for their family and an office for Dr. Rankin, a Civil War surgeon and Allegheny City medical examiner. Kate Irwin Rankin had grown up only a block away, her father, Henry Irwin, a partner in the rope walk. In 1898 the Rankins would sell their mansion to Dr. Roland Thatcher White for $18,000. Dr. White, a homeopath and "electro-therapeutist," also practiced medicine in the house while living there with his wife and his mother.

Although Ridge Avenue would come to be known as Allegheny's most illustrious address, it was home to only six millionaires in 1892: H. Sellers McKee, of the South Side glassmaking family; foundryman Abraham Garrison; and members of the Denny family, whose extensive landholdings in Allegheny and Pittsburgh extended back generations. James Laughlin Jr. of Jones & Laughlin, Pennsylvania Railroad purchasing agent William Mullins, and iron-forge owner Calvin Wells occupied handsome homes on North Lincoln Avenue, while Beech Avenue's millionaires in 1892 included two branches of the Denny family and John Porterfield, a retired grocer.

These wealthy families would continue to change the shape of Allegheny West until 1910, when the neighborhood's last great mansions were built.

Some commissioned additions that transformed large post–Civil War row-houses into palatial dwellings with fifteen or twenty rooms, or even more. Joseph Walton, for example, worked such a transformation, enlarging an 1860s rowhouse on North Lincoln Avenue into a Romanesque-influenced mansion for his daughter, Ida Walton Scully, and her husband, South Side glass manufacturer James W. Scully, in a series of incremental additions during the 1890s. The mansion's servants' wing featured an elevator from Pittsburgh's historic Marshall Elevator Company and an attached carriage entrance that faced Chapel Way. One block west, on North Lincoln Avenue, Elizabeth and William Thaw Jr. doubled the size of a rowhouse in the late 1880s. In 1899 Elizabeth Thaw, by then widowed, commissioned an addition of like size, creating a three-story brick mansion with approximately seventy-five feet of frontage. William, chairman of the Hecla Coal Company and a patron of the astronomers John Brashear and Samuel Langley of the Allegheny Observatory, was also a half brother of the notorious Harry Thaw of Pittsburgh's East End, who would murder famous architect Stanford White at Madison Square Garden in New York in 1906. Elizabeth, active in several civic groups, was a notable supporter of the Pittsburgh Orchestra Association. The house they left behind, at 930 North Lincoln Avenue, still stands, now used as offices and living space.

The southwest corner of Ridge and Galveston avenues saw the construction of what would be Allegheny's largest mansion between 1896 and 1898: the Byers-Lyon house, an enormous Flemish Renaissance–style double mansion. Ironmaster Alexander McBurney Byers was sixty-eight in 1896, when he asked the prominent architectural firm Alden & Harlow to design this L-shaped double house, whose form was unique in the area, with its courtyard facing the corner of Ridge and Galveston avenues and interior doorways connecting its two sides. The building itself, with brownstone trim, was clad in Roman (or Pompeian) brick, a long, thin, iron-flecked brick generally reserved for the homes of upper-middle-class and wealthy families. Byers was president of A. M. Byers & Company, which manufactured iron pipe on a five-acre site on the South Side and in Girard, Ohio. He was also president of the Iron City National Bank, a partner in the Girard Iron Company, and a director of three of George Westinghouse's companies and other corporations. He and his wife, Martha Fleming Byers, would live in the mansion's larger side, at 905 Ridge Avenue. Their daughter and son-in-law, Maude and John Denniston Lyon, would occupy the house's other side, at 901 Ridge.

The Thaw mansion on North Lincoln Avenue prior to its 1899 expansion. *Pittsburgh Illustrated*, pt. II, 1889. Courtesy of Historic Pittsburgh Full-Text Collection, Digital Research Library, University Library System, University of Pittsburgh

Lyon, a young banker when the house was built, was later vice-president of the Union National Bank and president of the Safe Deposit and Trust Company. The young couple's marriage in early 1896 was probably a factor in the house's construction.

Construction began in late 1896, when Byers received a permit to build a three-and-a–half story $80,000 brick mansion at Ridge and Galveston avenues. Newspapers later stated that the construction cost was $450,000, an unlikely sum at nearly twice what the Allegheny County Courthouse and Jail had cost in the 1880s. On January 21, 1899, the Byers and Lyon families threw open their doors for a housewarming party, welcoming families whose carriages brought them through the iron gates to the front entrance. "All of society," the *Pittsburgh Press* reported, "was present at the reception, both men and women being asked, as has become the custom at Saturday afternoon affairs." By the time he moved to Ridge and Galveston avenues, Byers had spent $766,625 to assemble what was reportedly the most significant art collection in western Pennsylvania. Alden & Harlow had designed the house in part to serve as a showcase for Byers's art, and undoubtedly, guests at the family's 1899 party were invited to view Peter Paul Rubens's *Saint Andrew;* Jean Baptiste Camillle Corot's *Danse des Nymphes;* and works by Van Dyke, Rousseau, Thomas Gainsborough, Adrian Lerrauly, and J. F. Raffaeli.

The Byers-Lyon home was perfectly designed to host such lavish entertainments: its sloping site made room for aboveground space at the rear of the house, which held the kitchens and other support areas. Notably, the Byers and Lyon kitchens were separate but adjoining, so that both could be used for large events. The 1900 census recorded six household staff living with the Byers family—a butler, a laundress, two cooks, and two chambermaids—while a butler and three other servants lived with the Lyon family. A Richardsonian Romanesque brick carriage house at the rear of the property, approximately one hundred by forty feet, contained living space for a driver, Henry Everard, his wife, Carrie, and their teenage children.

Byers, however, occupied his palatial home for less than two years, dying in a New York hotel in 1900. The *New York Times* noted that Byers had been depressed since the death of his son a year earlier. "Life without my son," he was reported to have said, "holds no joy for me." Appraisers valued his estate at $1,925,274.50. In 1901, Martha Byers gave Yale University $100,000 to build a social and religious center in honor of her husband and her son, the latter of whom had studied there. Today Byers Hall still stands on the Yale campus.

The Byers, of course, were not the only wealthy Alleghenians who entertained lavishly. Pittsburgh newspapers and two Pittsburgh society magazines, the *Bulletin* and the *Index,* reported on their housewarming parties, teas, charitable events, balls, card parties, club meetings, and weddings. In January 1895, the *Bulletin* observed that at "the height of the social season . . . fashionable people were kept going from one place to another so continuously that many members of the smart set [the social elite] were likely to become comparative strangers in their respective homes." Within one week, for example, Mrs. George E. Painter of Bidwell Street in Manchester had held both a Wednesday luncheon and a Saturday breakfast at the Duquesne Club, her guests including women from Allegheny's Semple, Watson, Chalfant, Layng, and Byers families.

The reach of the wealthy families who occupied Allegheny's Millionaires' Row stretched well beyond the enclaves of high society. The largest houses along Ridge and North Lincoln avenues and Brighton Road, for example, employed scores of servants. Census records show that the Jones family, at 801 Brighton Road, had eight live-in household staff persons in 1900; in 1910, when only Mary Jones and her daughter Mary Laughlin remained in the house, eleven servants attended their needs. The Jones servants included chambermaids, ladies' maids, butlers, laundresses, cooks, kitchen maids, a footman, and a groom. The 1900 census enumerator found five servants and two coachmen attending William and Alice Jones Willock and their only child, at 705 Brighton Road, and thirteen waiting on the A. E. and Mary Painter family in their stone mansion at 815 Brighton Road, dubbed "the Allegheny Palace" by newspapers when it was built in 1887.

Allegheny City servants were primarily of European origin or descent, more with roots in Ireland than in any other country. After 1900, the city's servants also included some Eastern European immigrants and a few African Americans. In Allegheny and Pittsburgh, most servants lived in the attics, although the largest houses of Allegheny West had rear wings with small rooms in which servants lived. Almost all servants were single women, most young, some middle-aged. Some of the wealthiest families employed men as butlers. Coachmen, typically single men, occupied rooms in carriage houses along alleys; some were African American. A small number were married, their families living with them in what were probably better living quarters than the rooms occupied by their unmarried peers.

One of the largest of these carriage houses and driver's quarters went up in 1895 at 713 Ridge Avenue. Matilda W. Denny had received a permit to construct the two-story, seventy-two-by-thirty-two-foot brick building for $4,700, comparable to the price of a brick single-family home of eight to ten rooms at the time, replacing three smaller stables. Matilda Denny, the eleventh of twelve children of Harmar and Elizabeth F. O'Hara Denny, owned considerable property in Allegheny and Pittsburgh through inheritance from Elizabeth's father, James O'Hara. She had lived in Downtown Pittsburgh until 1892, when she bought the Ridge Avenue property, which held a brick mansion that—like the new carriage house she would soon build—spanned

The Denny mansion on Ridge Avenue near Brighton Road, Allegheny West, in the Richardsonian Romanesque style. Courtesy of Pittsburgh History & Landmarks Foundation

its entire seventy-two-foot width. Denny never married, giving much of her time to the Pittsburgh chapter of the Daughters of the American Revolution (DAR), the First Presbyterian Church of Pittsburgh, and many society activities. She used her DAR position as a platform to advocate for transforming Pittsburgh's gritty Point into a park commemorating Fort Pitt, a dream that the DAR realized decades after her passing. She lived in her mansion, with a cook, a housemaid, and a waitress residing in its servants' quarters, until she died in 1918.

While each of the six houses in the 700 block of Ridge Avenue had a carriage house or stable at the rear of its lot, the one Matilda Denny built was by far the largest, and it would house coachman John Edelman and his family for twenty-five years. Edelman had started working for the Denny family when they lived on Penn Avenue, in or before the early 1870s. By the time the Edelmans moved to the new carriage house in 1895, John and Mary Edelman had named two of their four children—Harmar Denny Edelman and Matilda Denny Edelman—for John's employers. John, all told, would work for the family for more than half a century, and his son Harmar Denny Edelman would be a Denny family coachman as a young man. As employees of one of Pittsburgh's wealthiest families, the Edelmans lived better than most Pittsburgh servants. They were able to travel to visit relatives in England in the 1890s, a trip, later generations suspected, that Matilda Denny might have funded. When Matilda Denny died in 1918, her will left $1,000 to John Edelman and $50 to any other servant who had worked for her for more than a year. John and Harmar Edelman and their wives then moved to the Harmar and Elizabeth Denny mansion at 811 Ridge Avenue, where John, by then in his seventies, worked as caretaker and Harmar as chauffeur. John Edelman would work for the Denny family until a few years before he died in 1932, at age ninety-one; Harmar Denny Edelman would remain with the family into the early 1930s. Family members remembered daughter Matilda Denny Edelman as a woman who took care to observe correct manners and set a proper table, perhaps influenced by the trappings of upper-class life she had long observed. A member of the Allegheny City Epworth League and an enthusiastic elocutionist, Matilda Denny Edelman often gave readings at events sponsored by Allegheny's Methodist and Presbyterian congregations.

Western Allegheny City's wealthy and middle-class residents also commissioned handsome new church buildings throughout the 1890s. In 1892, the First Methodist Church of Pittsburgh amicably split into two congregations, based in Allegheny and the East End. The Allegheny group established Trinity

Methodist Protestant Church at 1018 Bidwell Street in Manchester (now Carter Chapel), designed in the Richardsonian Romanesque style by the firm of Riddle & Keirn. Their counterparts in Pittsburgh's East End founded the First Methodist Protestant Church of Pittsburgh at South Aiken Avenue and Howe Street, its building designed by Frederick Osterling. Calvary Methodist Episcopal Church (now Calvary United Methodist) at Beech and Allegheny avenues was also founded in the division of a Downtown congregation. The cornerstone of its beautiful Gothic Revival stone building, designed by architects Martin Vrydaugh and Thomas Wolfe, was set in place on May 18, 1893. The cornerstone for its sister church, Christ Methodist Episcopal (now First United Methodist Church of Pittsburgh), was placed at Centre and Liberty avenues in the East End. Calvary's stained-glass windows were produced by Louis Comfort Tiffany.

Calvary United Methodist Church, Beech and Allegheny avenues. Pittsburgh Steelers/Karl Roser

The social prominence of Calvary Methodist's members, marked by such beautiful accouterments, was evident in the lifestyles of congregants such as Albert and Ella Horne, who owned 924 Beech Avenue between 1878 and 1911. Albert Horne, a cousin of Joseph Horne, was a partner in the Joseph Horne Company, a Pittsburgh department store that operated for more than a century. In 1910, the Hornes' daughter Helen married real estate broker Edward J. House in a ceremony at Calvary Methodist. The *Bulletin* enthused about the details of the reception at Horne's home on Beech: "A small reception followed in the home of the bride, Mr. And Mrs. Horne receiving with the bridal party. White chrysanthemums with ferns were used in the drawing room, and the dining table was entirely in yellow. The center table had a centerpiece of yellow chrysanthemums tied with bows of yellow ribbon. The table for the bridal party was in an upstairs room, and had covers laid for 20. White orchids and chrysanthemums formed the centerpiece, and over the table were white satin bells and white chrysanthemums."

Next door to the Hornes, Charles and Mary Ann Machesney added one story and an attic to 922 Beech Avenue, remodeling the house with Colonial Revival features in 1899. Their son, attorney H. A. Machesney, was living there when he commissioned the construction of what is now the Benedum-Trees Building on Fourth Avenue, Downtown, in 1905. The granite, brick, and terra-cotta skyscraper was called the Machesney Building until 1913, when oilmen Michael Benedum and Joseph Trees bought it.

Other neighbors on the 900 block of Beech included the nationally known mystery writer Mary Roberts Rinehart and her husband, Dr. Stanley Rinehart, who rented the substantial McCook house (built in 1883) at Beech and Allegheny avenues between 1907 and 1911. While her husband practiced medicine on the North Side and in the Downtown Pittsburgh Jenkins Arcade, Mary Roberts Rinehart wrote her best-known work, *The Circular Staircase*, in 1907–8, in a small second-floor study. She was then thirty-one, and the success that she was starting to enjoy enabled her family to pay eighty dollars per month to rent the large dwelling, rather than the sixty dollars they had previously paid to rent an attached house on Western Avenue. The Rinehart sons, Stan Jr., Alan, and Frederick, were between ages four and nine when the family moved to the Beech Avenue house. The boys occasionally got into mischief, to their parents' embarrassment. Once they attached a rubber hose containing liquid soap to a household gas jet to blow bubbles, then lit the floating bubbles, burning the ceiling. They practiced marksmanship by

Benches in the interior of the Pittsburgh, Fort Wayne & Chicago Railway station in Allegheny City. Thomas & Katherine Detre Library and Archives, Sen. John Heinz History Center

shooting pigeons in the tower of Calvary Methodist, across the street, sending the birds to fall directly in front of a local police officer. The family left Beech Avenue in 1911, moving to a mansion in Osborne, next to Sewickley.

Pittsburgh Chronicle-Telegraph editor Joseph Siebeneck and his family also lived on Beech Avenue, at the corner of Galveston, moving there in 1891 or early 1892. Siebeneck, born in Germany, had come to the United States in 1852, becoming part owner of the *Pittsburgh Chronicle* in 1863 and acquiring the remaining interest in the newspaper in 1874. The paper had merged with the *Evening Telegraph* to become the *Chronicle-Telegraph* in 1884. (Siebeneck's father-in-law, Josiah King, was editor of the *Pittsburgh Commercial Gazette*.) Siebeneck purchased the Beech Avenue property in 1888, initially living in a house that had stood on the property since about 1869. In 1891, the Siebeneck family stayed with relatives at 851 Beech while their home at 855 was either

Mystery writer and Allegheny resident Mary Roberts Rinehart. Library of Congress
Prints and Photographs Division (LC-DIG-npcc-27413), Washington, D.C.

demolished and replaced or radically remodeled. The house that now occupies the property has a footprint similar to that of the original dwelling, but
the details of its construction—its round corner tower, shingled frieze, asym-
metrical façade, rough-cut stone lintels, and front door with strap hinges—
place it firmly in the 1890s.

Siebeneck's descendants would also leave their mark on the city. One of
his daughters, Mary Siebeneck, announced her engagement to the prominent Pittsburgh architect Thorsten Billquist in 1901, marrying him in 1904,
in a quiet ceremony in Cobourg, Ontario. Billquist, who had emigrated from
Sweden in 1887, first worked for McKim Mead & White, whose principals included the brilliant but erratic Stanford White. He had settled in Pittsburgh
in 1893, employed as a draftsman by Longfellow Alden & Harlow before
establishing his own practice on Sixth Avenue in 1895. After their marriage,
Billquist's practice continued to flourish; his best-known work may have been
the Allegheny Observatory in Riverview Park. Until both died, in 1923, Mary

and Thorsten lived at 855 Beech Avenue, with a rambling summer house on Linden Place in Sewickley. Henry Siebeneck, Mary Bilquist's unmarried brother and a Downtown attorney, lived with them, sharing ownership of 855 Beech after Joseph Siebeneck died in 1906. Henry Siebeneck estimated the home's value at $20,000 for the 1930 census. He sold the house in 1935, receiving only $5,500 after the Depression and changing residential patterns had eroded property values in his neighborhood. The house subsequently deteriorated, but it was rehabilitated as apartments in the early twenty-first century.

Another notable Allegheny address, now 849 North Lincoln Avenue, was built as an Italianate double house in 1866–67 by Pittsburgh flour merchant John W. Simpson, who sold both sides of the double house to separate owners in 1867. After a succession of owners, steel manufacturer William H. Singer of Western Avenue purchased the east half in 1895 and the west half in 1906. One of his four children, artist William H. Singer Jr., lived in the east half between

Newspapers nicknamed the Painter mansion at 815 Brighton Road "the Allegheny Palace" when it was built in 1887. *Art Work of Pittsburg*, pt. 3, 1893. Courtesy of Historic Pittsburgh Full-Text Collection, Digital Research Library, University Library System, University of Pittsburgh

1896 and 1901. Then, in 1907, at a family dinner celebrating his fiftieth wedding anniversary, Singer presented each of his children with property and in-
vestments worth $4 million. The gifts became public knowledge months later,
when a *New York Times* reporter examined documents that Singer had filed
in Allegheny County. "Mr. Singer," the *Times* reported, "has reached an age
when, although still prominent in business and financial circles, he desires to
see his children comfortably settled in life and to be relieved of the cares of his
large fortune." This transfer of fortune appears to have also been the catalyst
for the transformation of the forty-year-old double house into a single-family
home in 1907, an $8,000 project that created an imposing Colonial Revival
mansion. The garage at the rear of the property was also built in 1907, for
$3,700. The house was remodeled as a residence for Singer's son and business
associate, George Harton Singer. In 1910, George Harton Singer and his wife,
Charlotte, employed a laundress, a chambermaid, a cook, and a coachman,

Many of the area's wealthiest families lived on Brighton Road, seen here at its intersection
with Lincoln Avenue. *Art Work of Pittsburg*, pt. 7, 1893. Courtesy of Historic Pittsburgh Full-Text
Collection, Digital Research Library, University Library System, University of Pittsburgh

who all lived at 849 North Lincoln. The Singers and their children, however, remained in the house for only a few years before moving to Sewickley.

Elsewhere, property owners demolished viable houses that dated to the neighborhood's first period of rapid growth, in the 1860s, in their place erecting some of the largest dwellings ever built on either side of the river. In 1892, for example, Harry and Mary Elizabeth Darlington moved into a new four-story Richardsonian Romanesque house at 721 Brighton Road, on the site of an earlier dwelling that had stood for about thirty years. The architect George Orth had made the most of the twenty-five-foot-wide lot, designing a house that is more than one hundred feet deep, with a grand stairway. Fifteen years later, Harry Darlington removed three sizeable brick homes in order to build a Tudor Revival mansion for his twenty-year-old son, Harry Jr., at 709 Brighton Road. Joshua W. Rhodes, son of Joshua Rhodes of Western Avenue, removed a mansion at 920 North Lincoln Avenue so that he could commission an even larger Tudor Revival pile on its site in 1903. Rhodes, then thirty-one, had the new house built across the back alley from the Western Avenue home in which he had grown up. In 1908, second-generation steelman B. F. Jones Jr. replaced an older dwelling at the northwest corner of Brighton Road and Ridge Avenue with a forty-two-room steel-framed mansion designed by Rutan and Russell. The new house dwarfed the substantial house in which Jones had grown up, one block to the north.

Between 1909 and 1911, Allegheny West's last three mansions took shape at the northeast and northwest corners of Ridge and Galveston avenues. Two were on the site that the Graybar Electric Company now occupies. Until 1908–9, this site held the Pittsburgh and Allegheny Orphan Asylum, which at this point moved to Perry Hilltop, occupying the campus that the Western University of Pennsylvania had vacated when it moved to Oakland. Mary F. Jones Laughlin, a daughter of B. F. Jones, subsequently purchased the 1.64-acre asylum property for $100,000 in April 1909, a parcel measuring 250 feet wide along Ridge and North Lincoln avenues and about 286 feet deep along Galveston Avenue. Three weeks later, Laughlin gave the western 115 feet of the property to her daughter Mary Laughlin Robinson and gave the eastern 135 feet to another daughter, Madelaine Laughlin Alexander. The Laughlin sisters and their husbands then commissioned the construction of two of the largest and most elaborate dwellings ever built in the Pittsburgh area.

Mary Laughlin and William C. Robinson, president of the national Electric Products Company, which manufactured conduits, electrical wire, cables, and related products, hired society architect George Orth to design their house at Ridge and Galveston, not long before Orth designed the William Penn Snyder mansion directly across the street. The two-and-a-half-story house, built by the George A. Cochrane & Company for an estimated $65,000 in late 1909 and 1910, contained twenty-four rooms and measured about one hundred feet wide and ninety-five feet deep, with its rear ell. One year later, the Robinsons had a two-story secondary dwelling built toward the rear of the property. This smaller but still substantial house was of brick construction with a tile roof, about thirty-four by forty feet, and cost an estimated $6,000. The Robinsons would live at 900 Ridge Avenue until the early 1930s, spending summers at Franklin Farm, the Sewickley Heights estate that B. F. Jones had created, their five children all attending exclusive private schools.

Madelaine Laughlin Alexander and her husband, Rev. Maitland Alexander, received a permit to build 920 Ridge Avenue in August 1909. This two-and-a-half-story brick and stone house, said to be the first fireproof private dwelling in Pittsburgh, contained twenty rooms, measuring one hundred feet wide, with a rear ell that stretched eighty feet toward North Lincoln Avenue. The stated construction cost was $65,000, although years later the *Press* reported costs at $175,000. In 1910, the Alexanders had a substantial brick garage built on the property: constructed for $7,000, it cost as much as many of the single-family homes then being built in Pittsburgh's East End. The Alexander property was at least partly enclosed by a buttressed brick wall that was topped by carved stone ornamentation. The mansion's architect is not identified, but it is possible that George Orth, who designed the companion house for the Robinson family, designed the Alexander house as well.

However, although the Alexander house was among the largest and most ornate of Allegheny's mansions, it was also the shortest-lived: built in 1909–10, vacant from about 1931, and demolished in 1938. As thirty-five demolition laborers began their work at 920 Ridge Avenue, the *Pittsburgh Press* described the home as "one of the show places of a generation ago . . . doomed by the shifting sense of values that followed the World War." Then, in 1939 or 1940, the Robinsons had their former home at 900 Ridge Avenue demolished. The Robinson children inherited the property following the death of Mary Laughlin Robinson, in 1947, and less than a year later, they sold the property to the Graybar Electric Company, which also purchased the former Alexander property.

The third of the intersection's notable mansions, and the last to be built in Allegheny West, was the William Penn Snyder house, which rose at the northeast corner of Ridge and Galveston avenues between late 1910 and late 1911. George A. Cochrane & Company, of Columbus Avenue in Manchester, constructed the massive dwelling for an estimated $125,000. The firm had long enjoyed a sterling reputation on the North Side, having built Calvary Methodist Church and the Harry Darlington house, among others. The mansion's construction required the demolition of a substantial three-story brick dwelling and a two-story brick carriage house, both standing when William Penn Snyder bought the property for $40,000 in May 1910.

Snyder, born in 1861 in Hollidaysburg, Pennsylvania, had worked as a teenager for Schoenberger & Company, which operated an iron mill in Pittsburgh's Strip District. He eventually became a partner in Leishman & Snyder, iron brokers in Pittsburgh. Leishman (best remembered for having helped Henry Clay Frick fend off Alexander Berkman's 1892 assassination attempt) soon left the business, but Snyder remained an iron broker for the rest of his life, serving as president of the Clairton Steel Company and founding the Shenango Furnace Company and the Shenango Steamship Company. Now, to design their new family home, Snyder and his wife, Mary, like the Robinsons, hired George Orth, who had designed their Sewickley Heights country estate, Wilpen Hall, in the late 1890s. In addition, Orth had designed the Colonial Revival mansion on Ellsworth Avenue at Colonial Place in Shadyside that served as the Snyder family's city home during the first few years of the twentieth century. Now Orth created a mansion for the Snyders with Classical Revival features and a boxy form that may have fit in Manhattan but was a novelty in Pittsburgh. The house still stands, clad in brownstone, a dark brown sandstone that was used commonly in New York and elsewhere on the eastern seaboard but infrequently in western Pennsylvania. A 1910 *Pittsburgh Press* article reported that the brownstone had come from Longmeadow, Massachusetts, whose quarries supplied brownstone for some of H. H. Richardson's New England buildings and countless Manhattan and Brooklyn townhouses. Later sources said that the stone came from Hummelstown, Pennsylvania, a source of brownstone for thousands of notable buildings in the mid-Atlantic states.

Whatever the brownstone's source, the four-story mansion was ostentatious and impressive, occupying its entire 48-by-133-foot lot. Orth had included in his design an iron-gated quarter-circle interior driveway, reaching from Galveston Avenue to Chapel Way, that led to a six-car integral garage.

Ridge Avenue was
Allegheny's most
prestigious address.
Pittsburgh Illustrated, pt. 10,
1889. Courtesy of Historic
Pittsburgh Full-Text
Collection, Digital Research
Library, University Library
System, University of
Pittsburgh

Guests whose chauffeurs delivered them to that urban equivalent of a port-cochere would immediately gaze down upon the mansion's grand ballroom, lit by crystal chandeliers, in the front of what would otherwise be the basement level. The house's main floors featured elaborate woodwork, including a three-story stairway and ornate paneling, stained glass, ornamental wall and ceiling plaster, imported carved mantels, a pushbutton elevator, a pipe organ, and a third-story billiard room. A built-in vacuum system aided servants with housekeeping chores, and an air-filtering and -circulation system removed dirty particles from Pittsburgh's notoriously sooty air and cooled air in the basement before it circulated to the rest of the house.

The Snyder family moved into their new mansion around New Year's Day 1912 and held a formal housewarming party in mid-January. The party doubled as a coming-out ball for daughter Mary Black Snyder. The *Pittsburgh Press* called the brand-new mansion "one of the most magnificent homes in the city," noting that "the white and gold ballroom on the first floor of the house, with its ivory-beamed ceiling traced in gold, and yellow brocade paneled walls, has an ivory and gold balcony with a little den at the farther end." The newspaper added, "The ballroom, which will accommodate about 250 guests, is the largest private ballroom in the city and is a dream of ivory, crystal and gold. The rest of the house is perfect in detail and the decorations were arranged in simple effect, so that the artistic design of the rooms might not be obscured." William Penn Snyder died in 1921, still running the businesses he had founded; Mary Snyder remained in the brownstone mansion at Ridge and Galveston for a short time afterward.

Like other area elites, William and Mary Snyder purchased automobiles in the early twentieth century, cars then expensive enough that they were only rich men's playthings. Wealthy automobile enthusiasts soon formed the Pittsburgh Automobile Club, which began holding races in Allegheny City on a one-mile oval clay track on Brunot's Island, at Woods Run in the Ohio River, in 1904. The Brunot's Island racetrack had wide-banked lanes for safety, grandstands, and a clubhouse. A ferry brought Alleghenians to the track from a point on the shore about four hundred feet south of the Western Penitentiary property, while Pittsburgh spectators reached the island in boats that departed from the foot of Wood Street, along the Monongahela Wharf. The island was unrecognizable as the place that the famed explorers Lewis and Clark had visited 101 years earlier. In October 1904, Barney Oldfield, a twenty-six-year-old racecar driver, drove his eight-cylinder Green Dragon, with 120 horsepower, in a Pittsburgh Automobile Club event at Brunot's Island. Oldfield by then was nationally known, holding world speed records; he would go on to race at the opening of the 1909 Indianapolis Speedway and in later Indianapolis competitions. In 1904, when Oldfield raced against locals on Brunot's Island, the *Bulletin* reported, "Pittsburg will furnish several men who will drive their own cars and who can hold their own in almost any company."

The elite of Allegheny City founded and supported numerous area institutions, not just sporting groups like the Pittsburgh Automobile Club. Nearly all belonged to the venerable Duquesne Club in Downtown Pittsburgh, for example. The Allegheny Preparatory School opened in 1898 in a house that Mary F. Laughlin owned at the northwest corner of North Lincoln Avenue and Rope Way. A majority of the school's twenty-five charter members were Allegheny West residents, and the remainder lived within a few blocks of the neighborhood. During the school's first year, its trustees were Harry Darlington, banker James J. Donnell of North Lincoln Avenue, William R. Thompson of North Lincoln Avenue, patent solicitor William L. Pierce of Western Avenue, attorney Thomas H. Bakewell of Western Avenue, locomotive manufacturer Wilson Miller of North Lincoln Avenue, steelmaker David Parke of East North Avenue, Harmar D. Denny of Ridge Avenue, and iron manufacturer Richard G. Wood of Ridge Avenue. In 1900, the school's trustees commissioned the construction of the Allegheny Preparatory School at Lincoln and Galveston avenues, purchasing the property from the Nevin family for $28,000 and then having a row of small rental houses on the site demolished. The new school building was designed by Thomas H. Scott, with Classical Revival and Colonial Revival influences, and constructed by Cochrane & Davis of Allegheny City for an estimated $38,000. Henry Carr Pearson, a young Harvard graduate who had authored a textbook on writing in classical Greek, served as its first principal, from 1898 to 1903.

The Allegheny Preparatory School provided a classical education, its graduates virtually guaranteed admission to Ivy League colleges: it advertised that nineteen colleges admitted its graduates "on certificate," without requiring further proof of a student's qualification. The school, however, served the community for less than a generation before demographic changes rendered it obsolete. In 1917 or 1918, the school moved from its beautiful building to a house at 828 North Lincoln Avenue, where it remained for two years before ceasing operation.

Just before the prep school was founded, in 1895, prominent Alleghenians established the Allegheny Country Club on land bounded by California Avenue and Brighton Road in Brighton Heights. The club featured a six-hole golf course, and indeed, its members' enthusiasm for the sport contributed to the club's short stay in Allegheny, where there was little opportunity for expansion. Soon after its founding, in 1902, the club moved to a larger tract of land in Sewickley Heights, where it remains today.

The Allegheny Country Club's move to Sewickley Heights was typical of a growing trend in the area, as Allegheny City millionaires increasingly built large summer homes in that community. The trend accelerated in the late 1890s, when members of B. F. Jones's family began to create expansive summer estates on adjoining farm tracts in Sewickley Heights. By the middle of

The North Presbyterian Church at North Lincoln and Galveston avenues, Allegheny West, built 1896, designed by Vrydaugh & Wolfe. Courtesy of Pittsburgh History & Landmarks Foundation

the first decade of the new century, a score of Allegheny's wealthiest families had summer estates in and near Sewickley Heights, many of them designed by prominent architects who had worked in Allegheny West, such as Alden & Harlow and George Orth. The Pittsburgh, Fort Wayne & Chicago Railroad, along the north shore of the Ohio River, made it easy for these families to reach their summer homes in the years before local governments improved roads enough for automobiles to become a reliable means of transportation, and the area continued to increase in popularity. Allegheny department store partners Russell H. Boggs of West North Avenue and Henry Buhl Jr. of Western Avenue dubbed their summer places Hohenberg and Cloverton Hills. Elisabeth Jones Horne, the North Lincoln Avenue iron and steel heiress who had married into the Pittsburgh department store family, summered at Ridgeview Farm. Her parents, B. F. and Mary Jones, called their estate Franklin Farm, while James and Ida Walton Scully of 845 North Lincoln Avenue retreated to Oak Ledge to escape Pittsburgh's summer heat. Some of these Sewickley Heights summer mansions were larger than their owners' city houses, requiring support buildings like barns, servants' cottages, and water towers.

All of Allegheny's growth, however, all its wealth and expansion, was leading inexorably to the city's official demise in 1907, when it was annexed to the city of Pittsburgh.

CHAPTER 7

Annexation

1907

A
LLEGHENY CITY ceased to exist on December 9, 1907, the sixty-seven-year-old city's colorful and storied neighborhoods absorbed into the larger city across the river to become Pittsburgh's North Side. Allegheny's more than 130,000 residents were from that point on Pittsburghers, whether they liked it or not; its mayor, Charles F. Kirschler, became deputy mayor of Pittsburgh, and the rest of its government merged into Pittsburgh's as well, making it America's eighth-largest city. The annexation followed years of scheming by Pittsburgh's political power brokers, culminating in a controversial special election in 1906 and a lawsuit that extended into late 1907.

The nineteenth century had seen annexations on both sides of the river, as the two industrializing cities attracted immigrants from Europe and migrants from rural America. Pittsburgh grew from its four Downtown wards of 1850 to take in parts of the Strip and Hill districts; in 1868 it annexed Lawrenceville borough and nearly all of today's East End. Allegheny, meanwhile, annexed adjoining municipalities such as Manchester, Spring Garden, and Duquesne boroughs and the areas that would become Brighton Heights, Observatory Hill, Perry Hilltop, Summer Hill, Spring Hill, and Troy Hill.

Both cities' geographic expansion was comparable to that of other large northeastern and midwestern cities at the time: Boston, Chicago, Cleveland, Detroit, Minneapolis, New York. As Pittsburgh grew, however, its leaders and media spoke increasingly of also annexing the land and population of its smaller yet prosperous neighbor. As early as 1846, a Pittsburgh newspaper suggested consolidating the two cities, and the Pennsylvania legislature unsuccessfully attempted to unite Pittsburgh with Allegheny and other adjoining municipalities in 1854. Notably, in the same year the city of Philadelphia increased its land area from 4 to 135 square miles by annexing all of the boroughs and townships within Philadelphia County. Shortly thereafter, the Pennsylvania legislature, heavily lobbied by the Pittsburgh Board of Trade, passed the Consolidation Act of 1867, which permitted Pittsburgh to annex Allegheny City, the boroughs and townships to Pittsburgh's east, and several small South Side boroughs, provided that the electorates of both Pittsburgh and those communities voted in favor of annexation. Pittsburgh thus gained its eastern neighborhoods in 1868, through election. The referendum passed despite strong opposition from influential residents such as Judge Thomas Mellon, of the East Liberty banking family, and Thomas Howe, an industrialist and one of the creators of Woodland Road in Squirrel Hill. These two men and other annexation opponents spoke for suburban citizens who enjoyed their relatively undeveloped neighborhoods and suspected that Pittsburgh officials planned to raise taxes on their lands and business ventures.

At the same time, the voters of Allegheny City and the South Side rejected annexation, warning of Pittsburgh's significantly higher real estate taxes, alleging the likely devaluing of properties as a result of the opening of poorly planned new streets, and citing the rapid growth of Philadelphia's municipal debt since that city's 1854 expansion. The most prominent Alleghenian publicly opposed to annexation in 1867 may have been the venerable General William Robinson Jr., for whom one of the city's streets was named. Robinson, born in 1785 in a house on the site of the future city, had served as Allegheny City's first mayor in 1841, laid out part of his extensive landholdings in what is now called as the Mexican War Streets several years later, and was president of the Ohio & Pennsylvania Railroad and the Exchange Bank of Pittsburgh. Other prominent anti-annexation Allegheny residents in 1867 included Congressman Thomas Williams and Mayor John Morrison, who were neighbors on Stockton Avenue; Gottlieb Wettach, a Spring Garden tannery owner; George Bothwell, a paving contractor who lived on Palo Alto Street; and Arthur Hobson, a bank director and carpenter who would soon speculate in real estate on a new street called Beech Avenue.

While Alleghenians' opposition to annexation in 1867 was successful, in 1872 the Pennsylvania legislature authorized Pittsburgh's merger with the South Side boroughs, the West End, and Mount Washington without an election and despite South Side citizens' opposition, in an act that in some ways foreshadowed Allegheny City's eventual demise. As a result, prominent Allegheny City businessmen lobbied Harrisburg not to allow Pittsburgh to annex their city, and a rewrite of the Pennsylvania Constitution in 1873 prohibited the legislature from thenceforth enacting special laws that applied to a single city, such as the legislation that had brought the neighborhoods south of the Monongahela River into Pittsburgh. Pittsburgh thus took in no additional territory between 1872 and 1897.

By around 1890, though, Pittsburgh's business and political leaders had again begun to speak publicly of a "Greater Pittsburgh," a city whose boundary might be extended to take in Allegheny City, Homestead, Braddock, and even McKeesport and Sewickley. Pittsburgh boosters believed that adding the manufacturing works and populations of adjacent communities would enable the city to remain competitive with Chicago, New York, and other rapidly growing urban centers. The Pittsburgh Chamber of Commerce thus urged the consolidation of municipalities into "Greater Pittsburgh."

Pittsburgh political heavyweight Christopher Magee met with some success in this regard in 1895, persuading the state legislature, whose collective memory of the annexation controversies of 1867 and 1872 had faded, to compel a referendum to be decided by a majority of Allegheny and Pittsburgh's combined electorate. The initiative passed, but it was overturned as unconstitutional as the result of a suit filed by Allegheny City opponents of annexation. Nevertheless, a series of Allegheny executives all stated their support for merging the two cities, including William M. Kennedy, Allegheny's mayor between 1892 and 1896; Charles Geyer, mayor between 1897 and 1900; and James G. Wyman, who served both in the nineteenth century and from 1900 to 1906. The 1902 election of Samuel J. Pennypacker as Pennsylvania's governor strengthened the cause of annexation, since Pennypacker was allied with Pittsburgh mayor and annexation proponent George W. Guthrie.

In 1905, the Pennsylvania legislature passed yet another pro-annexation bill, which the state supreme court again found unconstitutional. Finally, in late 1905, Governor Pennypacker convened a special session in which the legislature passed a bill that provided for the consolidation of adjoining Pennsylvania municipalities upon approval of the majority of the combined electorates. In early 1906 the mayor of Pittsburgh formally requested an election on consolidation, a committee made up of Allegheny City officials and residents countering with a request that Pittsburgh's petition be dismissed. Judge Samuel McClung, a longtime Allegheny City resident who had moved to Squirrel Hill, found that this most recent bill, known as the Greater Pittsburgh Act, was legal, and on April 30, 1906, he ordered that the special election be held on Tuesday, June 12.

With the election looming in less than six weeks, those on both sides of the question moved quickly. On one side, the Allegheny Public Defense Committee represented city residents and businessmen who opposed annexation. Its chairman, William C. Gill, was a Downtown Pittsburgh attorney who lived on Hemlock Street in eastern Allegheny City. In addition to Gill, Allegheny's new mayor, Charles F. Kirschler, sworn into office on April 2, 1906, also opposed annexation. Kirschler, a Republican who pledged to give Allegheny "a clean, honest, Christian government," had defeated the pro-consolidation candidate, hardware manufacturer George B. Logan, of North Lincoln and Allegheny avenues. Kirschler himself, a former official of the D. Lutz & Sons brewery in Deutschtown, lived on Allegheny Avenue in Manchester. Other anti-annexation Allegheny City residents included Simon Kirschler, the mayor's brother and director of the Allegheny Department of Charities; public safety director Samuel Grenet, of Brighton Road and Woods Run Avenue; public works director John Swan Jr.; city solicitor Elliott Rodgers, of California Avenue; police superintendent John Glenn, of Perry Hilltop; Manchester building contractor Robert K. Cochrane; Christian Knaur, a horse shoer from Perry Hilltop; and John A. Sauer, a plumbing contractor, of Western Avenue. Attorney and former Pennsylvania governor William A. Stone, of West North Avenue in the Mexican War Streets, represented the Allegheny Public Defense Committee in legal matters.

The most significant pro-annexation organizations were the Pittsburgh Chamber of Commerce, the Good Government Party of Allegheny, and the Greater Pittsburgh Association of Allegheny. The Greater Pittsburgh Association of Allegheny opened a "headquarters" in Kenyon's Hall, on Federal Street near Ohio Street, and the Good Government Party of Allegheny met in a private home on West North Avenue in Manchester. Several organizations without Allegheny ties, such as the Civic Club of Allegheny County, the Oakland Board of Trade, and the Prohibition Party, announced their support for annexation as well. Interestingly, the long list of Allegheny City's prominent residents who favored the merger in 1906 was reminiscent of the roll call of those who had lined up to fight annexation thirty-nine years before. Alleghenians supporting the merger included B. F. Jones Jr., of the Jones & Laughlin Steel Company; Russell H. Boggs, of the famous Boggs & Buhl department store; astronomer John Brashear, of Perry Hilltop; Fourth Ward councilman John W. Robinson; and North Lincoln Avenue residents James Scully, a glass manufacturer, Joshua W. Rhodes, a tube manufacturer, and

Charles F. Kirschler
was Allegheny City's last mayor and
became deputy mayor of Pittsburgh
when the city was annexed in 1907.
Robert M. Palmer and Hartley M. Phelps,
*Palmer's Pictorial Pittsburgh and Prominent
Pittsburghers Past and Present, 1758–1905*, 1905.
Courtesy of Historic Pittsburgh Full-Text
Collection, Digital Research Library, University
Library System, University of Pittsburgh

James G. Wyman
former mayor of Allegheny City,
supported merging the two cities.
Percy F. Smith, *Notable Men of Pittsburgh and
Vicinity*, 1901. Courtesy of Historic Pittsburgh
Full-Text Collection, Digital Research Library,
University Library System,
University of Pittsburgh

William Glyde Wilkins, a prominent bridge engineer. H. J. Heinz, the owner of the famous food-processing complex in eastern Allegheny City, and Andrew Carnegie, who had lived in Allegheny during his boyhood, also supported Greater Pittsburgh.

The looming special election prompted a firestorm of public debate, sometimes noncredible attempts to sway public opinion, and accusations of corruption and fraud levied by both the Greater Pittsburgh backers and the "antis." Those who strove to preserve Allegheny as a separate city were at a disadvantage not only because of the planned combined vote counts but also because all of Pittsburgh's daily newspapers and the area's German-language newspaper, *Volksblatt und Freiheits Freund*, enthusiastically supported the Greater Pittsburgh movement. Indeed, the newspapers supported the merger

William C. Gill,
a Downtown Pittsburgh attorney
who lived in Allegheny City,
opposed annexation.
Robert M. Palmer and Hartley M. Phelps,
Palmer's Pictorial Pittsburgh and Prominent
Pittsburghers Past and Present, 1758–1905, 1905.
Courtesy of Historic Pittsburgh Full-Text
Collection, Digital Research Library, University
Library System, University of Pittsburgh

Elliott Rodgers
was another anti-annexation
Allegheny City resident.
Percy F. Smith, *Notable Men of Pittsburgh and*
Vicinity, 1901. Courtesy of Historic Pittsburgh
Full-Text Collection, Digital Research Library,
University Library System,
University of Pittsburgh

in a manner that would never be condoned today, each publishing front-page editorials and cartoons proclaiming the purported benefits of annexation and exhorting citizens of Pittsburgh and Allegheny to vote in its favor. Area newspapers cast the businessmen who led the Greater Pittsburgh movement as progressive men who knew what was best for the region, rarely reporting on the activities and arguments of those who wished to keep Allegheny City alive, save to characterize their leadership as self-serving politicians who feared losing their public paychecks. Indeed, the very labeling of these men and their allies as "antis" indicates that the Greater Pittsburgh force had successfully positioned itself as the status quo.

The three main arguments put forward by Greater Pittsburgh proponents were that the toll bridges that connected Pittsburgh and Allegheny would

Judge Samuel McClung
found the Greater Pittsburgh Act
to be legal and ordered the special
election on consolidation.
Percy F. Smith, *Notable Men of Pittsburgh and*
Vicinity, 1901. Courtesy of Historic Pittsburgh
Full-Text Collection, Digital Research Library,
University Library System, University of
Pittsburgh

Andrew Carnegie
who lived in Allegheny as a boy,
supported Greater Pittsburgh.
Library of Congress Prints and Photographs
Division (LC-USZ62-101767)
Washington, D.C.

become free; that all Allegheny residents would drink filtered water from
Pittsburgh's filtration plant; and that Allegheny's property taxes, then with
a higher millage than Pittsburgh's, would decrease. An April 29 editorial in
the *Dispatch* was straightforward in its assertion that Allegheny's water qual-
ity would improve: "The narrowness of Mayor Kirschler's view is illustrated
by the evident fact that his inability to see what Allegheny is going to get
out of it is due to the fact that he does not want to know. Is it nothing that
Allegheny will get filtered water without any taxation to pay for the plant?
Has the mayor ever taken the trouble to figure up what the typhoid fever and
other water-borne diseases cost Allegheny in loss of valuable lives and the
expenses of sickness?" Area newspapers also printed as fact a Pittsburgh real
estate organization's unlikely assertion that Allegheny City would experience

both higher property values and lower rents. The latter claim was intended to assuage the fears of Allegheny City's working-class citizens, who were expected to oppose the annexation. The *Pittsburgh Press* further claimed on June 10 that annexation would decrease crime in Allegheny City and that the city would "lose its unenviable repute as the Canada of the under world." Annexation, the *Press* assured its readers, would result in the founding of a free college for city residents and in upgrades to East and West parks, where, it said, "not a cent has been spent for improvement for many years."

In 1906, local members of the Grand Army of the Republic, a nationwide association of veterans of the Union Army in the Civil War, searching for a suitable site for a proposed Soldiers and Sailors Memorial, also weighed in on the coming election. The GAR's Pittsburgh leadership included some of Allegheny's leading annexation proponents, such as former mayoral candidate George B. Logan and Allegheny County recorder of deeds John A. Fairman, of Arch Street. The proposed new memorial was expected to generate considerable economic activity in whichever neighborhood it was built, and shortly after Judge McClung set the special election, the GAR exerted economic pressure by announcing that it was deferring its decision on its new hall's location until after the election. Allegheny's aging City Hall at Federal and Ohio streets, the GAR leadership explained, would not be needed after annexation, and its site would be an attractive location for the hall.

Consolidation forces also exerted pressure on Allegheny's German Americans: the anti-annexation Allegheny Public Defense Committee was counting on the support of the city's German American residents, and pro-annexation groups thus believed that winning German Americans to their cause was essential. The *Pittsburgh Dispatch* reported on May 10, 1906, that Allegheny select councilman John W. Robinson said, "The thing to do on the Northside is to proselyte the German vote east of Federal street. If we can break even with our opponents in the wards east of Federal street, Allegheny will be found on the side of annexation when the votes are counted." As noted earlier, Pittsburgh's German-language newspaper, *Volksblatt und Freiheits Freund,* also worked to persuade its readers to vote for Greater Pittsburgh. The newspaper reported extensively on the meetings and arguments of annexation advocates, its editorials leaving no doubt as to its stance. On Election Day, June 12, a banner headline in the *Volksblatt und Freiheits Freund* exhorted Pittsburgh's Germans: "BAHNFREI DEM FORTSCHRITT! JEDER STIMME

HEUTE FÜR GROß-PITTSBURG!" [Make Way for Progress! Every Vote Today for Greater-Pittsburg!]

Even as Allegheny and Pittsburgh residents debated the Greater Pittsburgh question, national and local events continued to attract attention. In late April 1906, residents read with horror about the San Francisco earthquake, which had killed more than three thousand people and destroyed many thousands of buildings. Mayor Kirschler telegrammed his San Francisco counterpart to seek information on Henry J. Lotz, of Lockhart Street in Deutschtown, a broker and a director of the German National Bank of Allegheny, who had been visiting San Francisco. Pittsburgh newspapers reported that he had died in the quake, but he later turned up alive. Allegheny citizens were moved to help the West Coast victims of the quake, whether or not a local had been injured. The Patrolmen's Relief Association donated $1,000 to earthquake relief, the Allegheny Common Council $2,500. In an interesting side effect of the disaster, the Pittsburgh-based American steel industry gained favorable publicity and market share as a result of the quake: San Francisco's buildings that were made of structural steel withstood the tremors far better than those of masonry construction.

Residents of eastern Allegheny City were further distracted from the annexation question on May 1, 1906, when Councilman Jacob P. Bupp, of 529 Suismon Street in Deutschtown, was arrested in Reserve Township. Bupp had allegedly stolen a horse and stated he would kill a farmer who had sold him another horse that had died. Bupp, according to the *Pittsburgh Dispatch*, became insane and struggled violently with Allegheny police when arrested. Area papers also reported that in late April the Allegheny police closed forty-six disorderly houses, most of which were on General Robinson, Lacock, Anderson, and Sandusky streets, in the lower city, forcing their residents to leave the city. Jacob Born and Jacob C. Born, tavern proprietors at Perrysville Avenue and East Street, were refused a liquor license because they had served a nineteen-year-old. Alleghenians also pondered the strange case of former councilman Henry Hettler of Troy Hill, who had vanished from Pennsylvania in 1895 and turned up in California in 1906. And Allegheny police captain Sidney Braff of Pennsylvania Avenue may have turned heads when he told the *Dispatch* on his forty-fifth wedding anniversary that public whipping of abusive husbands would solve modern society's marital problems, adding that Ober Park, at Federal and Ohio streets, was an ideal site for the proposed practice.

As Election Day drew nearer, however, local politics again took prominence in the minds of Alleghenians. Many of Allegheny and Pittsburgh's manufacturing and retail establishments told their employees they would have a half day off, urging their workers to vote for Greater Pittsburgh. Boggs & Buhl, the famous department store on Federal Street, and Haller Beck & Company, the salt works in lower Manchester, were among the workplaces that closed early that day. The Allegheny and Pittsburgh city governments also gave their employees the day off so that they could vote, Allegheny's Mayor Kirschler and his allies urging city workers to vote against annexation, Pittsburgh officials pressing the opposite. Also in favor of annexation were the Pennsylvania Railroad and the Pittsburgh & Lake Erie Railroad, one of whose officers told the *Pittsburgh Press* that he favored annexation but had not told his employees how to vote. An Allegheny City Roman Catholic priest, Father Francis Ward of Brighton Heights, avidly supported Greater Pittsburgh, publicly exhorting each of the 375 children in his parish school on Davis Avenue to bring their father or other male of voting age to the polls to vote in favor of annexation

EX-GOV. WILLIAM A. STONE.

A   ND here we sight a legal light
       Ten thousand candle-power bright,
         Whose hand has weight to regulate
The workings of a mighty State,
But though his store of legal lore
Is in demand the nation o'er,
    At times he dreams of purling streams,
    Where many a speckled beauty gleams,
And o'er his senses softly steal
The siren song of rod and reel
    And Blackstone's sterner law gives way
    To Isaak Walton's gentle sway.

Attorney and former Pennsylvania governor William A. Stone represented the Allegheny Public Defense Committee. George S. Applegarth, *Men of This Big Town of Ours as Seen by "Appy,"* 1911. Courtesy of Historic Pittsburgh Full-Text Collection, Digital Research Library, University Library System, University of Pittsburgh

and cancelling school on Election Day, June 12, so that the schoolchildren could do as he asked. In Pittsburgh, the pastor of the Third Presbyterian Church, on Fifth Avenue in Shadyside, gave a pro-annexation sermon just before the special election. Pittsburgh newspapers predictably identified few Allegheny City men who opposed the annexation, aside from the city's political leaders. The newspapers characteristically claimed that the only Allegheny residents who opposed annexation were Allegheny City government officials and city employees, particularly police and firemen. By Election Day, tensions were running very high; Mayor Kirschler even had a number of Pittsburgh residents arrested for posting Greater Pittsburgh flyers in Allegheny City neighborhoods.

Election Day itself was marked by both a festive atmosphere, a prancing horse pulling a wagon displaying a large banner that said "We are for Allegheny City" through that city's streets, and tense accusations. Pittsburgh police arrested men whom they accused of voting repeatedly against annexation, while Alleghenians alleged ballot-box stuffing in the city's Second Ward. R. H. Boggs, of Boggs & Buhl, hired private detectives, some of whom were plainclothes men, to look for anti-annexation vote fraud, and a *Pittsburgh Press* headline reported, "'Little' Pittsburghers, Seeing Defeat, Resort to Desperate Means to Steal Election from Consolidationists." Simon Kirschler prevented Allegheny General Hospital superintendent Peter K. Bechtel from voting in the hospital's election district, accusing him of living elsewhere and attempting voter fraud. Historical records, however, indicate that Bechtel did indeed reside at the hospital for a number of years.

In the end, the pro-annexation forces carried the election, thanks to the Pennsylvania legislature's act combining the vote counts of both cities. Eighty-five percent of Pittsburgh voters supported the measure, while only 35 percent of their Allegheny City counterparts voted in its favor.

A breakdown of the votes, on both sides of the river, reveals much about the area's demographics at the turn of the twentieth century. While every Allegheny City ward voted against annexation, the vote totals within each ward's various voting districts uncover differences along economic lines and the degree to which residents were personally associated with Pittsburgh's economic mainstream. The two districts containing most of prosperous Allegheny West, bounded by Ridge, Allegheny, and West North avenues and Brighton Road, voted in favor of annexation by a total of 177 to 48 (79 percent in favor of the merger). The Second Ward districts roughly corresponding to the middle-class Mexican War Streets voted for annexation by a total

THE ANNEXATION QUESTION IN ALLEGHENY

Pittsburgh newspapers ran cartoons like this one, hoping to persuade residents of both cities to vote for annexation. *Pittsburg Dispatch*, April 30, 1906

of 229 to 117 (66 percent in favor). Only a few blocks away, two working-class voting districts that were also in the Second Ward opposed annexation by a total of 270 to 160 (63 percent opposed). Manchester's voting districts in the vicinity of wealthy Western Avenue and the comfortable homes on Sheffield Street endorsed annexation, but residents in the more industrialized parts of the neighborhood voted against it. In the German enclaves of Deutschtown, Troy Hill, and Spring Hill, large majorities of voters also cast ballots against annexation. Allegheny City's Ninth Ward, which included the Woods Run neighborhood, home to many blue-collar workers, also voted heavily against annexation. The outer wards, which included developing middle-class neighborhoods like Observatory Hill and Brighton Heights, as well as established working-class areas, also had significant differences among election districts. Across the river in Pittsburgh, the greatest support for annexation came from the prosperous East End neighborhoods of Squirrel Hill, Highland Park, Shadyside, and Oakland, where more than 90 percent of voters favored Greater Pittsburgh. Elsewhere, as in Allegheny, Pittsburgh residents' votes revealed divisions along class and ethnic lines.

In the wake of the election, Mayor Kirschler announced that he considered Allegheny City's vote a success, because the number of votes that Alleghenians had cast in opposition to Greater Pittsburgh was greater than the number of votes that had elected him mayor. Allegheny Public Defense Committee attorney William A. Stone immediately appealed the election, and its results were placed on hold as the case proceeded through the courts. As the appeal wound its way through the legal system, even those who were most passionate about the election's outcome had little choice but to return to their routines. Through the rest of 1906 and most of 1907, then, the Allegheny City Select Council approved public works such as street grading and paving, discussed a proposed $1 million bond issue to finance a city reservoir, and elected Francis J. Torrance of Western Avenue as council president. In April 1907, Mayor Kirschler may have raised a few eyebrows when he recommended to the select council that Allegheny City build a new municipal building to replace its city hall. "The public at large," Kirschler said, "can be better served if all these branches of city government are under one roof." Kirschler also offered Allegheny schoolchildren a $50 prize for the design of an Allegheny City flag. Helen M. Meister, a student at the Thirteenth Ward School on Troy Hill, won for her design, which depicted the simple Robinson cabin of 1785 at what would become the foot of Federal Street.

In spite of the new city flag, and the hopes of Allegheny patriots, the Pennsylvania Superior Court, the Pennsylvania Supreme Court, and the US Supreme Court all eventually upheld the legitimacy of the Greater Pittsburgh Act, the US Supreme Court ruling in favor of the act in *Hunter v. Pittsburgh*. On November 20, 1907, two days after the Supreme Court decision, even Mayor Kirschler conceded that the merger of Allegheny into Pittsburgh was inevitable. Kirschler wrote to the select council:

Gentlemen:

After a conference with His Honor, Mayor Guthrie of Pittsburgh, and the Presidents of Select and Common Councils of the City of Pittsburgh and the Presidents of Select and Common Councils of the City of Allegheny it was deemed advisable, in view of the decision of the Supreme Court of the United States affirming the judgment of the Supreme Court of Pennsylvania, declaring the so-called Greater Pittsburgh Act constitutional, and in view of the urgent necessity of having the appropriation and tax levying ordinances of the enlarged city prepared as soon as possible, and there being but little time prior to the beginning of the new fiscal year for that purpose, that a request be made to the parties interested as appellants in the case of the Supreme Court of the United States that they take steps to have the mandate returned to the lower court as soon as possible, in order to make the actual consolidation effective at as early a date as possible. I, therefore, request Councils to take action on this matter, and present herewith a resolution for such purpose.

On December 9, 1907, the day of consolidation, newspapers later reported, the Pittsburgh City Council, accompanied by a marching band and carrying the Pittsburgh flag, crossed the Sixth Street Bridge. Pittsburgh officials then walked up Federal Street to the building that until that day had served as Allegheny City Hall. From there, according to one account, they escorted former Allegheny mayor Kirschler, former Allegheny City Council members, and their associates to Pittsburgh's City Hall. Mayor Kirschler, as noted earlier, would stay on as Pittsburgh's deputy mayor, but Pittsburgh mayor George W. Guthrie immediately requested the resignations of some members of Kirschler's cabinet who had opposed annexation.

During 1908, the expanded Pittsburgh city government tackled the logistics of merging two large cities while still carrying on its routine duties. The city reorganized its ward system, with Allegheny's fifteen wards becoming Pittsburgh wards 21 through 27. In dozens of instances where street names were duplicated, the city sometimes changed North Side street names and other times changed street names in what was called "old Pittsburgh." Most new street names were similar to the old ones, or at least started with the same letter. Liberty Street in Deutschtown, for example, became Lockhart Street, to avoid confusion with the avenue in Downtown Pittsburgh's whole-sale district; Manchester's Frazier Street was renamed Fontella because a Frazier Street already existed in Pittsburgh's Oakland neighborhood. Across the river, the city changed Cedar Street in Bloomfield to Cedarville, leaving intact the name of the North Side avenue of elegant homes facing East Park. Preble Street on Polish Hill became Paulowna Street, deferring to the well-known avenue near the Ohio River in Manchester.

The former Mayor Kirschler, despite potential antagonism remaining from his strenuous opposition to Greater Pittsburgh, served out his term as deputy mayor of Pittsburgh, remaining in the post through 1909. He then returned to the private sector and was later associated with brewing and banking firms. In 1940, seven years after the death of the last mayor of Allegheny, North Siders honored his son, Charles F. Kirschler Jr., on the occasion of the hundredth anniversary of Allegheny's incorporation as a city.

CHAPTER 8

Middle-Class and Working-Class Allegheny

1890–1910

A MID THE CHAOS and controversy brought by annexation, daily life for most citizens continued as usual, whether they were called Alleghenians or Pittsburghers. Area millionaires' ability to escape to their summer homes in Sewickley Heights seems to have lengthened their stay on the North Side and even encouraged the construction of Ridge Avenue's last great mansions. Lower Allegheny City was becoming ever noisier and more crowded at the end of the nineteenth century, and the elites' summer homes ensured that solace was always nearby. In the meantime, Allegheny's middle- and upper-middle-class families, who enjoyed discretionary income but did not own summer estates, began to move out of the city.

Property values along Beech Avenue and the middle-class streets of Manchester and the Mexican War Streets declined for the first time in the 1890s. All three areas lost residents to developing East End streetcar suburbs, primarily Friendship and Shadyside. The first conversions of Beech Avenue houses to apartments took place in the 1890s, several more becoming flats in the following decade. A block away, more than half of the houses in Denny Row on West North Avenue were divided into apartments or became rooming houses between 1900 and 1910. The area's demographics were shifting: although some middle-class families remained in the homes of Beech Avenue, Manchester, and the Mexican War Streets into the 1920s or later, many other dwellings, converted into apartments or rooming houses, now housed blue-collar occupants or entertainers. These new working-class residents and their elite neighbors were aware of one another's presence, but they inhabited separate worlds.

A few middle-class Alleghenians of the time, although somewhat transient, would become nationally known for their accomplishments. The civil engineer George Washington Ferris settled in the Pittsburgh area in 1887,

Famous dancer and choreographer Martha Graham was born in Allegheny. Martha Graham
Collection, Music Division, Library of Congress, Box 250/15, #387; Martha Graham Resources, a division of
The Martha Graham Center of Contemporary Dance, www.marthagraham.org

opening a consulting office at 553 Grant
Street, Downtown. Ferris lived in a modest
brick dwelling at what is now 1318 Arch Street
in the Mexican War Streets area between 1887
and 1890 and then may have moved to the
Downtown building where his office was located. He became nationally known in 1893,
when his towering new contraption called a
Ferris wheel delighted and scared thousands
in its debut at the Chicago World's Fair. He
died in Pittsburgh in November 1896. Several blocks from Ferris's home in the Mexican War Streets, Dr. George and Jane Beers
Graham lived in a middle-class enclave on
Brighton Place near California Avenue. The
couple's daughter Martha, born in 1894,
would one day become the famous American dancer and choreographer, her talents
discovered and nurtured in California after
her family moved west in 1904.

George Ferris, inventor of the
Ferris wheel, lived in the Mexican
War Streets area. Carnegie Library of
Pittsburgh Pennsylvania Department,
Pittsburgh Photographic Library

The area's ethnic demographics were also
undergoing dramatic shifts, as many families left the area and many more moved in.
Nearly all of Allegheny West and Manches-
ter's wealthy and middle-class German Jewish families left the North Side between 1902 and 1908. Most relocated to Squirrel Hill, Oakland, and Friendship, near the new Rodef Shalom synagogue, which moved from Downtown
to Fifth Avenue in Oakland in 1907. The Concordia Club also left the North
Side for Oakland in 1913. Despite this migration of upper-class Jewish residents to the East End, dozens of less prominent Jewish families, generally of
Eastern European origin, remained on the North Side. In 1907 one of the
leaders of this Jewish community, Herman Jacob, a Deutschtown livestock
dealer, led a group of Alleghenians in establishing Congregation Beth Israel,
an Orthodox synagogue that moved into a former Baptist church at the corner of East and Foreland streets. Jacob served as the congregation's first president. Six years later, several Beaver Avenue shopkeepers and other residents of
Manchester founded Congregation Beth Jehuda, which occupied a converted

A bridge across Kilbuck Pond in Riverview Park, which opened in 1894. Pittsburgh City Photographer Collection, 1901–2002 (715.3732994.CP). Archives Service Center, University of Pittsburgh

dwelling on Nixon Street until 1926, when it purchased a former Lutheran church at Chateau and Adams streets. It remained there until about 1960.

Just as Allegheny's wealthiest German Jewish families were beginning to move to the East End, four ethnic groups that were fairly new to the area— Slovaks, Italians, Lithuanians, and Croatians—started creating fledgling

communities in the city's westernmost sections. Slovak immigrants, from sixteen counties in northern Hungary, clustered in the Woods Run neighborhood in the late nineteenth century. In 1890, Peter V. Rovnianek, who published the Slovak newspaper *Amerikansko Slovenske Noviny* and owned a small Pittsburgh bank, along with other community leaders, founded the National Slovak Society in Allegheny City. The National Slovak Society, a mutual beneficial organization, eventually grew to include eight North Side lodges among hundreds across the country. Rovnianek would serve as its national president for its first eleven years. Some members of Allegheny's Slovak community attended the Bohemian Roman Catholic St. Wenceslaus Church on Progress Street before founding St. Gabriel Archangel parish in Woods Run in 1903. The parish built a substantial church on California Avenue in 1906.

Italian immigrant families also began to settle in Allegheny City in the last years of the nineteenth century. By 1900, most of them lived close to the intersection of Federal and Ohio streets, in Manchester, where a number ran shoemaking shops, and in Deutschtown. The 1900 census recorded ten families living in what was described as "Italian colony bank of Ohio River, between Greenwood and Fayette [West North Avenue] sts." With no Italian Catholic parish in Allegheny City, many of these Italian immigrants at first attended mass at St. Peter's Church, on West Ohio Street. In 1906, however, in response to Allegheny's growing Italian population, the Diocese of Pittsburgh founded Regina Coeli parish. Regina Coeli celebrated mass in a rented space on Chateau Street in Manchester until 1908, when it purchased a modest former Lutheran church that stood nearby, on Juniata Street. The parish gained population and expanded its complex of buildings incrementally in subsequent decades.

Among Allegheny's Italian immigrant families were Felice and Augustina Pivirotto, who moved to North Taylor Avenue in the Mexican War Streets in the first decade of the twentieth century. Felice Pivirotto had been unsuccessful as a Pittsburgh tavern proprietor during the depression of the mid-1890s, but he had quickly recovered to found the Italo-French Produce Company. Pivirotto's new business, which manufactured pasta and imported groceries and produce, operated on Sampsonia Way in Allegheny by 1900. By about 1910, the company was grossing $500,000 per year. The Pivirottos continued to enlarge their business property at least into the early 1910s, by which point a six-story warehouse towered over the rest of the neighborhood. The building, which later housed bedding manufacturing, is now known as the Mattress Factory.

The area's Lithuanian immigrants founded Ascension Roman Catholic parish in Manchester in 1906. The parish purchased and remodeled the former Second Presbyterian Church at Metropolitan and North Franklin streets, remaining there until it disbanded in 1962. Ascension, one of the North Side's smallest Roman Catholic congregations, did not have a school. A rowhouse across Metropolitan Street from the church served as its rectory.

Croatian immigrants had also begun to come to eastern Allegheny City in significant numbers in the late 1880s. The first Croatian families settled in a residential neighborhood immediately east of the present Sixteenth Street Bridge, on and around what would become the site of the H. J. Heinz Company complex. In 1894, Allegheny's Croatian immigrants founded St. Nicholas parish, the first Croatian Roman Catholic church in America. The parish converted an aging house on East Ohio Street to a church building and worshipped there for several years before hiring the prominent Pittsburgh architect Frederick Sauer to design a church on East Ohio Street, completed in 1901. With their landmark church and its adjacent rectory anchoring the community, Croatians came to occupy nearly all of the houses, tenement buildings, and storefronts along the two-mile stretch of East Ohio Street between the Sixteenth Street Bridge and Allegheny's border with Millvale borough. The neighborhood became known as Mala [Little] Jaska, named for the Croatian village where many of its residents had been born. In the late nineteenth and early twentieth centuries, houses lined both sides of East Ohio Street in the vicinity of St. Nicholas. Those on the southern side of the street were but a few feet from the busy tracks of the Western Pennsylvania Railroad and surely provided hellish living conditions. That they remained occupied for decades testifies to the demand for housing in Pittsburgh's turn-of-the-century immigrant neighborhoods.

Mala Jaska remained the heart of Pittsburgh's Croatian community even after Croatian settlement spread up East Ohio Street to Millvale and Shaler Township and across the Thirtieth Street Bridge to the upper Strip District and Lawrenceville. Many of St. Nicholas parish's men worked in the tanneries, foundries, and other factories along adjacent River Avenue or in the yard of the Western Pennsylvania Railroad on River Avenue; some walked across the bridge to the Black Diamond steel mill in the Strip District. Women employed outside the home felt fortunate if they landed jobs at the nearby H. J. Heinz plant, widely known for its exceptional working conditions. Company founder Henry John Heinz provided his employees with a library, a dining room, an auditorium, rooftop garden, and company picnics, and he even sent them on occasional trips.

Some Mala Jaska residents also worked in Pittsburgh's Central Stock Yards, which moved to Herr's Island in the first decade of the twentieth century. The stockyards had previously been located in East Liberty in Pittsburgh's East End, where they occupied a site adjoining Penn Avenue and the Pennsylvania Railroad for decades. Herr's Island had also housed stockyards for years, interspersed among small manufacturing plants and modest frame homes during the second half of the nineteenth century. Other, smaller Allegheny stockyards could be found along Brighton Road and Buena Vista Street, above West North Avenue, and on Preble Avenue at Woods Run. Now, however, the new consolidated Herr's Island stockyards were among the largest in the United States. Swine from these stockyards were slaughtered at packing plants on Spring Garden Avenue, workers having herded them over Troy Hill along the most direct available route: up steep, narrow Rialto Street and then down Wicklines Lane into the Spring Garden Valley. Rialto Street thus earned the nickname Pig Hill, by which it is still known today.

Coexistence between the city's working-class immigrants and its elites was not always easy. Perhaps the most extreme example of this came in 1892, when the area that Alleghenians still called Deutschtown gained notoriety in the wake of anarchist Alexander Berkman's attempt to assassinate the wealthy industrialist Henry Clay Frick. Berkman had tried to kill Frick in protest against the Carnegie Steel Company's treatment of striking workers at its

Homestead plant, including the deadly conflict between armed Pinkerton guards and mill hands, shooting and stabbing Frick in his Downtown office before Frick's associates subdued him. Pittsburgh police, investigating the crime, quickly learned that Berkman, of New York, had boarded in a house on Chesbro Street in Deutschtown for several days before the assassination attempt. A *Pittsburgh Commercial Gazette* reporter visited the small red-brick rowhouse where Berkman had stayed, one block west of the Sixteenth Street Bridge and one hundred feet north of River Avenue. He called the dwelling "one of the most slovenly and filthy to be found," noting in particular its "dark, foul-smelling staircase."

Pittsburgh police subsequently arrested the keepers of the boardinghouse, anarchists Paul Eckert and Carl Knold, and charged them with aiding the assassination attempt. Attorney Joseph M. Friedman of Liverpool Street represented Knold and another Deutschtown man, Henry Bauer. Police spent considerable time interviewing alleged Deutschtown anarchists and nihilists and brought Marcus Albrecht, a shoemaker on Spring Garden Avenue and

Exposition Park. Carnegie Library of Pittsburgh Pennsylvania Department, Pittsburgh Photographic Library

an anarchist group founder, in for questioning. Albrecht disclosed considerable information on Allegheny anarchists' activities and beliefs and identified
Theodore Rohm, who had a shoe store on East Street, as a Berkman associate.
Whether Rohm supported Berkman's actions or Albrecht simply wished to
cause trouble for a business rival is unknown.

In any event, Pittsburgh newspapers devoted considerable space to the assassination attempt and the ensuing investigation. Five hundred anarchists reportedly lived in Allegheny, according to the papers, mostly in Deutschtown
and at Woods Run. This estimate may not have surprised residents who
recalled that in 1883, Allegheny had hosted a convention of the socialist-
anarchist International Working People's Association. Indeed, in Allegheny,
sympathy for anarchism and socialism was strong in working-class neighborhoods, where some workers distrusted factory owners and feared new machinery that might diminish demand for their skills. Significantly, and not
surprisingly, the Allegheny neighborhoods where socialism and anarchism
had a toehold in 1892 were the same ones that voted most strongly against
Allegheny's annexation in 1906.

At Deutschtown's western end, development of Cedar Avenue in the
Schenley leasehold, between East North Avenue and Avery Street, lagged behind that of the sections of North Avenue, Ridge Avenue, and Brighton Road
that faced the Allegheny parks. In and before the 1880s, the majority of the
Schenley lots along Cedar had contained modest frame dwellings, although
a few held small commercial enterprises, including a bakery, a lumberyard,
and a stained-glass shop. The 1880–81 construction of the landmark William
Mohrmann house at Cedar and East North avenues for a thirty-one-year-
old liquor dealer and his family, however, signified that prosperous families
might choose to build large dwellings on Cedar despite the lot-leasing system. Increasing demand for property in lower Allegheny also played a role
in Cedar Avenue's subsequent popularity and development, and between
about 1890 and the first few years of the twentieth century, lot lessees built
about fifteen substantial brick dwellings on Cedar Avenue, replacing earlier,
smaller frame buildings. These new houses, primarily built with Queen Anne
and Richardsonian Romanesque influences, were on Cedar's 800 and 900
blocks, between Foreland and Tripoli streets. Although all of their façades
were primarily brick, some also used considerable quantities of carved limestone. Nearly all of the new houses going up on Cedar were built for German
families who already made their homes in Deutschtown, including Cedar
Avenue's last two grand houses, which went up in 1906 and 1907. These urban

FEDERAL ST. STATION-ALLEGHENY, PA.
VIEW FROM SOUTH EAST. NO 3482
3-23-07 - 9.10 AM.

The Pittsburgh,
Fort Wayne &
Chicago Railway
station in
Allegheny City.
Thomas & Katherine
Detre Library and
Archives, Sen. John
Heinz History Center

mansions, built by Victor Meyer's Sons, a contracting firm from Brighton Road in Brighton Heights, stood at opposite corners of Suismon Street, built for a brewery president and a doctor, both prominent in eastern Allegheny's German community.

Theodore Huckestein, the president of the Mutual Union Brewing

The H. J. Heinz complex, about 1904; it had expanded considerably since opening in 1889.
Thomas & Katherine Detre Library and Archives, Sen. John Heinz History Center

Company, and his wife, Anna, had 820 Cedar Avenue built in 1907. The house, with more than five thousand square feet but relatively unornamented, cost $18,000 to build. Huckestein, although born in Germany, had lived in Deutschtown his entire adult life. He operated saloons in Deutschtown and Downtown Pittsburgh and was a partner in a Sharpsburg liquor store

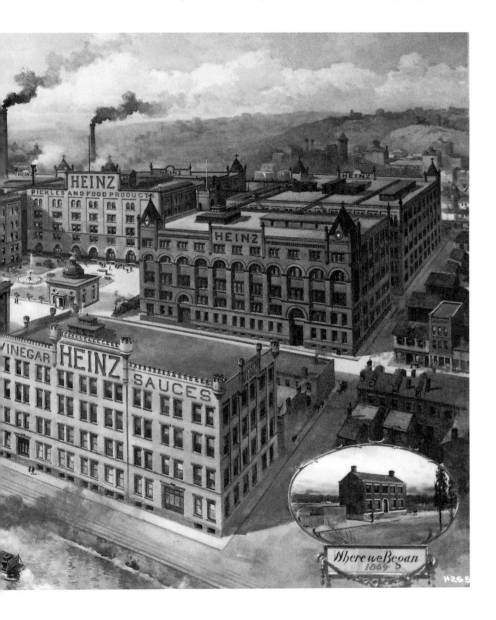

before he founded the Mutual Union Brewing Company with other brewers in 1906. The company ran a brewery in Aliquippa and had an office in Downtown Pittsburgh. After Prohibition began in 1920, Huckestein served as president of the North Pole Ice Company on West Carson Street in the West End. Huckestein ran the ice company and lived at 820 Cedar Avenue until he died in early 1933, nine months before Prohibition was repealed. Two of his children remained in the house into the 1940s.

Dr. John and Ida Hierholzer had 900 Cedar Avenue built in late 1906 and early 1907, for $14,000. John Hierholzer had grown up above his German

H. J. Heinz workers loading a rail car, about 1904; two rail lines served the plant.
Thomas & Katherine Detre Library and Archives, Sen. John Heinz History Center

immigrant father's dry goods store on East Ohio Street, between East and Middle streets. The family belonged to St. Mary's Church on Lockhart Street, which Hierholzer's father, Charles, had helped found. The senior Hierholzer was also president of the Real Estate Loan and Trust Company on East Ohio Street, and the family had the resources to allow John Hierholzer an education at St. Vincent's College, at Jefferson Medical College, and in Vienna. He practiced at Mercy Hospital before he established his own medical offices in Downtown Pittsburgh and at 900 Cedar. He also served as medical director and vice-president of the Knights Life Insurance Company, which moved its offices into the former William Penn Snyder mansion at Ridge and Galveston avenues about 1930. Dr. Hierholzer practiced medicine at 900 Cedar Avenue until about 1950 and lived in the house until he died at age ninety-six, in 1958.

Other prominent Deutschtown families bought existing homes on Cedar Avenue. Charles and Sophia Blumhage Hanna, for example, born in Pennsylvania to German immigrants, bought the house at 910 Cedar Avenue in 1901. By that time, Charles Hanna had operated a successful shoe store at East Ohio and East streets for several years. They would own and live at 910 Cedar Avenue until 1920. Their son Howard W. Hanna worked as chief clerk for the Jones & Laughlin Steel Company and lived in Mount Lebanon for much of his adult life; their grandson Howard W. Hanna Jr. founded Howard Hanna Real Estate Services in 1955.

After 1890, Allegheny's population growth, together with new streetcar lines, also abetted development in the city's newer neighborhoods, and many families moved further out from the city's center. Some Mexican War Streets and Deutschtown residents moved outward to Perry Hilltop, Observatory Hill, and Fineview; Deutschtowners were also likely to move north along the East Street Valley. Subdivision and home construction in Reserve Township eased crowding on Troy Hill and in Spring Garden. A number of Manchester residents put down new roots in Brighton Heights, as land-owning families subdivided large tracts off California Avenue. Some of the upper North Side's largest homes went up along California and along Perrysville Avenue, on Perry Hilltop and Observatory Hill. The prominent architect Frederick Osterling designed houses for himself and some neighbors on California, while a group of stately Perrysville homes became known as Judges' Row. Still other families found room to build across the city line, in Bellevue borough. Indeed, Bellevue, incorporated in 1867, experienced a population boom in the 1890s and the first years of the twentieth century as middle-class and working-class

Alleghenians flocked there. Others went yet further, to boroughs like Ben Avon and Sewickley, where rail stations enabled their commute to Allegheny and Pittsburgh.

New schools and other public buildings like firehouses followed the population booms in the outer neighborhoods. The city commissioned John

Brown Chapel A.M.E. Church at Boyle and Hemlock streets, built 1903; the congregation was established in 1837. Jesse Belfast

Morrow School, built on Davis Avenue in Brighton Heights, in 1895, along with handsome new fire stations on Observatory Hill and Troy Hill. Allegheny's older communities also received new public buildings. The Fifth Ward Manual Training School went up at Page and Manhattan streets in Manchester in 1894–95, featuring elaborate stone carvings by the prominent artisan Achille Giammartini of Page Street. In 1907–8, the Italian Renaissance–style Fifth Ward School No. 1 (now Conroy School) was built on the same block of Page. Manchester architect Frederick Sauer designed Deutschtown's 1898 Latimer School (restored in the 1980s as the Schoolhouse Apartments).

Two landmark churches began serving Allegheny's African American community in the first years of the twentieth century. Allen Chapel African Methodist Episcopal Church (originally Chartiers Street A.M.E.) purchased a former Lutheran church at Columbus Avenue and Fulton Street in Manchester for $10,000 in 1905. Brown Chapel A.M.E. Church was built in 1903 at Boyle and Hemlock streets, replacing an earlier building that the congregation had used. The two Gothic Revival edifices were not the only black churches in Allegheny, but their presence spoke to the community's stability and its respect for religion.

Inspired by all the growth and prosperity, Alleghenians looked across the river with envy at Schenley Park, which had begun with a 300-acre donation to Pittsburgh in 1889. In response, the city's current mayor, William Kennedy, led a fundraising drive to purchase the 202-acre Watson dairy farm near Perrysville Avenue in Allegheny's western uplands, for use as a municipal park. City government quickly established Riverview Park, and twenty-five thousand residents attended its dedication ceremony on Independence Day, 1894. The park remained popular with city dwellers, who made their way there on foot and via Perrysville Avenue streetcars. Public works crews had created winding roads and footpaths throughout the park, cleared land, and created a picnic area. An amphitheater, a zoo, an aviary, and a carousel would soon follow, opening in the park soon after the turn of the twentieth century. The new Allegheny Observatory, designed by architect Thorsten Billquist of Beech Avenue with guidance from astronomers John Brashear and James Keeler, went up around the same time; it occupies the park's highest point, 1,220 feet above sea level.

Alleghenians, with their new neighborhoods and their city's new amenities, relied heavily on public transportation, and area providers struggled to keep pace with the demand. The Pittsburgh, Fort Wayne & Chicago Railroad, part of the Pennsylvania Railroad system, constructed a new passenger depot on Federal Street between 1905 and 1907. The three-story brick Flemish Revival building with stone trim, which replaced a smaller Italianate facility, rose on the west side of Federal Street between the railroad's right-of-way and Stockton Avenue. The Fort Wayne Railroad, as the line was called, had still crossed Federal Street and the West North Avenue and Brighton Road intersection at grade when the old station was in use. Now, with the construction of the new station, the railroad built a new bridge over the Allegheny River and changed track grades, replacing the Federal Street crossing with an overpass and depressing its tracks to below grade at West North and Brighton.

These changes were a long time coming. Both of the at-grade intersections had been hazardous for years. In 1887, a Fort Wayne locomotive had hit a streetcar at Federal Street, killing bank teller John Culp of Sherman Avenue and Harriet Weyman, who lived on West North Avenue near Sherman. William Price of Beech Avenue, an electrical contractor and former Allegheny council member, had been struck by a Fort Wayne locomotive as a pedestrian at Brighton and West North in 1904. These Allegheny railroad fatalities were among hundreds of such accidents in urban America in the late nineteenth and early twentieth centuries, leading to track-grade changes across the country.

As the railroads improved, property on and above West North Avenue, west of the Fort Wayne Railroad, became valuable for manufacturing and other activities that benefited from rail sidings. The industrial 800 block of West North Avenue took on much of its present appearance between 1894 and 1902, as the Denny Estate and its tenants erected multistory factories and warehouses. Many of these buildings remain today, the block one of Pittsburgh's best examples of a turn-of-the-century urban manufacturing corridor.

As late as 1890, most of the manufacturing buildings along the block had been of wood-frame construction. The Allegheny Transfer Company occupied one of these frame buildings until 1894, when it built a seventy-foot-wide brick stable and storage building at 839 West North Avenue for $7,000. Across the street, the Allegheny City Department of Public Works commissioned a three-story, 20,000-square-foot brick stable for the city's horses in 1895–96. The façades of both these buildings show Richardsonian Romanesque influences.

The Hipwell Manufacturing Company had the brick building at the southwest corner of West North Avenue and Rope Way built in 1896 and

1897. Hipwell initially made telephones, electrical products, brass goods, and other metal products. In the 1920s, it became known for manufacturing metal flashlights, which it produced on the premises until the early twenty-first century. The Iron City Pharmacal Company, chemists, occupied the adjoining building, at 837 West North Avenue, in the late 1890s and the first few years of the new century. The Sands-Richey Company, chewing gum manufacturers, succeeded them as tenants.

The McCormick Harvester Company built a warehouse of red brick and structural steel on the north side of West North Avenue at the Fort Wayne Railroad tracks in 1902. The three-story building cost $33,000 and measured eighty-one feet wide. McCormick's successor, the International Harvester Company, added the building's fourth story in 1913. Peter and John Katsafanas moved the Katsafanas Coffee Company from Downtown Pittsburgh to a two-story brick building at 828 West North Avenue, next to International Harvester, in about 1925. The partners remodeled the façade with a metal sign that still spells "Katsafanas Coffee." Elsewhere on the 800 block, the North Avenue Stair Company made stairways for Allegheny's and Pittsburgh's houses and commercial buildings, and the North Side Transfer Company stood across the street from its competitor, Allegheny Transfer. Both the stair company and North Side Transfer buildings are now gone.

Industry and warehouses eventually took over part of the 900 block of West North as well. The Polar Water Company built a truck depot on the former site of a lumberyard there in the 1920s, and on the opposite side of the street a warehouse replaced a row of spacious rental houses that the Denny Estate had commissioned in the nineteenth century. The most ignominious blow to the neighborhood's earlier character may have come in 1929, when a catering company bought the Second Church of Christ, Scientist (the former Ninth United Presbyterian Church), at West North and Galveston avenues. The new owner removed a large part of the church, reducing it to one story for use as a factory. The former church still stands today, with part of its original first story evident to attentive passersby.

A short distance away in the same neighborhood, Recreation Park (originally Union Park) provided a place for Alleghenians to attend baseball and football games, fairs, and other events. The park occupied Denny family property, extending from about one hundred feet east of Allegheny Avenue to Galveston Avenue, and from Behan Street north to Pennsylvania Avenue. Recreation Park already existed by 1876, when the Alleghenys beat another

The Pittsburgh Alleghenys of 1888. Library of Congress Prints and Photographs Division (LC-DIG-ppmsca-18835), Washington, D.C.

local team, Xanthas, there in their first game. The Alleghenys, soon to be re-named the Pirates, left Recreation Park for the larger Exposition Park on the Allegheny River, in the present vicinity of Heinz Field, in 1891, but amateur and professional baseball teams continued to play at Recreation Park into the early twentieth century. Recreation Park also hosted fairs, bicycle races, and football games for amateur and professional teams and for the Western University of Pennsylvania. The Allegheny Athletic Association and the Pitts-burgh Athletic Club played the first professional football game at the park on November 12, 1892, when the Allegheny team paid twenty-four-year-old William "Pudge" Heffelfinger $500 to play. Heffelfinger, who had been an All-American at Yale, made the game's only touchdown and helped the Alle-gheny team to victory.

Exposition Park remained the Pirates' home until midseason 1909, when the team moved to the new Forbes Field, in Oakland. The earlier ballpark had faced perpetual flooding problems because of its proximity to the Al-legheny River. In one frightening incident early in the twentieth century, a neighborhood youngster named Art Rooney had nearly drowned in the

William Heffelfinger became the first professional football player in 1892, when the Allegheny team paid him $500 for a game. Carnegie Library of Pittsburgh Pennsylvania Department, Pittsburgh Photographic Library

flooded park. Less ominously but still problematically, the Pirates sometimes played baseball games with the field covered in water. Forbes Field, on the other hand, provided a site that was dry, had considerably larger capacity, and was close to Pittsburgh's emerging middle-class population center. After the Pirates left, Exposition Park still hosted semiprofessional baseball, college football, and other sporting events for several years before being demolished. Recreation Park vanished around the same time, its site converted to industry. No physical traces of Recreation Park exist, but the cobblestone paving of Behan Street is the surface on which countless Alleghenians walked on the way to the area's first baseball and football games.

Although professional baseball's popularity continued to increase in the late nineteenth and early twentieth centuries, players still received relatively modest paychecks. The Alleghenys, for example, were renamed the Pirates after the club quietly recruited second baseman Lou Bierbauer following the collapse of the upstart Players League in 1891. In 1892, however, Bierbauer, in spite of his fame, lived in a boardinghouse on Lacock Street off Federal Street, a neighborhood of aging homes, industry, and railroad tracks. Many of his teammates rented living quarters in the same neighborhood, and others boarded at the Hotel Boyer across the river, at Seventh Street and Fort Duquesne Boulevard. One Pirate who would remain a lifelong Pittsburgher, pitcher Frank "Lefty" Killen, lived in an unostentatious brick home at 1226 Resaca Place in 1897. In the 1896 season, he had led the National League with thirty-six wins.

While Alleghenians, including, perhaps, Bierbauer and Killen, happily rode streetcars to places like Recreation and Exposition parks, they could have easily chosen to stay in their immediate neighborhoods for daily necessities.

The Troy Hill Firehouse, built in 1901, housed Engine Company 39 until it closed in 1905 despite residents' protests. Pittsburgh Steelers/Karl Roser

The first decades of the twentieth century were probably the nation's best years for small groceries, bakeries, and the other family businesses that typically occupied neighborhood corners—or sometimes stood in the center of the block. Population density was high in the older, fully built-up parts of the city, and the early chain stores that would soon begin to take the place of the smallest mom-and-pop stores were not yet part of the retail scene.

In 1902, Manchester was home to nearly one hundred grocery stores, and Deutschtown contained more than seventy. Most of these stores had only a few hundred square feet of stock, and many proprietors and their families used not only the buildings' upper floors but the rear of the first stories as personal living space. Together both neighborhoods also had more than twenty barbershops and over fifteen bakeries. Although both neighborhoods covered significantly more area before post–World War II urban renewal and highway projects, the sheer number of such small retail businesses emphasizes the difference that a century can make in the urban streetscape: groceries, to illustrate, stood on nearly every block in Deutschtown and on most Manchester blocks that did not hold mansions. Troy Hill, which occupied the same area then that it does now, had more than twenty groceries, five dry goods stores, and three pharmacies; the residents of Perry Hilltop could choose from among around twenty groceries, five dry goods stores, three barbershops, and three bakeries.

All the population growth and commercial development in Allegheny highlighted the fact that the city's street-numbering system varied from neighborhood to neighborhood. Thus, in 1899 Allegheny City government superimposed a methodical house-numbering grid on most of the city. Numbers would henceforth run east and west from Federal Street, and north from the Allegheny River. They were now uniform on parallel blocks; for example, all blocks immediately north of East and West North Avenue began with 1100 and 1101, and Allegheny Avenue at the Allegheny West–Manchester border marked the beginning of the 1000 block of each street to its west. Despite the city's hilly topography, the new system extended into Allegheny's outer neighborhoods. Allegheny's 1899 house numbering remains in place today, even though some homeowners declined to change or conceal the carved stone house-number plaques that were typical of late nineteenth-century dwellings. Indeed, more than a century later, the original house number plaques that remain on some North Side brick façades reveal their pre-1899 construction.

In 1910, soon after annexation, the North Side's most significant and storied growth period came to a close. Its last mansions were about to be completed and occupied, and much of the remainder of the former lower Allegheny had settled into the stability that would characterize the North Side for about half of the twentieth century. During the next two decades, the area would experience steady public and private investment, transforming its main commercial district and filling in its newer residential neighborhoods.

CHAPTER 9

Maturity and Stability

1910–1930

A FTER SEVERAL DECADES of expansion, the second decade of the twentieth century marked the end of the North Side's steady growth. Between 1910 and 1930, the North Side's commercial districts and residential neighborhoods matured with the help of a healthy economy, greater Pittsburgh's growth, public works projects, and the new city zoning law. Natural disasters helped shape the North Side as well.

Pittsburgh always has been most flood-prone in March, as rains and melting snow and ice along the Allegheny and Monongahela rivers and their tributaries produce high waters. In the first years of the twentieth century, many Alleghenians and Pittsburghers recalled the flood of 1884, when the rivers reached a 33.3-foot flood stage, as the worst in their lifetimes. A few elderly residents had also witnessed the 35-foot flood of 1832, which remained the worst on local record. In the new century, destructive flooding became a near-annual occurrence, thanks to shoreline infill and upstream timber cutting. Thus, on the morning of March 14, 1907, when the *Pittsburgh Gazette* warned that a 28-foot flood was about to hit Pittsburgh and Allegheny and that waters might rise as high as 30 feet, residents may not have been surprised. This flood, however, surpassed expectations, breaking the 1884 mark in the early afternoon; the waters peaked at 36.5 feet on March 15.

The enormous 1907 flood hit Allegheny particularly hard, the *Pittsburgh Press* on March 15 calling Allegheny "one of the most disconsolate cities in the country." Area newspapers likened the Federal Street area, from the river north to Lacock Street, to canal-based Venice. Water reached the tops of the first stories of some buildings; families huddled on upper stories without heat, electricity, or food; police officers in skiffs brought bread and coffee to some of those who were stranded. Fire companies abandoned their stations

Lower Federal Street flooded on March 15, 1907. Pittsburgh City Photographer Collection, 1901–2002 (715.133438.CP). Archives Service Center, University of Pittsburgh

on River Avenue and at Martin and Corry streets, and Federal Street hotel porters carried guests to safety on their backs. Officials at the Western Penitentiary at Woods Run evacuated first-floor inmates to the upper stories. John Adley, who worked on a riverboat that was moored near the foot of Allegheny Avenue, apparently died when the boat capsized.

As the waters receded, Allegheny's lower streets were covered in eight inches of mud. The oozing sediment contained household goods, pieces of homes, and huge chunks of ice from a floe that had come down the river from Armstrong County. To add to Allegheny's woes, Downtown Pittsburgh's stores were able to reopen earlier than those in the Federal Street shopping district, and Allegheny's merchants could only watch as their customers crossed the river for food and dry goods.

In the wake of the 1907 flood, the Pittsburgh city government formed a commission to find solutions to this perennial problem, perhaps spurred on by the recent annexation of its neighbor across the river. H. J. Heinz, the food

Lacock Street looking east from Grantham Street, July 8, 1911, before street raising.
Pittsburgh City Photographer Collection, 1901–2002 (715.112144.CP). Archives Service Center, University of Pittsburgh

manufacturer, served as president of the commission; other members included department store partner Henry Buhl Jr.; James D. Callery, who owned a River Avenue tannery; and William J. Carlin, president of the Thomas Carlin's Sons foundry on River Avenue. The Pittsburgh Flood Commission's 1910 report found that experts accepted the possibility of a forty-foot flood, noting that property values in the affected areas would be $50 million higher if flooding were less of a threat. The commission recommended solutions including construction of reservoirs to contain floodwaters, reforestation, and raising grades of lower North Side streets. Although expense and landowner opposition made reservoirs unfeasible, the city raised the level of lower North Side streets in the summer and fall of 1911.

The area where the city raised North Side streets extended along Federal Street from the Sixth Street Bridge to the Fort Wayne Railroad tracks, and from Federal Street five blocks east to Grantham Street. Work crews deposited nine feet of fill in the lowest area, around Federal and Robinson streets; some sections were raised by only one foot. The project required relaying

Lacock Street looking east from Grantham Street, September 19, 1912, after street raising.
Pittsburgh City Photographer Collection, 1901–2002 (715.122882.CP). Archives Service Center, University of
Pittsburgh

streetcar tracks and natural gas and water lines and raising manholes and storm sewers, in addition to repaving streets. North Siders who commuted to jobs in Pittsburgh were forced to detour, and the *Pittsburgh Press* noted that many residents who attempted to walk through the construction area found their shoes ruined. The city placed temporary boardwalks along the streets for the 1911–12 winter, then laid new sidewalks after the fill had time to settle.

Many property owners hired contractors to raise their buildings to the new street level. On the south side of Robinson Street just east of Federal Street, workmen painstakingly elevated the party-wall houses of Jackson's Row, by then more than eighty years old, nearly a full story. The owners of a row of aging houses on Lacock Street, on the other hand, did not raise them: after the city finished changing the street grades, the new sidewalks came to within a few feet of the tops of the houses' front entrances, and tenants had to climb in and out of the openings. The houses nevertheless remained occupied for years. Elevating the buildings along Federal Street also inconvenienced merchants and shoppers. In December 1911 the *Gazette Times* reported that

Cremo and Martindale streets during the flood of March 28, 1913. Pittsburgh City Photographer Collection, 1901–2002 (715.133267.CP). Archives Service Center, University of Pittsburgh

store owners, fraternal lodges, and the keepers of rooming houses planned to ask the city for damages to compensate for the losses that the grading project had caused. The newspaper noted that the courts were also still reviewing the case of merchants on Ninth Street in Downtown Pittsburgh as a result of a grade-raising project there.

In spite of the short-term inconveniences it caused, raising street grades in the North Side also led to considerable private investment in the neighborhood over the next few years. Russell H. Boggs of Boggs & Buhl, for example, soon commissioned the three-story Boggs Building, with storefronts and apartments, occupying an entire block at the southeast corner of Federal and Robinson streets; its northernmost section incorporated a three-story hotel from the late nineteenth century that had been raised to the new street level. Charles Bickel had designed the building in the Classical Revival style, with terra-cotta ornamentation. Boggs also commissioned the William Penn Theater at Federal and Isabella streets and a three-story commercial building at 210 Federal Street. Across Federal Street from the Boggs Building, a four-story store and office building went up.

Boggs & Buhl itself moved to a spacious new four-story store building on Federal Street at the corner of the Diamond in 1914, also commissioning an adjacent laundry building in 1915. The same corner held the six-story bank and office building of the Dollar Savings Fund and Trust Society, constructed in 1913. Although both the new Boggs & Buhl buildings and the bank occupied higher ground than the former flood zone, and thus might have escaped flooding's hazards, it appears that the commercial development that took place after Federal Street was raised nevertheless contributed to these buildings' construction and to the area's overall increase in property values.

Meanwhile, east of Federal Street, new wholesale and rail-transport buildings soon dwarfed decades-old houses and small manufacturing shops. The wholesale paper manufacturer Ailing & Cory commissioned a six-story warehouse of reinforced concrete on River Avenue just east of Federal Street in September 1913. Frick and Lindsay, a distributor of supplies for steel mills and for oil-well and mining operations, moved into a just-completed seven-story building at Robinson and Sandusky streets in 1912 or 1913. The building, now the Andy Warhol Museum, contained enormous spools of wire rope and countless shovels, wheelbarrows, and lengths of metal pipe. One block away, the Pennsylvania Railroad and the Baltimore and Ohio Railroad constructed large new freight stations. The neighborhood's new role as a warehouse and transportation area came as a logical extension of Pittsburgh's warehouse district, directly across the Allegheny River. Warehouses had clustered along Liberty Avenue above Seventh Street, Downtown, since the days of the Pennsylvania Canal and had expanded into the lower Strip District in the late nineteenth century.

The rampant industrial development also spread to areas west of lower Federal Street that were safer from flooding. A seven-story brick warehouse that may have been the area's largest new structure, with a 1.4-acre footprint, went up at the corner of Allegheny and South avenues in 1917. A few blocks away, the D. L. Clark Company moved its candy-making operation from McKeesport back to the North Side in 1911, first occupying a former cracker factory on Martindale Street. The Clark candy plant grew during the next decade with additions and with the construction of a new factory across the street that produced Clark Bars, Zagnut Bars, and Teaberry gum until late in the twentieth century.

Public works projects also continued to change the face of the North

Side in the 1920s. As early as 1910, the nationally prominent landscape architect Frederick Law Olmsted Jr. had recommended widening busy East Ohio Street between the H. J. Heinz plant and the city's northeast boundary with Millvale, to benefit motorists living to the northeast. The city executed the 1.4-mile project in 1920 and 1921, at a cost of $555,000. Pittsburgh mayor Edward Vose Babcock and public works director Norman Brown shepherded the East Ohio Street widening, along with other transportation improvements that included creating the Boulevard of the Allies and widening West Carson Street and Second Avenue.

The widening of East Ohio Street, of course, led to other neighborhood changes. St. Nicholas Croatian Roman Catholic Church had to be moved back twenty feet and raised eight feet, relocated by the John Eichleay Company, a South Side firm that was nationally famous for moving large buildings. Other buildings along East Ohio were treated with less dignity: the front section of the Duquesne School, immediately east of St. Nicholas, was

The beginning of the East Ohio Street widening project in 1920. Carnegie Library of Pittsburgh Pennsylvania Department, Pittsburgh Photographic Library

simply removed, a new façade added to the part of the building that was left behind. This reconstruction dismayed neighborhood children, who lost the use of the schoolyard during much of 1920. Some houses and small stores along East Ohio also had their front sections removed, while others remained untouched. The small rental houses that lined part of the street's southern side were demolished.

Ambitious public works continued. When lumber baron and former Pittsburgh mayor Edward Vose Babcock became an Allegheny County commissioner in 1925, he hired Norman Brown to head the county's Public Works Department. During the next several years, Brown built bridges and roads at Babcock's direction, constructing new suspension bridges linking Downtown and the North Side at Sixth, Seventh, and Ninth streets just between 1925 and 1928. Those bridges and other new spans that provided access to the North Side—the Sixteenth Street, Thirty-first Street, West End, and McKees Rocks bridges—complied with federal standards for river navigation clearance. Ohio River Boulevard, linking the North Side with suburban boroughs, also emerged. All of the new bridges and the new roadway, together with the creation of North and South parks and the Allegheny County Airport, established Babcock's legacy as an aggressive modernizer of the county's transportation network and recreation facilities.

Just before Babcock became a county commissioner, a calamity had highlighted the need for newer and safer bridges. On the morning of January 18, 1924, a large deck section of the Thirtieth Street Bridge at Herr's Island collapsed into the icy Allegheny River. John Richard of Scriba Place on Troy Hill and John Rimensnyder of Mount Troy Road were in a truck carrying livestock for the William Zollar Packing Company on Spring Garden Avenue; the truck fell through the hole in the bridge deck into the river. Rimensnyder, thirty-six, reportedly grabbed the tail of one of the hogs that the truck had been carrying and held on as the animal swam to land. Richard, the twenty-two-year-old truck driver, drowned. A coroner's jury found the city responsible for the tragedy, and Pittsburgh newspapers blasted Mayor William A. Magee and the city's Public Works Department, pointing out that local bridges now routinely carried heavier loads than the nineteenth-century ones for which they had been designed.

Changes in urban activity also led to Pittsburgh's first zoning ordinance, in 1923. Well before that time, the North Side had arguably lost residents as a result of the lack of land-use controls. The neighborhoods from which

St. Nicholas Church on East Ohio Street being raised eight feet and moved back twenty feet to accommodate street widening, 1921. John W. Eichleay Jr.

Allegheny City's middle class had fled in the late nineteenth and early twentieth centuries—primarily Allegheny West, Manchester, and the Mexican War Streets—had previously had no means to prevent property owners from converting single-family houses to flats or from demolishing houses to build factories or warehouses. In contrast, many developers in the East End neighborhoods to which middle-class Alleghenians moved imposed deed covenants requiring single-family residences with minimum lot sizes and construction costs. A few developers in newer North Side neighborhoods like Brighton Heights and Observatory Hill had also begun to impose similar deed restrictions in the late nineteenth century. The North Side, however, was otherwise long free of land-use constraints, except for those that courteous neighbors might extend one another.

In 1917, however, the Pittsburgh Voters League and the Civic Club of Allegheny County both recommended that the city implement a zoning ordinance, a year after New York City became the first large American city to regulate land use. The Civic Club specifically predicted that factories would eventually replace dwellings in the North Side's oldest residential areas. Land use on the North Side and throughout Pittsburgh received further attention in 1921, when the city hosted 275 US city planners for the Thirteenth Annual Conference on City Planning. Then, in 1923, during final discussions of Pittsburgh's first zoning ordinance, the Denny Estate successfully appealed to the City Council to zone its residential property in what is now Allegheny West for light industrial use, an estate representative testifying that houses near West North Avenue and Brighton Road were still renting for about the same amounts as they had in 1882.

The 1923 zoning code designated the North Side's heart, a twenty-block area around Federal and Ohio streets, for commercial activity. The fringes of that central area, as well as the Mexican War Streets, half of Deutschtown, slivers of Allegheny West, a third of Manchester, and Perry Hilltop and Troy Hill, were zoned as "A Residence Districts." Ridge and North Lincoln avenues in Allegheny West and most of Brighton Heights, Observatory Hill, Summer Hill, and Spring Hill were termed "B Residence Districts." At the same time, city planners, in a move that many North Siders would later regret, zoned about half of residential Manchester and its Beaver Avenue shopping district and half of Deutschtown for light industry, along with the neighborhood that extended for several blocks west and east of lower Federal Street. Planners zoned the rest of Manchester and Woods Run, fronting on the Ohio River, for heavy industry.

The western North Side's mansion district had started to change within several years after the neighborhood's last great houses went up, in about 1910, and its decline was evident by 1919, when a dearth of new families over the past several years caused the Allegheny Preparatory School to close. Soon after World War I ended, in 1918, more and more prominent families began living full-time at their Sewickley Heights estates or otherwise left the North Side. In 1921, the *Blue Book*, Pittsburgh's directory of affluent society families, listed 181 North Side households; 96 were in Allegheny West, in Manchester, and on or near West North Avenue on the Mexican War Streets, and 13 were in the North Side's old core, between East and West parks. By just 1932, the *Blue Book* listed only 94 North Side households: 38 in Allegheny West and Manchester and 8 in the old core.

Some families occupied their Allegheny West homes, at least part-time, well into the 1920s or 1930s. When those owners eventually moved, wealthy families rarely stepped forward to buy or rent their mansions. By the late 1920s, the remaining families of Millionaires' Row were disproportionately represented by elderly homeowners, many of them the aging unmarried children of the elite who had built or purchased homes in the neighborhood decades earlier. The widow Elizabeth Thaw remained in her old home at 930 North Lincoln after her husband's death, staying there until 1923, then resided in Squirrel Hill and Sewickley Heights, selling her North Side mansion for $27,500 to an elocutionist who operated the Pittsburgh School of Speech there. The mansion became a boardinghouse in about 1930. The former Letitia Holmes house, at 719 Brighton Road, became a boys' home in 1923, after Holmes's granddaughter moved to the Sewickley area and sold the property. Charlotte and George Harton Singer sold their mansion at 849 North Lincoln Avenue in 1920 to hardware manufacturer John McGinley and his wife, Jennie, in one of the neighborhood's few post-1910 purchases by prosperous owner-occupant families. Jennie McGinley and others, however, converted 849 North Lincoln Avenue to a rooming house in 1932. Beginning in the 1920s, rooming-house operators purchased many of the neighborhood's old mansions.

The death of one of the old Ridge Avenue millionaires made national headlines. Eben M. and J. Frederic Byers, the sons of A. M. and Martha Fleming Byers, had remained in the family home at Ridge Avenue and Galveston Street after their widowed mother moved to her Sewickley Heights estate, Poplar Hill. Eben, a lifelong bachelor with a reputation as a ladies' man, earned international recognition as an amateur golfer. He began taking

Radithor, a solution of radium and water, after a 1927 arm injury, drinking fourteen hundred bottles of the patent medicine in 1930 and 1931, causing his lower jawbone, much of his upper jaw, and parts of his skull to dissolve and brain abscesses to form. Grossly disfigured, Eben Byers died of radium poisoning in 1932 and now lies in a lead-lined coffin in Allegheny Cemetery. The *Wall Street Journal,* noting his death, ran a memorable headline: "The radium water worked fine until his jaw came off." The Federal Trade Commission had interviewed the ailing Byers a few months before he died and subsequently forced Radithor's New Jersey manufacturer and similar firms to cease operation.

The Byers-Lyon mansion, still containing its original furnishings and art collection, sat empty for years after Eben Byers's death, until Pittsburgh demolition contractor and salvage dealer Austin Givens, Inc., bought it for $25,000 in 1939, planning to remove valuable interior architectural items for resale and demolish what remained of the building. Givens did not carry through with these plans, however, and in 1941 sold the mansion to the Eastern Star Temple Association, a women's organization.

When Harmar D. Denny died in 1918, Elizabeth Denny inherited his interest in the Denny Estate. She remained in her hulking stone mansion at 811 Ridge Avenue long after nearly all of her prominent neighbors had left for Sewickley and the East End, and in 1935 she held Ridge Avenue's last society debut, presenting her debutante granddaughter Elizabeth Marshall Denny with a formal tea party. Limousines delivered society guests to the home, gliding past mansions that had long before been converted to business use or to crowded rooming houses. Mrs. Denny told the *Pittsburgh Press,* "I was born here. I intend to remain on this avenue for the rest of my days. I don't care how many move." The Allegheny Centennial Committee visited her in 1940, to take advantage of her recollections of the nineteenth century's "Millionaires' Row" for a book it was compiling.

When Mrs. Denny proclaimed her allegiance to Ridge Avenue in 1935, she may in fact not have been able to afford to move. The Denny real estate fortunes suffered increasingly from residential and industrial vacancies as the Great Depression worsened in the early 1930s and as estate managers adopted a policy of not charging rent to unemployed tenants and not requesting back rent once tenants found work. The Denny Estate evicted no tenants for nonpayment during the Depression and also assigned about 150 properties to social-service agencies that provided housing for unemployed families between 1932 and 1935. The Denny family, with its diminished rental income, ran up tens of thousands of dollars in property tax delinquency to the City of Pittsburgh, Allegheny County, and Pittsburgh School District. Mrs. Denny thus owed back taxes on 811 Ridge by 1935, when the city, county, and school district initiated proceedings to collect the debt. Whether because of her family's prominence, the Denny estate's kindness toward tenants, or the dismal prospect of trying to resell the mansion, the taxing entities did not follow through with foreclosure until 1947. By then, Mrs. Denny had lived in the East End for about four years. When she died in 1950, she left behind a personal estate worth $35,561 and real estate in Downtown, the Strip District, the lower Hill District, and on West North Avenue.

The migration of the wealthy, abetted by continuing industrial encroachment on the lower North Side, reliable new automobiles, and road improvements, was also hastened by a natural gas explosion. On November 14, 1927,

Reedsdale Street after a gas tank explosion on November 14, 1927. Pittsburgh City Photographer Collection, 1901–2002 (715.275496.CP). Archives Service Center, University of Pittsburgh

workmen using acetylene torches accidentally ignited a five-million-cubic-foot tank that the Equitable Gas Company owned on Reedsdale Street, at the foot of Fontella Street in Manchester. Two smaller gas tanks on the property caught fire as well. The US Weather Bureau reported on the incident: "What seemed to be a dense mass of dust and smoke [rose] from the ruins . . . burst into flames and a ball of fire apparently 100 feet in diameter separated from the dense mass and began to rise. It rose rapidly, the volume growing smaller with ascent until finally it burned itself out at an estimated height of 1,000 feet." The explosion was audible throughout Allegheny County and in parts of bordering counties. At a comfortable home on Western Avenue, Susan Cooper Walker felt the blast: "Unaware that I had just regained consciousness, I opened my eyes and was amazed to see the pictures from the walls lying broken on the floor. . . . I heard a commotion in another part of the house and rushed out to find windows broken, the air full of plaster dust from fallen ceilings, and everything in a jumble. The twelve big plate glass windows in the end of the dining room were shattered. Most of the windows in the house were out. Nearly all the ceilings were down."

All told, the blast killed twenty-eight people, including Equitable Gas superintendent Charles S. Michaels of 917 Beech Avenue, and injured hundreds more. In addition to Equitable Gas employees, some of the dead had worked for the Riter-Conley Company, which had been working on the gas tank; the Joseph Horne Company, whose warehouse was across Reedsdale Street from the blast; and the Pittsburgh Clay Pot Company, whose ruined plant was immediately west of the gas tanks. After the blast, thousands of Pittsburghers mobbed the Allegheny County morgue, anxious to learn the identities of the dead.

In a front-page story, the *New York Times* described the blast: "The crash of rending metal, the jangle of shattered glass in windows within a radius of five miles, the rasping of broken timbers and the rumble of crumbling walls, and then the shrieks of dying, the groans of the hundreds of injured and the cries of persons who fled from their ruined homes—these were the sounds and scenes throughout the Manchester district after the tanks let go." Within a two-block radius, the explosion damaged many buildings irreparably, toppling walls and chimneys and causing roofs to collapse, rupturing water mains, and causing floods. Buildings as far away as Pennsylvania Avenue, Brighton Road, and West North Avenue, about a mile away, sustained lesser structural damage. The blast blew out the windows of storefronts and

homes and upset furniture and other goods in several North Side neighborhoods, Downtown Pittsburgh, the West End, and the South Side, effects
felt as far away as East Liberty, Carrick, and Homestead. Along Downtown
streets, plate-glass windows dropped and cut office workers. In the West End,
one thousand windows broke in the Lawrence Paint Company's seven-story
building facing the Point, and windows blew out at the Duquesne Incline and
in nearby factories.

In the explosion's chaotic aftermath Father Devlin of St. Peter's Church
on West Ohio Street converted the parish elementary school to an emergency
hospital, Boggs & Buhl contributing beds to the effort. The Salvation Army
set up operations on Reedsdale Street, and iron-pipe manufacturer J. Frederic
Byers allowed the Red Cross to set up a temporary headquarters in his home
at 911 Ridge Avenue. Presbyterian Hospital, then at Sherman and Montgomery avenues, treated 210 of the wounded; Allegheny General Hospital treated
191 people; and St. John's Hospital in Brighton Heights cared for 43. The roll
call of the injured included students of the Conroy School on Page Street in

Kenyon Theater and Café, Federal and Erie streets. Pittsburgh City Photographer Collection, 1901–
2002 (715.3950405.CP). Archives Service Center, University of Pittsburgh

Manchester, who had been showered with glass shards while they played in their schoolyard.

In spite of the chaos caused by the explosion, the decline of the North Side's Millionaires' Row and the lower North Side's middle-class neighborhoods was largely quiet. In the meantime, other areas thrived. The largely German and Italian northern half of Manchester had greater residential stability than the more prosperous southern half, as families headed by contractors, shopkeepers, Fort Wayne Railroad workers, and skilled and unskilled workers in the Pittsburgh Locomotive Works and other factories remained in their Manchester homes well after their wealthier neighbors had left the North Side for the East End. Employment in stockyards and tanneries and at H. J. Heinz anchored Spring Garden, Troy Hill, and Spring Hill. The latter two neighborhoods, unlike Manchester, also had room for new home construction during the prosperous 1920s. Perry Hilltop and Fineview remained middle-class and working-class communities, with new residents moving uphill from the Mexican War Streets and the central North Side. The area's northernmost neighborhoods—Brighton Heights, Observatory Hill, and Summer Hill—also still had undeveloped land, and the healthy 1920s economy enabled the construction of hundreds of new homes for middle-class families.

One notable Brighton Heights home, at 3710 California Avenue, was built in 1927 for Dr. J. Wade Elphinstone, a well-known physician. Decades later it would house Dan Rooney, a young jack-of-all-trades with his father's football team, the Steelers, and his wife, Patricia, along with their growing brood. This house was designed by the prominent architect Benno Janssen and his business partner, William Y. Cocken. Architect Janssen was distinguished by both his talent and his professional lineage: before settling in Pittsburgh, he had worked as a draftsman with the Boston architectural firm Shepley, Rutan & Coolidge, the successor to H. H. Richardson's office. He first came to Pittsburgh in 1904 to work for McClure & Spahr. Janssen and Cocken did most of their work in the East End, but while the records of early twentieth-century Pittsburgh construction suggest that few upper North Side families hired upper-echelon architects such as Janssen, many of the Craftsman, Tudor, Prairie, and Colonial Revival houses that went up in Brighton Heights, on Observatory Hill, and in the outer East Valley were designed by other talented architects, like Charles Bartberger, Frank Smart, C. G. Mentel, William Snaman, and C. W. Hodgdon. Benno Janssen did also design the North

Side's Annunciation Roman Catholic School at North Charles Street and Norwood Avenue with Edward Hergenroeder in 1926. Later on, in the early 1940s, Edward Hergenroeder would design North Catholic High School on Troy Hill.

All the churches and other institutions founded by area newcomers continued to change the shape of the neighborhood. Nativity Roman Catholic parish was founded to serve the Observatory Hill neighborhood in 1916. Its congregation worshipped in a former Lutheran church for ten years, then moved to a new edifice on Franklin Road. St. Cyprian, the North Side's first Polish Roman Catholic congregation, was founded in 1920. That year, the congregation acquired the former Concordia Club building at 204 East Stockton Avenue and remodeled the structure as its church, rectory, school, and convent. Brighton Heights residents established St. Cyril of Alexandria in 1924, promptly commissioning a church building on Brighton Road.

The North Side's growing African American population established Bidwell Presbyterian Church around 1917, constructing a church building at

Oliver High School on Brighton Road. Pittsburgh Steelers/Karl Roser

the northwest corner of Bidwell and Liverpool streets in Manchester. Most of the congregation's charter members lived in Manchester, with others coming from the Charles Street Valley, the Mexican War Streets, Allegheny West, and as far away as Millvale and Bellevue. S. T. Campbell, one of these charter members, was a real estate agent working out of his home on Strauss Street in the Charles Street Valley, while his neighbor and fellow trustee Joseph Bowman owned a delivery service. The other charter trustees included laborers and drivers. Pastor Benjamin F. Glasco shepherded the Bidwell Presbyterian congregation from its beginnings into the 1930s.

The North Side's commercial districts matured in the second decade of the century, and entrepreneurs opened silent motion picture theaters in most neighborhoods. Russell H. Boggs's William Penn Theater, at Federal and Isabella streets, may have been the best-known early North Side theater because of its location. In 1914, Crucible Steel owner David E. Park commissioned the construction of the Garden Theater on West North Avenue, designed by Thomas H. Scott. Park lived nearby on East North Avenue, in a mansion that occupied part of the present site of Allegheny General Hospital. More North Side theaters quickly followed. James and Charles Walker of Juniata Street in Manchester closed their family's longtime feed business at 1625 Beaver Avenue and had the Academy Theater built on its site in 1913. The Hippodrome Theater opened directly across the street from the Academy about five years later. The Keystone Theater at 528 East Ohio Street began to present silent pictures in 1915 or 1916. Deutschtown residents could also visit the Arcadia, Century, and Gould theaters, all on East Ohio Street between East and Chestnut. By the mid-1920s, most of the North Side's commercial strips had at least one theater. Troy Hill residents saw shows at the Lowrie Theater at 1713 Lowrie Street and at the Colonial at 1733 Lowrie Street; they could walk down the Basin Street city steps to the Jewel Theater, at 1201 Spring Garden Avenue. The Happy Hour Theater at 3202 McClure Avenue and the Morris Theater served the Woods Run neighborhood. Perry Hilltop residents attended shows at the Atlas Theater at 2603 Perrysville Avenue; the Brighton Theater at 1812 Brighton Road was convenient to neighbors in the Charles Street Valley and Manchester. Multiple streetcar lines led to the Garden Theater and to the Novelty, Elite, and New Kenyon theaters on Federal Street, in the North Side's central shopping district. Some of the theaters in less affluent neighborhoods, particularly in earlier years, had unpretentious exteriors and interiors, while those in major shopping areas, like lower Federal Street and East Ohio

Street, conformed more closely to the popular image of classic movie houses.

The social fabric was also enriched by thriving fraternal and veterans' lodges and by ethnic, sporting, and musical associations. The North Side's population peaked in 1920, with 142,322 residents, a large number of whom seem to have belonged to one or more organizations. In the 1920s, the lower North Side neighborhoods with fully developed commercial streets—Deutschtown, Manchester, and the central Federal Street area—contained multiple halls in which well-known fraternal lodges and independent organizations held meetings. Numerous Masonic lodges shared space in the Masonic Hall at West North Avenue and Reddour Street, while other chapters convened at Madison and Pressley streets in Deutschtown. The Socialist Lyceum at Foreland and James streets in Deutschtown housed the Allied Slavonic Singing Society, the Swiss Singing Society, the Justice Building and Loan Association, the Daughters of America's Allegheny Council, and the Allegheny Commandery of the Knights of Malta. Rodgers Hall, at 105 Federal Street, on the present site of PNC Park, leased meeting space to the Knights of Pythias, the Knights of Malta, three International Order of Odd Fellows lodges, the Ladies of the Maccabees, the Sons and Daughters of Liberty, and railroad signalmen and painters' unions.

The North Side was also home to numerous athletic associations. Turner halls, where residents of German descent practiced "physical culture," thrived in Deutschtown and Manchester. Some residents formed groups that took advantage of the local rivers: the Columbia Boat Club was at the foot of Mendota Street, on the Allegheny River, and the Manchester Aquatic Club's home was at the foot of Franklin Street. The Irish-American Athletic Association used space at David B. Oliver High School in Brighton Heights. Residents also supported the Union Camping Club on Foreland Street in Deutschtown, the Orient Camping Club at 701 East Ohio Street, and the Venus Star Hunting and Fishing Club on Spring Garden Avenue, although the most popular sport at some of those establishment consisted of outsmarting Prohibition.

Various social and ethnic clubs also thrived, some giving their members the opportunity to drink during the Prohibition years (1920–33). The Army and Navy Club met in the former Allegheny City Hall at Federal and Ohio streets. Some Manchester residents belonged to the Columbus Italian Political Club on Columbus Avenue, the Slavonic Evangelical Union at 1601 Beaver Avenue, or the Aurora Club at 1800 Beaver Avenue. To the east were

Deutschtown's German-American Beneficial Club at 510 Suismon Street, the National Croatian Society at 1012 Peralta Street, the Kennelworth Club at 422 East Ohio Street, and the Optimist Social Club at 1126 Brabec Street on Troy Hill. The decades before television would lure many Americans away were the heyday of such associations.

Of course, some Pittsburghers pursued less wholesome recreation on the North Side. Many visited women who worked for the infamous madam Nettie Gordon, who owned "resorts" on the lower North Side between about 1910 and 1934. Gordon had been born in or near Keyser, West Virginia, in 1875, to Sydney and William H. Gordon, a carpenter. She moved to Pittsburgh about 1900 and found work as a waitress on Fourth Avenue, Downtown. By about 1910, she had emerged as a key figure in the North Side's underworld, arguably becoming Pittsburgh's most prominent "resort" keeper. Gordon, apparently prosperous, invested her earnings in valuable real estate on the North Side and Bellevue. She never married and lived comfortably with servants in an apartment building that she owned at 10–12 East North Avenue, now the Light of Life mission. She donated generously to political campaigns, and although she was arrested on a few occasions, she reportedly had bought off enough city officials and judges that she had little fear of landing in prison. She eventually became a Republican committeewoman in the Twenty-second Ward, helping poor North Side families with donations of groceries and coal. After Gordon died in 1934 in St. John's Hospital in Brighton Heights, following gallstone surgery, she was buried in Uniondale Cemetery on the North Side and eulogized in Pittsburgh's daily newspapers and in the venerable society magazine the *Bulletin Index*. She left behind a $200,000 estate, equal to well over $1 million in the early twenty-first century.

Nettie Gordon's success is best viewed within the context of the freewheeling lower North Side of her day. Prohibition drove alcohol distribution and sales into the hands of racketeers who enjoyed the protection of Pittsburgh police. Speakeasies that offered beer and whiskey, slot machines, and other illegal entertainment did business openly, particularly on General Robinson and Sandusky streets. On the North Side, drinking was widespread and open during Prohibition. Pittsburgh reporter Ray Sprigle wrote regularly about the North Side's speakeasies and gambling dens and the police officials and politicians who protected and profited from them. The crusading Sprigle would go on to gain national fame when he won a Pulitzer Prize in 1938 for documenting Supreme Court justice Hugo Black's past Ku Klux Klan membership; he later wrote about spending a month in the South disguised as a black man. In the 1920s Sprigle, however, devoted particular attention to North Side police inspector Charles Faulkner, who was able to move to a substantial red-brick house that still stands on Chateau Street at Pennsylvania Avenue in Manchester, ostensibly on his $3,000 annual city salary. In Deutschtown, Sprigle quietly trailed a beer salesman on his collection route to a host of bars on East Street and Madison Avenue, at Middle and Tripoli streets, at Chestnut and Peralta streets, and on a side trip up Spring Garden Avenue. The *Pittsburgh Post* identified dozens of the "vice resorts" targeted in "Sprigle's Roll of Shame," calling the Delmont Hotel in the Boggs Building at Federal and General Robinson streets a "bawdy house" where women openly solicited beer-drinking customers. On East Ohio Street, patrons drank, played slot machines, and consorted with prostitutes at the Island Hotel (later Lambros Lounge). The adjacent Green Front Inn offered its customers both booze and women. Edward J. Detzel operated slot machines in his auto parts store at 3607 Evergreen Road, near the city's northern border. Patrons at Schmidt's Hotel at Lowrie and Lager streets on Troy Hill drank beer and played slot machines; a nearby pool hall at 1723 Lowrie Street also had slots.

Sprigle's persistence earned his newspaper the enmity of police officials, who retaliated by arresting and jailing photographers snapping shots of a fire at the Cyclorama Building at Beech Avenue and Brighton Road. Soon, however, the times would shift yet again, as federal charges against many of the liquor dealers in 1928 and Prohibition's subsequent end helped weaken the North Side rackets. The neighborhood went on to shift further in the wake of national depression and global war.

CHAPTER 10

The Great Depression and World War

1930–1950

THE AMERICAN STOCK MARKET crashed on October 29, 1929. On a single day, stocks lost 12 percent of their value. North Siders and other Pittsburgh residents may have been worried, but few, if any, anticipated the difficulties to come. And indeed, Pittsburgh was spared the early brunt of the crash. Mills and factories continued to run on existing orders, and local construction remained active in 1930. In and after 1931, however, Pittsburghers, like citizens across the nation, felt the effects of the Great Depression.

Events on the North Side mirrored conditions in greater Pittsburgh and in the United States: job losses and pay cuts, sheriff's sales of family homes and business properties, bank failures, and the closing of familiar neighborhood businesses. Unemployment and shrinking paychecks left some families unable to pay mortgages or rent, and many of those families doubled up with relatives or strangers in crowded living quarters. Banks found few buyers for foreclosed houses, instead renting many abandoned dwellings to tenants or letting them stand empty for years. Banks would remain reluctant owners of some area foreclosures until the early 1940s. Compounding banks' difficulties, some depositors feared closings and withdrew their savings. The resulting bank runs—many withdrawals in a short time—caused some financial institutions to suspend operation. Before the federal government began to insure deposits in 1934, depositors in failed banks lost considerable amounts of money.

Before the beginning of the Great Depression, ten banks operated on Pittsburgh's North Side. Nearly all were in the lower Federal Street commercial corridor, on Beaver Avenue in the Manchester business district, or along East Ohio Street in Deutschtown. In these decades before branch banking, such independent financial institutions scattered along community business corridors were sources of community stability and pride, their boards of directors typically made up of neighborhood retail merchants, manufacturers, doctors, and contractors.

The Depression brought devastating changes to the nation's financial landscape. The Bank of Secured Savings, at Beaver Avenue and North Franklin Street, a Manchester mainstay since 1893, closed its doors permanently on July 12, 1932. With the closing, the bank's 7,670 depositors lost their savings, which totaled $1,333,232, an average of $174 per person. The 4,100 depositors at the Perry State Bank, on Perrysville Avenue in Observatory Hill, lost an average of $133 apiece. The Real Estate Savings & Trust Company, on Federal Street, just south of the Diamond, closed on November 16, 1932, as a result of large withdrawals. Its 12,466 depositors lost an average $188. The closed institutions managed to make sporadic payments to depositors during the 1930s. By 1939, the Bank of Secured Savings had returned 64 percent of its outstanding deposits, the Perry State Bank 91 percent, and the Real Estate Savings & Trust Company 59 percent. The *Pittsburgh Press* reported, however, that there was "scant prospect that [the depositors] will ever collect much more of their money." This prediction would turn out to be accurate.

Nevertheless, over time, some of the injured institutions did recover. The Real Estate Savings & Trust Company eventually reorganized and reopened as the North Side Deposit Bank, predecessor of today's Northside Bank. The National Bank of America in Pittsburgh, at 709 East Ohio Street in Deutschtown, remained closed for about eighteen months in 1933 and 1934, reopening with an agreement that its depositors would waive 50 percent of their savings and accept gradual repayments as the institution returned to stability. The Bank of Secured Savings never reopened; one of the North Side's first state-owned wine and spirits stores occupied its former space after Prohibition was repealed in 1933.

The Great Depression also left many area residents unemployed. To assist in the emergency, the Allegheny County Emergency Association (ACEA) organized in January 1931 to provide work to unemployed men and women. During the next two years, the association hired county residents to improve various public facilities, some on the North Side. At Emmanuel Episcopal Church at West North and Allegheny avenues, for example, the fund paid unemployed congregation members and other workers to construct a basement auditorium. ACEA workers also labored at Allegheny General Hospital on Stockton Avenue, St. John's Hospital in Brighton Heights, the Woods Run Settlement House, Holmes Hall for Boys on Brighton Road, and the YMCA on West North Avenue.

In the midst of the Depression's ravages, most North Side neighborhoods fell on the side of Democrat challenger Franklin D. Roosevelt in the 1932 presidential election. Six of the seven North Side wards went for Roosevelt, who garnered more than two-thirds of ballots in the Twenty-third Ward (Deutschtown) and more than three-quarters in the Twenty-fourth (Troy Hill and parts of Spring Garden and Spring Hill). The Twenty-seventh Ward (Brighton Heights and Woods Run) was the only one to side with Herbert Hoover, its residents casting their ballots for the Republican incumbent by a nearly two-to-one margin. Hard times may have been less evident in middle-class Brighton Heights, if not in blue-collar Woods Run.

As economic conditions deteriorated, more and more North Side residents also became at least temporarily homeless. About twenty unemployed, homeless men built a group of crude huts, which the *Pittsburgh Post-Gazette* dubbed "Boxtown," on Monument Hill in the winter of 1932. City government soon burned Boxtown, along with the larger and better-known "Hooverville," along Penn Avenue in the Strip District. The homeless remained, of course, even if their temporary residences were eradicated. Susan Cooper Walker, of Western Avenue, noted that "each morning, even after the coldest nights, Allegheny Park would be carpeted with a mass of newspapers on which the homeless had slept. Sometimes we would feed as many as thirty men a day who stopped at our door, but I decided that was not fair to the cook, so we got meal tickets from restaurants in Pittsburgh and Woods Run and gave those to the men . . . rather than food or money."

Around the same time, about fifty World War I veterans who had neither work nor homes took over a row of vacant, dilapidated storefronts with upstairs apartments at 1120–24 Pennsylvania Avenue in Manchester. The veterans made some repairs to the property and agreed to pool any wages or relief checks they received. The settlement became known as War Veterans Industries and remained there until at least 1934. Other unemployed men congregated at the Brighton Woods Community Center, at 1223 Woods Run Avenue. In 1933, the *Post-Gazette* appealed to readers to donate money so that this community center and others like it around the city could purchase athletic equipment to provide recreation for an estimated ten thousand jobless residents.

Many area families' income fell well below subsistence level. A 1937 study found that a working-class family of four in Pittsburgh needed to earn at least $1,366 per year to live comfortably. Some families had no choice but to get by on less, and charitable groups and government cobbled together various forms of assistance for residents unable to provide for themselves. Pittsburgh government and the Allegheny County Emergency Association distributed $50,000 worth of free shoes to the aid effort, handed out by Boggs & Buhl, on lower Federal Street, and by the shoe stores of Charles Wanetick at 513 East Ohio Street, John Berberich at 523 East Ohio Street, and James Simon at 1614 Beaver Avenue. The Pittsburgh Surplus for the Needy Committee reopened a former food-processing plant on Spring Garden Avenue, producing thousands of cans of vegetables per day for distribution to impoverished families.

Civic leaders also simply tried to cheer city residents. In mid-1933, arguably the worst year of the Depression, city officials, marching bands, nationality groups, and mummers staged a "funeral parade for Hard Times." City council president and North Sider Harry A. Little, of 621 Allegheny Avenue, was among the parade planners. The procession, before a reported one hundred thousand cheering spectators, marched from Oakland to Downtown and the North Side, along Federal Street and Stockton Avenue, and ended at Brighton Road. Pallbearers wore coveralls to suggest the revival of Pittsburgh's factories.

The Pittsburgh economy did begin to show signs of life toward the mid-1930s. Sears, Roebuck and Company opened a new store at East Ohio and Sandusky streets in August 1934, and home construction started to revive where undeveloped land remained on the upper North Side and in some other Pittsburgh neighborhoods. Property owners erected thirty-one houses on the North Side in 1935 and twenty-nine more in 1936. Most of the new dwellings were in the Twenty-sixth Ward, covering Observatory Hill, Perry Hilltop, and part of Spring Hill. Prohibition's end in 1933 had also allowed the old Eberhard & Ober brewery at the foot of Troy Hill, by then a Pittsburgh Brewing Company facility, to reopen. Taverns and clubs could now begin to sell alcohol openly again.

Still, as late as 1938, public assistance and federal works programs such as the Works Progress Administration (WPA) and the Public Works Administration (PWA) supported 61 percent of residents in the lower North Side. (In a telling comparison, public funds supported 2 percent of Squirrel Hill's population but 82 percent of Hill District residents.) In addition to employing North Siders, the WPA and PWA maintained the community's infrastructure and recorded local history. The PWA contributed $71,000 toward the city's $281,000 renovation of the aging North Side Market House in 1935 and 1936, with improved structural support and new refrigeration equipment, floors, marquees, and lighting. The city used WPA funds to grade and pave streets; to build water lines, storm sewers, city steps, and retaining walls; to repair public safety buildings and parks; and to plant trees. Using federal funds, teams of unemployed architects also documented the physical features and history of significant older buildings in Pittsburgh, as they did in other cities across the nation. The Brewer Mansion, then still standing on Western Avenue near Allegheny, was apparently the first North Side building documented in the project, which continues today as the Historic American Buildings Survey. In 1936, WPA workers recorded the physical features of every North Side building and of most buildings in Allegheny County. In 1939, the WPA-funded Pennsylvania Writers' Project compiled *The Story of Old Allegheny City*, a history of the North Side.

The nascent recovery was dealt a temporary setback by the catastrophic St. Patrick's Day 1936 flood. The floodwaters crested at 46 feet on March 18, nearly 10 feet above 1907's high-water level of 36.5 feet. Downtown Pittsburgh's devastation received national media attention, but the North Side was particularly hard hit. The fetid waters inundated homes and businesses within three blocks of the Allegheny and Ohio rivers, leaving twenty-five thousand residents temporarily homeless in Deutschtown, the lower Federal Street area, Manchester, and Woods Run. The *Pittsburgh Press* called the lower North Side a "little hell . . . a silt-covered ghost town." The Red Cross used the YMCA at West North Avenue and Monterey Street as its temporary North Side headquarters, and the Carnegie Library, the Sarah Heinz House in Deutschtown, and most churches, schools, firehouses and police stations on dry land became shelters.

Some residents tragically never reached area shelters: nearly half of Allegheny County's thirty-eight flood casualties died on the North Side. Albert Folan, a twenty-one-year-old laborer, drowned when his skiff capsized near his home. Oscar Beckert, age fifty-five, died while trying to keep inventory dry in the seed store that he owned at the northwest corner of Federal and Isabella streets. Rising waters on Saw Mill Way, an alley near the H. J. Heinz complex, also imperiled the massively built Marco Markovich, age twenty-eight, a 625-pound former meat cutter who had contracted pneumonia. A

Red Cross rescue team broke down part of a brick exterior wall of Markovich's house because he could not fit through a second-floor window and took him to the Sarah Heinz House on a hastily improvised raft made by joining three skiffs. Markovich later died at Presbyterian Hospital, then located at Sherman and Montgomery avenues. Presbyterian and Allegheny General hospitals each treated more than one hundred flood victims.

In the meantime, more than 125 firefighters struggled in icy, waist-deep water to contain a $100,000 nighttime blaze at a three-story Crucible Steel warehouse that occupied a city block at Reedsdale Street and Ridge Avenue. The *Pittsburgh Press* reported that "driftwood, huge empty steel drums and anything else the raging river could pick up swirled through the streets." Police discovered fifty barrels of explosives that had floated to the foot of McClure Avenue, near the Western Penitentiary at Woods Run, and were thankful that the material had not ignited.

As floodwaters finally receded, WPA workers joined residents in cleaning mud and debris from streets. Boggs & Buhl on Federal Street reopened on March 20, and nearby businesses followed. Some of the largest North Side businesses—H. J. Heinz, Ailing & Cory, McKinney Manufacturing, and the Standard Sanitary Manufacturing Company—had lost $25,000 each, mostly in cleanup costs and ruined equipment. The D. L. Clark candy factory was also badly damaged. Heinz, despite its losses, donated food to shelters. The makeshift accommodations for North Siders emptied steadily, and the *Pittsburgh Press* reported on March 26 that most flood refugees wanted to remain in their neighborhoods.

Although crime in the area may not have increased during the Depression, newspapers in Pittsburgh and the rest of the nation seemed fascinated with daring bank robberies and career criminals. Newspapers had a field day in late 1930, when robbers hit two North Side banks in four days. Four young men held up the Perry State Bank for $5,085 on December 13, a week after a robbery had killed a bank employee in Verona, a suburb east of the city. Police recovered $1,560 of the take in a rooming house on Tripoli Street in Deutschtown a few days later and later arrested all or most of the group in New York. Then, on December 16, six men wielding sawed-off shotguns robbed the Manchester Savings Bank on Beaver Avenue of $52,000. The group threatened to kill eighty-year-old bank president G. C. Gerwig and assaulted the seventy-five-year-old bank manager, Adam Hoffman. The *Pittsburgh Press* reported that one bank customer, Kenneth Behannan of West North Avenue, fled when he heard a robber say he should be killed because he had seen the getaway car's license plate. The group left the scene in a late-model Packard, which police later found abandoned at Woods Run.

Some area criminals gained a degree of local notoriety, thanks to the newspapers' fascination with aberrant behavior. Thomas Sords had been born on the North Side in about 1911. His Irish immigrant parents had run saloons on Beaver Avenue and North Charles Street and been involved in North Side politics. After a stint in reform school, Sords had embarked on a crime spree that earned him the nickname "bellboy bandit." He died at age twenty-one outside an Allegheny Avenue grocery that he attempted to rob on December 30, 1931. Police arrested one of his associates, Harry Mitchell of Beech Avenue, in the ensuing investigation. Grocer Carl Lange, who had exchanged gunfire with Sords, helped police track down another stickup artist just four weeks later. In this second instance, Lange followed a store customer who had acted suspiciously to his rooming house. Lange called police, and the suspect confessed to four local robberies.

Some businesses seemed to be cursed by crime. Stickup men, for example, visited the W. L. Douglass Shoe Store at 419 East Ohio Street in Deutschtown seven times between 1927 and 1932. In 1930, store manager G. J. Smith shot one of the assailants and helped North Side police to arrest him. In a particularly brazen 1932 robbery, armed men entered the fifth-story suite of the John Hancock Mutual Life Insurance Company in a Federal Street office building and took $160 from employees and a customer. Newspapers described the criminals as well dressed; whether they were apprehended is unknown.

Police investigated the 1937 death of the eccentric Deutschtown hermit Pete Liebach as a murder. Liebach lived alone on the hillside above Madison Avenue near Vista Street, in a two-room wood-sided house that his German immigrant parents had owned. He had worked as a laborer in Allegheny City in his youth, but by his middle age, in the early twentieth century, he supported himself by selling herbs that he gathered in the woods. When Liebach's brother, Andrew, killed himself in 1906, newspapers reported that Pete was widely believed to be a wealthy miser. Police in fact found $25,000 in silver coins in the house in 1909, after a neighbor complained that he had argued with and frightened local children. Liebach remained a subject of North Side speculation and gossip, remaining in his hillside shanty for decades. The aging hermit was frequently inebriated, and neighbors avoided him because of his unpleasant disposition. Then, in 1937, the eighty-year-old man died in his

Groundbreaking
for the Buhl
Planetarium in 1938.
Carnegie Library of
Pittsburgh Pennsylvania
Department, Pittsburgh
Photographic Library

The Buhl Planetarium was only the fifth planetarium in the United States at the
time it was built. Pittsburgh City Photographer Collection, 1901–2002 (715.4160593.CP).
Archives Service Center, University of Pittsburgh

squalid home. Police believed that Liebach had been killed by someone who intended to rob him, but his death was later found to be from natural causes. In the wake of Liebach's death, newspapers reported that he had been worth more than $50,000. Part of his wealth, ironically, was held in mortgages on other people's houses.

The police worked in the North Side City Hall, the aging building that had once housed Allegheny City government offices. As early as 1929, Pittsburgh officials discussed replacing the structure with a modern public safety building. The idea finally became reality in 1937, after city government accepted the Buhl Foundation's offer to construct a planetarium. The city then purchased and remodeled the former Burry bakery on Arch Street, adjacent to the old city hall, and moved the police station and other offices there in 1938.

The Buhl Planetarium thus went up on the old city hall site in 1938 and 1939. The architectural firm Ingham & Boyd designed the building, constructed at a cost of $1,100,000. The facility was then one of only five planetariums in the United States and one of twenty equipped with a Zeiss Model II Planetarium Projector built by the Carl Zeiss Optical Works of Germany—as of 2012, the Zeiss projector is still in operation, making the Buhl Planetarium home to the oldest operating major planetarium projector in the world. Before its construction, the nearest planetarium had been in Philadelphia, and the Buhl Planetarium was immediately popular. When it opened, Mayor Cornelius Scully expressed hope that "in the Northside we may eventually have a second civic center which will favorably compare with the great edifices in Oakland."

The planetarium followed by three years the completion of the new Allegheny General Hospital on East North Avenue. The hospital had outgrown its seven-story Stockton Avenue building, which the *Pittsburgh Press* had called a "shack" in 1930. Hospital president Reverend Maitland Alexander, of Ridge Avenue and Sewickley Heights, officiated at the 1930 groundbreaking at the hospital site, which took the place of three mansions facing East North Avenue. A tunnel connected the hospital to its nursing school at the rear of the property along Hemlock Street, which replaced several brick rowhouses. In spite of its ambitious beginnings, the hospital project ran out of money when construction was 75 percent complete, in 1931. The unfinished building then sat vacant for nearly three years, a twenty-two-story symbol of the Depression's power to thwart progress and hope. The hospital board finally

Allegheny General Hospital, built from 1930 to 1936. Pittsburgh Steelers/Karl Roser

secured a $2 million Public Works Administration loan in 1934, and three hundred skilled workers completed the project over the following two years, the new six-hundred-bed facility opening on June 28, 1936.

In 1939, as the recovery continued to gain pace, a new coalition representing North Side business associations proposed a comprehensive modernization program. This group, called the Federation of Civic Bodies, recommended improving existing main roadways in the area and building a new bridge across the Allegheny River to Bigelow Boulevard, clearing slums and addressing vice, creating new recreational facilities near the Allegheny and Ohio rivers, constructing apartments and hotels, and marketing the North Side to potential residents and businesses. The arrival of World War II would put these ideas on hold for several years.

Before the war came, North Side residents and business owners, proud of their new public facilities and optimistic about the improving economy, celebrated the centennial of Allegheny City's incorporation in 1940. Charles

Kirschler Jr., son of Allegheny's last mayor and his father's successor as president of the Provident Trust Company on East Ohio Street, chaired the Allegheny Centennial Committee. Pittsburgh's Mayor Scully was honorary chairman. The festivities included plays by Alleghenians Mary Roberts Rinehart and Bartley Campbell, fashion shows featuring antiquated clothing, and a concert at the Carnegie Music Hall. A July 17 parade marked the centennial celebration's grand finale. The committee also published *The Story of Old Allegheny City.* While the WPA writers who had worked on the project believed that a comprehensive North Side history would have to include the story of the notorious madam Nettie Gordon, they were overruled by the centennial committee: the book did not mention Gordon.

The new mood of optimism was interrupted when the Japanese attacked Pearl Harbor on December 7, 1941. Joseph E. Good, of 1039 Woods Run Avenue, who held the rank of staff sergeant in the Seventy-second Pursuit Squadron of the US Army Air Force, died in the attack. Good had graduated from Oliver High School in 1939, the son of laborer Melvin Good and Nellie Good, enlisting soon after graduation. Good's family, of course, was not the only one profoundly affected by the coming of war: World War II would have far-reaching effects on all of America, including the North Side, over the next three and a half years.

Life on the North Side was soon marked by the rationing of essential goods like meat, gasoline, coffee, baby food, and sugar; the absence of loved ones who might not return from the service; and the primacy of industries that produced goods for the war effort. The war helped revitalize Pittsburgh manufacturing and attracted skilled and unskilled workers to the city, their arrival changing the city's shape yet again. The Pittsburgh Housing Authority reclassified the Allegheny Dwellings public housing project as defense housing in 1942, after its construction had already begun. The Allegheny Dwellings, nearly three hundred units on a twenty-acre site in Fineview, had originally been intended to provide low-rent housing for families of modest means. The H. J. Heinz Company, internationally known for its food products manufacturing, reconfigured its Cereal Building to turn out airplane parts. Herbick & Held's printing plant hummed around the clock, printing war-ration stamp books. The D. L. Clark candy factory qualified as an essential war industry, sending countless thousands of Clark Bars to US troops. The LaBelle steel plant on Reedsdale Street in Manchester, the Pennsylvania Transformer Company, Duff-Norton on Preble Avenue, the American Radiator and Standard

Manufacturing Company, and Heyl & Patterson also supplied the war effort. North Side housewives and single women went to work in many of these factories as area men joined the armed forces.

North Siders also contributed to fundraisers and scrap-metal drives to support the war effort. The scrap drives yielded old appliances, ornate iron fences, plumbing, and even lawnmowers, guns, and athletic trophies, all to be melted down. A pile of assorted metal items on the former Exposition Park site reached four million pounds in late 1942, leading the *Pittsburgh Press* to name it Scrap Mountain.

The wartime boom was not without its hazards. At least one of the many wartime contracts led to tragedy when a 1942 explosion and fire at the Watson-Standard Paint Company plant on Galveston Avenue killed firefighter Howard Rubaker of Fineview. He and twenty-five other firemen who were injured

Alleghenian playwright Bartley Campbell. Billy Rose Theatre Division, The New York Public Library for the Performing Arts, Astor, Lenox and Tilden Foundations

Businesses on Federal Street, looking north from in front of old Allegheny City Hall, 1935. The Great Atlantic & Pacific Tea Co. Pittsburgh City Photographer Collection, 1901–2002 (715.3524687.CP). Archives Service Center, University of Pittsburgh

Manchester's Beaver Avenue business district looking south from Columbus Avenue, 1937. Pittsburgh City Photographer Collection, 1901–2002 (715.3732968.CP). Archives Service Center, University of Pittsburgh

Looking down Beech Avenue from Brighton Road, 1929: the automobile's effect on North Side street scenes. *Pittsburgh City Photographer Collection, 1901–2002 (715.298739.CP). Archives Service Center, University of Pittsburgh*

in the blaze had been unaware that the plant was engaged in secret chemical production for the war effort. After the fire, the Pittsburgh public safety department asked the army and navy for notification of hazardous materials manufacturing.

Overseas, thousands of North Siders served their country with distinction. Charles "Commando" Kelly of Deutschtown may have been the best known of these. Kelly, an army corporal, was from Shawano Street, where he had lived with his mother and siblings in a second-floor apartment in an unpainted wood-frame house that lacked hot water, electricity, and a bathroom. During the war, he won the Congressional Medal of Honor for repelling German soldiers under fire while his fellow soldiers evacuated an ammunition storehouse in Italy in 1943. Mayor Scully subsequently declared April 26, 1944, Commando Kelly Day, presenting Kelly with the key to the city in front of the City-County Building as thousands watched. Misfortune, including business failure and unstable relationships, would mark his later life, but his wartime heroics instilled pride and hope in his fellow Pittsburghers.

Charles W. Tate and James T. Wiley were members of the famous Tuskegee Airmen, America's first black fighter pilots. Tate had been born and raised in Manchester, where his father, William, was a truck driver and laborer. He

James T. Wiley, a member of the Tuskegee Airmen, America's first black fighter pilots. He is shown here with his parents. © 2004 Carnegie Museum of Art, Charles "Teenie" Harris Archive

flew ninety-nine missions in the war and received the Distinguished Flying Cross. Tate later also served in the Korean War, then worked as a post office supervisor and manager for many years. Wiley had lived in a home that his parents owned at 706 Woods Run Avenue; his father, James, was a letter carrier. He had received a bachelor's degree in physics from the University of Pittsburgh and was taking graduate-level classes at Carnegie Tech when he enlisted. Wiley served with distinction in Italy. During Wiley's 1944 visit to Pittsburgh, Mayor Scully praised him as an example of achievement in adverse circumstances; he was also a guest at a United Negro College Fund event at the Duquesne Club. He later earned an MBA at the University of Chicago and was an executive with the Boeing Company in Seattle.

After the war ended, returning veterans and their families created unprecedented demand for housing. The lower North Side neighborhoods had virtually no room for new homes, and some sections were no longer regarded as proper or safe for women or families. Landowners thus subdivided scattered tracts into building lots in the upland sections of the North Side—Brighton Heights, Perry Hilltop, Troy Hill, Observatory Hill, Spring Hill, and Summer Hill. Some new subdivisions used land that had managed to remain in agricultural use: Rialto Place on Troy Hill, for example, occupies the former greenhouses of John Bader, who sold flowers in the North Side and Downtown market houses for many years. Others, such as a cluster of postwar homes on the Federal Street extension in Fineview, went up on the large residential estates of earlier decades.

The North Side and the rest of Pittsburgh, however, simply did not have enough developable land or preexisting homes to satisfy postwar demand. Some North Side families thus crossed the city's border to move into Ross and Reserve townships. The loss of residents and shoppers to the suburbs exacerbated the lower North Side's deterioration and its perceived obsolescence in the early postwar era. City planners and community organizations would try many revitalization schemes, some more successful than others, in the following decades.

CHAPTER 11

Decline and Rejuvenation
1950 to the Present

A T MIDCENTURY, Pittsburgh, like so many American cities, had an aging stock of buildings that had suffered disinvestment during the Great Depression and World War II. The city's business leaders and its new Urban Redevelopment Authority recognized the need to address Downtown deterioration, launching the Renaissance project, which removed a railyard and old buildings at the Point and replaced them with Gateway Center. Pittsburgh planning agencies and the Pennsylvania Department of Transportation also presented plans for North Side redevelopment and highway construction.

By 1950, the century's midpoint, Pittsburgh's population was peaking, at about 677,000. The North Side's housing, commercial buildings, and factories were at this point among Pittsburgh's oldest, however, and the area was already losing population. The Pittsburgh Regional Planning Association thus decided to study the North Side in particular as early as 1951. The resulting report, published in 1954, spoke bluntly of "the burden of obsolescence and decay which afflict[s] the lower North Side." Specifically, the study noted that of the lower North Side's 18,756 housing units, 56.6 percent were "without private bath or dilapidated." It described the lack of parking facilities adjacent to businesses and the fact that many of the area's streets were inefficient for automobiles. It criticized the business district around Federal and Ohio streets as disreputable, terming some of its stores old-fashioned and plain.

To address the many problems the planning association found, the study proposed sweeping changes to the lower North Side's land use and transportation corridors. Industrial districts, it proposed, should be created west of Chateau Street, within a four-block swath, through which railroad tracks already ran through Manchester and along the Ohio and Allegheny rivers. New highways should run along Chateau Street in Manchester and along

206

The doomed Allegheny Center area in the early 1960s, looking northwest; Stockton Avenue is at left. Courtesy of Pittsburgh History & Landmarks Foundation

Reedsdale and Lacock streets, parallel with the Allegheny River, East Street, and East Ohio Street. The flat and hillside residential area north of North Avenue between Brighton Road and East Street, containing the Mexican War Streets and several blocks eastward, should be redeveloped. This scheme would eliminate all of the area's 50- to 120-year-old houses, stores, and churches, and almost all of its streets, in favor of high-rise apartments, parking lots, and a shopping plaza. A new limited-access highway just above the redeveloped community would connect California Avenue in Manchester with East Ohio Street, proceeding through northern Manchester, the Mexican War Streets, and Deutschtown, hugging the hillside below Perry Hilltop, Fineview, and Troy Hill. The area around the Diamond should be revitalized with women's and children's clothing stores, restaurants, clean and modernized commercial buildings, promotional efforts, parking lots, and new and updated housing. Farther south, below Ohio Street, the association called for a group of new one-story retail buildings with rooftop parking, elevated walkways connecting the new stores. The historic Market House and many other nineteenth- and early twentieth-century buildings would be razed to make way for parking and new commercial space.

The sweeping 1954 plan sat on the shelf until 1958, when the closing of the eighty-nine-year-old Boggs & Buhl department store added impetus to the call for redevelopment. The Buhl Foundation, a charitable organization, had sold the store ten years before, shortly after announcing the closing of the Federal Street business and its branch stores in Dormont and on Mount Washington. A group of investors had bought Boggs & Buhl from the foundation and reopened the Federal Street store after just a month of remodeling, to acclaim from shoppers and from city and state officials. But this did not last: now, ten years later, the new owners blamed the store's more recent closing on a steady loss of market share to suburban retail outlets. The city demolished the vacant building in 1960.

Even as Boggs & Buhl came down, the doomed North Side commercial district retained a variety of businesses that today's city enthusiasts would envy. The 1960 Pittsburgh directory shows that the thirty-six city blocks around the historic Allegheny Diamond included approximately fifteen churches, eight barbershops, seven pharmacies, two print shops, six hotels, two dry cleaners, two bookstores, five furniture stores, two automobile dealerships, eleven beauty shops, four jewelers, five cigar stores, and twenty-two restaurants, among scores of other businesses. The area also contained more than three hundred rented apartments, seventy-three owner-occupied homes, and twenty-two boardinghouses, most of which were likewise owner occupied. More than forty doctors, dentists, optometrists, and chiropractors maintained offices in these blocks as well, as did five architectural firms.

Allegheny Center changed everything, reshaping the old city's downtown forever. Pittsburgh corporate leader ALCOA owned 80 percent of the Allegheny Center project; the Oliver Tyrone Company of Pittsburgh and Lewis E. Kitchen of Kansas City owned the remainder. Demolition for Allegheny Center began in 1962, with the Market House coming down in 1965. Nearly all traces of the old neighborhood were removed, and even the Diamond's historic street grid was altered. Federal and Ohio streets, the two main thoroughfares of old Allegheny, no longer met. The new shopping mall and high-rise office building blocked Federal Street, and the formerly bustling intersection was reduced to a pedestrian crossing. The new high-rise also took away about one-third of Ober Park, where countless North Siders had relaxed and socialized for decades. Project planners built a one-way traffic circle named the North, South, East, and West commons on or near the cartways of what had previously been secondary streets. Most of Montgomery Avenue and parts of Sandusky and Arch streets were replaced with grass, while several secondary streets and all of the neighborhood's alleys disappeared altogether.

A few of the 850 families removed from an area in which 80 percent of the houses were declared substandard moved to the Northview Heights public housing project on the North Side, which opened in 1962. Only about ten

The first baseball game at Three Rivers Stadium in 1970. Thomas & Katherine Detre Library and Archives, Sen. John Heinz History Center

of the hundreds of buildings that once stood between East and West parks remained. The Carnegie Library, Buhl Planetarium, and the North Side Post Office still clustered at the historic center. To the west, St. Peter's church and rectory, Allegheny High School, and Divine Providence Hospital remained standing. The former Christ Episcopal Church parish house and the adjacent Community House survived among the many buildings that were demolished along Union Avenue. The Civil War–era Reformed Presbyterian Church on Sandusky Street still stands as a Duquesne Light Company facility on the East Commons. All of the surviving buildings are above Ohio Street, in the northern half of the redevelopment area.

Allegheny Center opened its doors in 1966, the complex including a Sears, Woolworth's, A&P grocery, and Roth Carpet, with an underground parking garage. Its retail component, unfortunately, was only partially successful even in its earliest years, with considerable vacant space by the early 1980s. The developers originally planned to build approximately twelve hundred high-rise and two hundred townhouse rental units, but by that time had put up only about eight hundred apartments and fifty townhouses.

The related changes to downtown roadways also had profound effects on the North Side. The Pennsylvania Department of Transportation began to study proposed highway routes through the North Side in the 1950s. It proposed a California Avenue–East Ohio Street connector just above the Mexican War Streets that it called the Upper Belt and an interchange at Monterey and Jacksonia streets, along with a highway that would run south, cutting a swath through West Park, and then go on to Downtown Pittsburgh. A more costly proposed southern alternative, called the Lower Belt, would use Chateau Street in Manchester, cutting through the lower North Side past a proposed stadium site on Monument Hill. The Upper Belt would remove 7,700 residents and 2,300 buildings, the Lower Belt 2,700 residents and 830 buildings.

Both public opinion and Pittsburgh officials favored the Chateau Street route over the West Park alternative. Building the highway through Manchester was more attractive because it required displacing fewer people: this was an era when public agencies strained to find acceptable housing for residents displaced by a seemingly endless parade of redevelopment projects. The Manchester alternative also coordinated with the proposed industrial park and stadium. In addition, the competing scheme would have ruined West Park, one of the few lower North Side resources that mid-twentieth-century planners valued, in association with the era's emphasis on open spaces. The North Side Board of Trade, whose membership was drawn mostly from Manchester's Beaver Avenue retail district, opposed the Chateau Street plan and advocated for the Upper Belt, but state government also opted for the Chateau Street alternative in 1960, and the federal government concurred in 1961. By then the city had started purchasing land for the Chateau industrial district. Demolition for the new roadways began in mid-1961, when workers pulled down a late nineteenth-century brick house at 1512 Liverpool Street, once the home of riverboat captain William B. Dravo. Industrial firms began to move into the area in 1964, and the city soon announced plans for a shopping plaza on

East Street at Royal Street, about 1970; St. Boniface Catholic Church peeks over the tops of commercial buildings. Courtesy of Pittsburgh History & Landmarks Foundation

Beaver Avenue. Planners shifted the proposed stadium site from Monument Hill southward to the flood plain, and the facility, named Three Rivers Stadium, opened in 1970 as the home of the Pirates and the Steelers.

The East Street Valley Expressway met with much more citizen opposition than the highway through Manchester, perhaps because the East Street project took place a decade later, at a time when speaking out against government initiatives had become more common. Citizen advocates persuaded the Department of Transportation to alter the highway route to spare St. Boniface Roman Catholic Church, originally slated for demolition, and Dr. Martin Krauss, an East Ohio Street optometrist, was among the leaders of HEART, the East Street Highway Emergency and Relocation Team. This group accepted that the Pennsylvania Department of Transportation would build the roadway, but it advocated for fair treatment for affected property owners along the East Street valley floor, on the slopes on each side, and in part of Deutschtown. During the ensuing, often contentious planning process

PNC Park, home of the Pittsburgh Pirates, opened in 2001. Pittsburgh Pirates/Dave Arrigo

that took place between about 1967 and 1982, Krauss and HEART sparred with city and state officials; convinced PennDOT to stop sending homeowners purchase offers with eviction notices, which it called "scare tactics"; and fought for better compensation for homeowners. HEART also pushed for safer demolition practices, particularly after one Lockhart Street demolition sent building materials crashing into an occupied home. City, county, and state officials and other dignitaries finally broke ground for the expressway in 1982 on East Street, near Hazlett Street. Steelers broadcaster Myron Cope served as master of ceremonies, and team owner Art Rooney and Steelers Hall of Famer Franco Harris—both North Side residents—also attended. The North Shore Expressway, stretching across the lower North Side, was completed a few years later, linking the Fort Duquesne Bridge with Route 28 near the H. J. Heinz plant.

The overwhelming changes coming to their city had inspired fourteen Pittsburghers with roots in the old North Side to charter the nonprofit Allegheny City Society back in 1958. Highway plans may have been a factor in the society's founding, as its charter stated that one of its goals was to "support efforts to preserve the Commons, monuments and land marks in Allegheny City." The society does not seem to have engaged in advocacy efforts in its early years. Rather, its primary purpose was to preserve the memories and social ties of former Allegheny residents and their descendants. Its members held quarterly meetings with speakers who presented programs on topics of interest. While the society eventually fell dormant, new members revived it in the 1990s, and it remains active to this day, keeping the North Side's history alive and advocating for preservation of its landmarks.

James D. Van Trump of Point Breeze, in Pittsburgh's East End, first earned recognition as a champion of the city's nineteenth-century building stock in the 1950s, as renewal efforts accelerated. In a 1962 letter to the *Pittsburgh Press,* Van Trump, then associate editor of *Charette,* an architecture magazine, called attention to the 1300 block of Liverpool Street, declaring it "without any doubt the finest surviving Victorian street in Pittsburgh." Soon thereafter, in 1964, Van Trump and Arthur P. Ziegler Jr., an English teacher, founded the Pittsburgh History & Landmarks Foundation (PHLF) to defend Pittsburgh's built environment, including the North Side.

One of the foundation's early successes was saving the old North Side Post Office, which lay within the Allegheny Center redevelopment area.

Heinz Field has hosted the Pittsburgh Steelers and the University of Pittsburgh Panthers

since 2001. Pittsburgh Steelers/Karl Roser

The Carnegie Science Center opened in 1991. Pittsburgh Steelers/Karl Roser

The foundation also championed preservation plans for Manchester and the Mexican War Streets that included purchasing and updating some houses and retaining rather than displacing low-income residents, including Manchester's substantial black population. Although Van Trump had long spoken in favor of preservation as a sole voice, the numbers of PHLF were able to raise greater awareness of the value of Pittsburgh's older buildings and communities for their architectural and cultural significance, which its members believed inseparable from the fabric of the city and the surrounding region. As part of their advocacy efforts, Van Trump and Ziegler also authored *Landmark Architecture of Allegheny County, Pennsylvania* (1967), which pointed out the architectural value of the North Side, particularly the lower North Side neighborhoods and Troy Hill.

As the 1960s began, the Mexican War Streets had settled into quiet decay. The neighborhood's population included apartment dwellers, rooming-house tenants, and homeowners. A few residents with neighborhood roots in the nineteenth century now rubbed shoulders with Italian and Greek immigrants,

The interior of the National Aviary in West Park. Carnegie Library of Pittsburgh
Pennsylvania Department, Pittsburgh Photographic Library

African Americans, and others relatively new to the North Side. Because
most property owners were of modest means, the community's streetscapes
remained nearly identical to their appearance in the early twentieth century.

Carl and Marilyn Detwiler moved to the Mexican War Streets in 1962, the
young couple buying a visually striking red-brick corner house with a turret
on Resaca Place. Carl Detwiler had grown up in a rambling home on West
North Avenue in Manchester, then studied architecture at Carnegie Tech and
city planning at Harvard. While working at the Pittsburgh Regional Planning Association, he met Marilyn, a city planner from Illinois. Rather than
moving to the East End or the suburbs like many of their peers, the Detwilers
settled in the Mexican War Streets, determined to demonstrate their belief in
the North Side. They were among the first of many new residents to move to
the area in and after the 1960s, early enough to watch the destruction of the
North Side commercial district across West Park from their home. With time,
the Mexican War Streets' architecture and proximity to Downtown attracted
more new residents, who eventually founded the nonprofit Mexican War

Federal Street looking south from Park Way, early 1960s; businesses had begun to vacate for urban renewal. Courtesy of Pittsburgh History & Landmarks Foundation

Streets Society in 1969. The society held the first annual Mexican War Streets house tour in 1970, to publicize the community's assets and its resurgence.

Van Trump and Ziegler's *Landmark Architecture of Allegheny County, Pennsylvania* also identified a small North Side neighborhood that it called Lincoln-Beech as a priority for preservation efforts. This area, soon better known as Allegheny West, was by then comprised largely of rooming houses that had been subject to benign neglect for decades after their affluent early owners had moved away. During the next few decades, owner-occupants

The Andy Warhol Museum occupies the former Frick & Lindsay warehouse at Sandusky and Isabella streets. Pittsburgh Steelers/Karl Roser

purchased homes of manageable (and some not so manageable) size on Beech, North Lincoln, and Galveston avenues and adjacent streets. The new residents restored these dwellings and in many cases returned them to single-family configuration. While most of the houses on Beech and Galveston avenues generally ranged from eight to twelve rooms, some of the properties returned to single-family use were much larger, containing twenty rooms or even more. Residents of Allegheny West, like those in the Mexican War Streets and eventually other North Side neighborhoods, also began conducting annual house

The Allegheny Market House interior, just before the building was demolished in 1965. Courtesy of Pittsburgh History & Landmarks Foundation

tours to show off their restoration work and to market their revitalized communities. Some preservation projects were particularly challenging. In about 1980, a three-story brick party-wall house at North Lincoln and Galveston avenues partially collapsed into the street. Such an event would have resulted in demolition in most neighborhoods, but the Pittsburgh History & Landmarks Foundation worked with community leaders to save the house and its attached neighbor, and both were restored as condominiums.

In the mid-1990s, seven of the once-fashionable Denny Row's houses on West North Avenue still stood vacant and abandoned. The Allegheny West Civic Council, in association with the Community Design Center of Pittsburgh, acquired most of the houses and restored their façades, then sold them to owners who would follow through with interior rehabilitation. The row, now mostly restored, brightens a corner of the North Side that many had assumed beyond hope.

Despite the best efforts of residents and PHLF, however, some of Millionaires' Row's largest houses nevertheless fell to the wrecking ball. The neighborhood had begun to lose its mansions even before midcentury, possibly with the demolition of the brick Walker house in the 1200 block of Western Avenue in about 1932. Soon, the Robinson and Alexander houses in the 900 block of Ridge Avenue were destroyed, replaced with the Graybar Electric building. In the late 1950s, the former B. F. Jones mansion, the former Painter mansion, and other substantial dwellings on the block of Brighton Road between North Lincoln and Western avenues also came down. Two of the relics of Millionaire's Row, the B. F. Jones Jr. House, at Ridge Avenue and Brighton Road, and the Byers-Lyon House, at Ridge and Galveston avenues, were incorporated into the new campus of the Community College of Allegheny County, opened on Ridge Avenue in 1966, augmenting educational opportunity for county residents. The college, however, demolished many other houses to make way for modern buildings and parking. Yet other Ridge Avenue houses fell for highway construction and to meet the increased demand for surface parking.

While the Mexican War Streets and Allegheny West began to rejuvenate, Manchester's troubles continued to grow. The neighborhood had remained relatively stable after its wealthier residents left in the late nineteenth and early twentieth centuries, with working-class and some middle-class families living in homes they owned and renting apartments in the larger houses. When a substantial number of Manchester's white families fled to the suburbs in the 1950s, some black families who remained were able to purchase homes for the first time. Others, however, had no choice but to rent substandard living quarters. During the 1960s, Manchester residents grew frustrated with city government's seeming indifference to neighborhood needs. Community members complained of absentee landlords, rats, and dilapidated homes, and in 1967 they interrupted Mayor Joe Barr's visit to the North Side to demand that the city construct a playground in Manchester. Pittsburgh newspapers pointed out that unemployment and heroin were pervasive in the neighborhood.

Racial tensions also flared. At Oliver High School in Brighton Heights, black students from Manchester fought white students from Brighton Heights in 1967. In 1968, Manchester having visibly deteriorated, unrest following the assassination of Martin Luther King included looting of some local businesses, vandals burning businesses in the new Chateau Plaza shopping center on Beaver Avenue and also striking older storefronts in Manchester. National Guard troops patrolled Manchester, the Hill District, and Homewood in the wake of King's death. Although the disruptions took greater tolls on the Hill

The Mattress Factory contemporary art museum opened in 1977. Pittsburgh Steelers/Karl Roser

and in Homewood, they nonetheless contributed to Manchester's continuing decline and to public perception of the neighborhood as a slum. Then, in June 1970, an elderly white woman living in a deteriorating Pennsylvania Avenue mansion shot and killed a twelve-year-old black neighbor boy who was playing in her yard. Within two days, violence followed violence, with firebombings, the retaliatory murder of a sixty-year-old Italian immigrant bartender

outside his Pennsylvania Avenue home, and other incidents. City government went so far as to demolish the elderly woman's mansion within a few weeks of the shooting, fearing that it too would be firebombed.

Even at its worst moments, however, Manchester held a core of residents who retained hope for and faith in their community. These residents, who had formed advocacy organizations before the dark days of the late 1960s, began working on revitalization strategies with the Urban Redevelopment Authority (URA) in 1969. In 1970, Manchester representatives, together with the URA, embarked on an ambitious plan to build new for-sale and rental housing and to restore some of the neighborhood's grand nineteenth-century dwellings. Over time, the Manchester Citizens Corporation (MCC) was organized, succeeding earlier groups as an advocate and development partner with city government and eventually emerging as a strong local voice. The group's early activities including shutting down more than a dozen nuisance bars. Recognizing the architectural significance of their neighborhood's housing stock, MCC members also visited other cities to learn about historic preservation. Embarking on a restoration and preservation program that would retain Manchester's longtime low-income residents, rather than price them out of their own neighborhood, the MCC worked to help stabilize the community. Today, the Manchester Historic District covers most of the neighborhood and is listed on the National Register of Historic Places, as are all or much of Allegheny West, the Mexican War Streets, and Deutschtown.

Yet another ambitious but ultimately discouraging attempt to revitalize old Allegheny came in 1978, when city government, at the request of two community organizations, the North Side Civic Development Council and the Central North Side Neighborhood Council, held a lottery to sell abandoned houses on the Mexican War Streets and in the neighborhoods immediately to the north and east. This event, dubbed the Great House Sale, offered deteriorated homes for one hundred dollars, together with architectural advice and assistance with insulation and sidewalk repairs. The sale required that buyers rehabilitate the houses and live in them. The nearly eleven hundred potential buyers who competed for the thirty-two available dwellings—including four hundred who vied for one three-story brick rowhouse on Boyle Street—initially gave hope to North Siders and to Mayor Richard Caliguiri's administration. Ultimately, however, the Great House Sale highlighted the many barriers to reinvestment in the North Side's deteriorating homes. Bankers weren't ready to make loans in the neighborhood, so lottery winners found it hard to finance and insure their rehabilitation projects. Some also may have underestimated construction costs. Thus, in January 1980, more than a year and a half after the lottery, buyers had claimed only eight of the thirty-two vacant houses.

Then, after decades of slow decline, Pittsburgh and southwestern Pennsylvania's manufacturing base collapsed in the early 1980s. Although the regional steel industry was most important to the economy of the Monongahela and Ohio River valley communities, the loss of hundreds of thousands of jobs in steel and other industries affected virtually every community's commercial district, residential areas, and spirit. Pittsburgh-area newspapers reported on mill closings, home foreclosures, and food lines seemingly every week. The North Side, of course, received its share of the economic bad news, particularly in working-class neighborhoods like Deutschtown, Troy Hill, Spring Garden, Manchester, and Woods Run.

In response to the needs highlighted by the Great House Sale and other early housing reclamation efforts, which exacerbated the industrial collapse, the URA began offering low-interest loans to buyers to purchase and rehabilitate older homes in many North Side neighborhoods and in some other sections of the city. It also enabled the construction of new houses for owner-occupants in Manchester, Deutschtown, Spring Garden, the Central North Side, and the Charles Street Valley. Architects designed the homes built in historic districts to complement the façades of adjacent older dwellings. The URA also worked with North Side community groups in commercial development, speculatively renovating obsolete buildings as space for offices, light manufacturing, and retail space. For example, an old River Avenue flour mill was reused as a small business incubator, a former Greyhound bus terminal on California Avenue as manufacturing and office space, and the Victorian-era Hollander Building on East Ohio Street as offices and commercial space.

Four North Side organizations joined forces with the URA, the Pittsburgh History & Landmarks Foundation, and private and public lenders to renovate the conspicuously abandoned Eberhardt & Ober brewery at the foot of Troy Hill Road, the project anchored by Western Pennsylvania's first microbrewery and brewpub, the Penn Brewery. Other small startup companies were now neighboring tenants in the sprawling red-brick complex.

Then, in 1988, more than twenty community-development and -advocacy nonprofits established the Pittsburgh Community Reinvestment Group (PCRG), a coalition whose purpose was to advocate for fair lending practices in low- and moderate-income Pittsburgh neighborhoods. Among the PCRG's founders were community groups from most of the neighborhoods on the struggling North Side. The PCRG invoked the federal Community Reinvestment Act, which required that lending institutions make credit available in all neighborhoods from which they accepted deposits, in conformance with sound lending practices. Working with a dozen Pittsburgh banks and the Urban Redevelopment Authority, the reinvestment group worked to develop loan products and marketing campaigns tailored for these neighborhoods. Their combined efforts helped a significant number of longtime North Siders and new residents buy their first homes, contributing significantly to neighborhood stability. The PCRG, housed in the Manchester Citizens Corporation offices in its first few years, quickly became a national model.

In 1993, Pittsburgh voters elected as the city's fifty-seventh mayor the first North Side resident to fill that post: State Representative Tom Murphy of Perrysville Avenue. Most of his twentieth-century predecessors had hailed from the East End. Murphy's background was in community service; he had served as a Peace Corps volunteer, a North Side Civic Development Corporation staffer, a state representative, and a longtime Meals on Wheels volunteer. Murphy's appointments to city posts included a handful of veteran North Side community activists with whom he had worked since the 1970s. During his three terms, Pittsburgh continued its slow recovery from the mill closings, and national media occasionally spotlighted the city's comeback. The city, however, continued to experience fiscal difficulties, and Murphy's own Perry Hilltop neighborhood suffered from seemingly intractable gang violence and disinvestment. Still, although he was at times a polarizing figure, Murphy remained popular on the North Side throughout his time in office. His legacy includes the construction of new stadiums for the Pirates and the Steelers along the Allegheny River shore: PNC Park, a classic baseball park, and Heinz Field, designed specifically for football. The new stadiums together replaced the aging Three Rivers Stadium, which came down in a spectacular controlled implosion in 2001.

The North Side gained more regional attractions in the late twentieth century. The Carnegie Science Center went up in 1991, near the foot of Allegheny Avenue. In 1993 Congress designated the Pittsburgh Aviary in West Park as the country's National Aviary. In 1994 the Andy Warhol Museum opened in the former Frick & Lindsay warehouse, at Sandusky and Isabella streets. Nearby, on Herr's Island, townhouses, a marina and restaurant, and offices replaced the stockyards that had operated for nearly a century. The Priory, a boutique hotel, and its companion the Grand Hall opened in a former Benedictine monastery and the neighboring St. Mary's Catholic Church in Deutschtown in the late 1980s. These buildings had been slated for removal before a shift in the East Street Valley Expressway's planned alignment made their demolition unnecessary.

In the late twentieth and early twenty-first centuries, the North Side also benefited from residents' tenacity and their deep appreciation of their neighborhoods. North Siders, both those with ancestral roots in nineteenth-century Allegheny City and newcomers, strove to maintain and improve their neighborhoods. Residents worked hard to support their public and parochial schools, to foster public safety, to strive for racial harmony, and to assist low-income and homeless families. They didn't always succeed, but as the twenty-first century's second decade begins, the North Side appears poised to thrive, thanks to the strength of its institutions, its businesses, and its people.

The Future

WHERE DOES THE NORTH SIDE go from here? As we all must remember, "We are Pittsburgh." Once before Allegheny City put everything together in a uniform effort to move forward, to be successful; it brought experts in architecture, construction, banking and many other businesses to cooperate in the process, and it was successful. From its beginnings, when people ventured across the Allegheny River to the North Side, Allegheny has been a good place to live and work. At the city's start, everyone contributed whatever they could, including their talents. They risked capital and worked hard, keeping up the pace as Allegheny City began to take shape, with homes and businesses emerging along the newly constructed roads and streets, aligned with the rivers.

Still, today there are many positives on Pittsburgh's North Side. Allegheny General Hospital is an excellent facility. The Community College of Allegheny County (CCAC) offers a fine education to the general public. The North Shore, along with the Rivers Casino, built in 2009 and the subject of some controversy, also holds Heinz Field, where the Steelers and the University of Pittsburgh football team play, as well as the Pirates' PNC Park, the most beautiful baseball diamond in the country.

The area also houses three new hotels, two excellent office buildings, and many dining and entertainment spots along Federal Street and in its environs, an area with strong potential for revitalization. The children's museum stands nearby, as does the Old Carnegie Library, which is now being used for civic meetings and charitable organizations. Some places might be removed to allow better land use. Allegheny Center could be made more open and inviting. If Federal Street and North Avenue were revitalized, the way north up Federal could be revitalized to the top of the hill at Perrysville Avenue, moving out to Riverview Park and neighborhoods with many fine houses and small business. East of Allegheny Center are Deutschtown, the Heinz

Plant, the hill communities, Troy Hill and Spring Hill, and Millvale, Etna, and Sharpsburg. Route 28 North showcases the small, lovely towns along the Allegheny River. Closer to the city center lies the National Aviary, a point of local pride whose footprint was part of the original West Park. While the aviary, like many other local landmarks, needs additional land for expansion and parking, its growth must be carefully shepherded.

Politicians in Pittsburgh and Harrisburg must know more about the city than its topography if a feasible plan that takes the city as a whole into account is to be devised. We must work together to educate our politicians and to make our region strong. We must encourage business leaders to join in our effort with a positive attitude and a willing spirit. The potential of a wonderful community has always been here. While the costs of realizing this potential seem daunting, the necessary investment would soon pay off: the community would be reinvigorated, the tax benefits would be substantial, and new places to shop and eat would inevitably appear. Indeed, the North Side could become the pride of Pittsburgh.

Back in 1840, at Allegheny's founding, everyone worked together in the dream of creating such a vital and engaging community. This remains the dream today, provided that people of different economic statuses and varied talents can come together with a strategic plan to thoughtfully develop the entire area. We all must come together with a common purpose: to make the North Side a grand place to work and live. If we believe that this dream can become a reality, we will be successful. Let us begin, with God's help.

BIBLIOGRAPHY

Allegheny City Councils. "Minutes of Select and Common Councils Meetings." Allegheny (Pittsburgh): 1906, 1907.

Allegheny City Society. *Allegheny City 1840–1907.* Chicago: Arcadia Publishing, 2007.

Allegheny County, Pennsylvania. "Deed Books." Pittsburgh: 1830–present.

Allegheny Fire Department. *History of the Allegheny Fire Department as Gleaned from Its Earliest Inciniency and from Fire Department Records.* Allegheny (Pittsburgh): Allegheny Fire Department, 1894–95.

Allegheny Select and Common Councils. *Annual Reports of the Various Officers and Standing Committees of the City of Allegheny.* Pittsburgh: Bakewell & Marthens, 1876.

Applegarth, George S. *Men of This Big Town of Ours as Seen by "Appy."* Pittsburgh: Iron City Trades Journal Printing, n.d.

Arnold, Bion J. *City Planning for Pittsburgh: Outline and Procedure: A Report by Bion J. Arnold, John R. Freeman, Frederick Law Olmsted.* Pittsburgh: Pittsburgh Civic Commission, 1910.

Bennet, Joseph. *The Life of an Immigrant.* Pittsburgh: privately printed, 1937.

Boucher, John Newton. *A Century and a Half of Pittsburg and Her People.* 4 vols. New York: Lewis Publishing, 1908.

Brashear, John A. *John A. Brashear; The Autobiography of a Man Who Loved the Stars.* Edited by Lucien Scaife. New York: American Society of Mechanical Engineers, 1924.

Bridge, James Howard. *The Inside History of the Carnegie Steel Company: A Romance of Millions.* New York: Aldine, 1903.

Burgoyne, Arthur Gordon. *All Sorts of Pittsburgers / Sketched in Prose and Verse.* Pittsburgh: Leader All Sorts, 1892.

Burstin, Barbara S. *Steel City Jews 1840–1915.* Apollo, PA: Closson, 2008.

Butko, Brian, and Nicholas P. Ciotola, eds. *Industry and Infantry: The Civil War in Western Pennsylvania.* Pittsburgh: Historical Society of Western Pennsylvania, 2003.

Carlisle, R. C., comp. *Phase I Archaeological Examination of the Brighton-on-the-Park Site (36AL261), Pittsburgh, Pennsylvania.* Pittsburgh: University of Pittsburgh Cultural Resource Management Program, 1985.

Casson, Herbert Newton. *The Romance of Steel: The Story of a Thousand Millionaires.* New York: Barnes, 1907.

Catholic Historical Society of Western Pennsylvania. *Catholic Pittsburgh's One*

Hundred Years: A Symposium Prepared by the Catholic Historical Society of Western Pennsylvania. Chicago: Loyola University Press, 1943.

Citizens Committee on City Plan of Pittsburgh. *A Major Street Plan for Pittsburgh: A Part of the Pittsburgh Plan.* Pittsburgh: Municipal Planning Association, 1921.

———. *Pittsburgh Playgrounds: A Part of the Pittsburgh Plan.* Pittsburgh, 1920.

———. *Railroads of the Pittsburgh District: A Part of the Pittsburgh Plan.* Pittsburgh: Municipal Planning Association, 1924.

Concordia Club. *Constitution, By-Laws and Rules of the Concordia Club of Pittsburgh with List of Members.* Pittsburgh: Concordia Club, 1914.

Consolidated Illustrating Company. *Allegheny County, Pennsylvania.* Pittsburgh: Consolidated Illustrating, 1896.

Cowin, Verna. *Pittsburgh Archaeological Resources and National Register Survey.* Pittsburgh: Carnegie Museum of Natural History, 1985.

Dahlinger, Charles William. *Old Allegheny.* Pittsburgh: Historical Society of Western Pennsylvania, 1918.

Dickson, William Brown. *History of Carnegie Veteran Association.* Montclair, NJ: Mountain Press, 1938.

Diocese of Pittsburgh School Board. *Fifteenth Annual Report of the Parish Schools of the Diocese of Pittsburgh 1918–1919.* Pittsburgh: Pittsburgh Observer, 1919.

Duquesne Borough Council. "Meeting Minutes." Duquesne (Pittsburgh): 1850–55.

Durant, Samuel W. *History of Allegheny Co., Pennsylvania: With Illustrations Descriptive of Its Scenery, Palatial Residences, Public Buildings, Fine Blocks, and Important Manufactories.* Philadelphia: L. H. Everts, 1876.

Feldman, Jacob S. *The Jewish Experience in Western Pennsylvania: A History, 1755–1945.* Pittsburgh: Historical Society of Western Pennsylvania, 1986.

First Presbyterian Church of Allegheny. *The Work of a Century: History of the First Presbyterian Church of Allegheny.* Pittsburgh: First Presbyterian Church of Allegheny, 1930.

Fleming, George Thornton. *History of Pittsburgh and Environs, from Prehistoric Days to the Beginning of the American Revolution.* 5 vols. New York and Chicago: American Historical Society, 1922.

Floyd, Margaret Henderson. *Architecture after Richardson: Regionalism before Modernism—Longfellow, Alden, and Harlow in Boston and Pittsburgh.* Chicago: University of Chicago Press, 1994.

Foster, Morrison. *My Brother Stephen.* Indianapolis: privately printed, 1932.

Fox, Arthur B. *Pittsburgh during the American Civil War, 1860–1865.* Chicora, PA: Mechling, 2002.

Frasure, William Wayne. *Longevity of Manufacturing Concerns in Allegheny County.* Pittsburgh: University of Pittsburgh Press, 1952.

Gazi, Stjepan. *Croatian Immigration to Allegheny County, 1882–1914*. Pittsburgh: Croatian Fraternal Union of America, 1956.

Gerold, B. *Golden Jubilee, St. Joseph's Church, N.S., Pittsburgh, Pennsylvania, June 17, 1917*. Pittsburgh: St. Joseph Church, 1917.

Glasco, Laurence A., ed. *The WPA History of the Negro in Pittsburgh*. Pittsburgh: University of Pittsburgh Press, 2004.

Hall, J. Morton. *America's Industrial Centre: Pittsburgh's Great Industries and Its Enormous Development in the Leading Products of the World*. Pittsburgh: W. G. Johnston, 1891.

Harper, Frank C. *Pittsburgh of Today, Its Resources and People*. 5 vols. New York: American Historical Society, 1931–32.

Hopkins, G. M. *Atlas of Greater Pittsburgh, Pennsylvania: From Official Records, Private Plans, and Actual Surveys*. Philadelphia: G. M. Hopkins, 1910.

———. *Atlas of the Cities of Pittsburgh and Allegheny: From Official Records, Private Plans and Actual Surveys*. Philadelphia: G. M. Hopkins, 1882.

———. *Real Estate Plat-Book of the City of Allegheny: From Official Records, Private Plans and Actual Surveys*. Philadelphia: G. M. Hopkins, 1890.

———. *Real Estate Plat-Book of the City of Allegheny: From Official Records, Private Plans and Actual Surveys*. Philadelphia: G. M. Hopkins, 1901.

———. *Real Estate Plat-Book of the City of Allegheny: From Official Records, Private Plans and Actual Surveys*. Philadelphia: G. M. Hopkins, 1902.

———. *Real Estate Plat-Book of the City of Allegheny: From Official Records, Private Plans and Actual Surveys*. Volume 1. Philadelphia: G. M. Hopkins, 1907.

———. *Real Estate Plat-Book of the City of Pittsburgh: From Official Records, Private Plans and Actual Surveys*. Philadelphia: G. M. Hopkins, 1925.

Hopkins, G. M., & Co. *Atlas of the Cities of Pittsburgh, Allegheny, and the Adjoining Boroughs: From Actual Surveys & Official Records*. Philadelphia: G. M. Hopkins, 1872.

Jordan, John W., ed. *Genealogical and Personal History of Western Pennsylvania*. 2 vols. New York: Lewis Historical Publishing, 1915.

Kelly, John M. *J. M. Kelly's Handbook of Greater Pittsburg: Historical, an Encyclopedia, Political and Statistical, the Proposed Ship Canal, Directory and Guide; Including a Comprehensive Street Directory and Lithographed Map in Colors*. Pittsburgh: J. M. Kelly, 1895.

Kidney, Walter C. *Pittsburgh's Landmark Architecture: The Historic Buildings of Pittsburgh and Allegheny County*. Pittsburgh: Pittsburgh History & Landmarks Foundation, 1997.

Knowles, Morris. *The Flood Menace and Its Remedy: What Is Being Done to Prevent the Annual Great Loss to Property and to the Industrial Interests of the Busy Pittsburgh District: A Carefully Prepared Analysis of the Situation*. Pittsburgh: Pittsburgh Flood Commission, 1910.

Kussart, Sarepta Cooper. *The Allegheny River.* Pittsburgh: Burgum Printing, 1938.

Lambing, Andrew Arnold. *Brief Biographical Sketches of the Deceased Bishops and Priests Who Labored in the Diocese of Pittsburgh from the Earliest Times to the Present, with an Historical Introduction.* Pittsburgh: Republic Bank Note, 1914.

———. *A History of the Catholic Church in the Dioceses of Pittsburg and Allegheny from Its Establishment to the Present Time.* New York: Benziger Brothers, 1880.

Leonard, John William. *Pittsburgh and Allegheny Illustrated Review: Historical, Biographical and Commercial. A Record of Progress in Commerce, Manufactures, the Professions, and in Social and Municipal Life.* Pittsburgh: J. M. Elstner, 1889.

Lubove, Roy. *Twentieth-Century Pittsburgh.* 2 vols. Pittsburgh: University of Pittsburgh Press, 1996.

Martinek, Jason. "The Amazons of Allegheny: The Fire, the Riot, and the Textile Strike of 1845." *Western Pennsylvania History* 94 (Spring 2011): 38–48.

McMillan, W. H. *The Second United Presbyterian Church of Allegheny, Pa.: A Historical Sermon Preached July 16th and 23rd, 1876.* Pittsburgh: Stevenson & Foster, 1877.

Mercantile Illustrating Company. *Pittsburgh: The Distributing Point for the West and South; Allegheny County, Destined to Be the Greatest Manufacturing Center of the World.* Pittsburgh: 1900.

Miles, Lisa A. *Resurrecting Allegheny City: The Land, Structures & People of Pittsburgh's North Side.* Pittsburgh: 2007.

Morneweck, Evelyn Foster. *Chronicles of Stephen Foster's Family.* 2 vols. Pittsburgh: University of Pittsburgh Press, 1944.

Most Holy Name Church. *Sixtieth Anniversary of the Dedication of Most Holy Name Church, Troy Hill: North Side, Pittsburgh, Pennsylvania, 1868–1928.* Pittsburgh: 1928.

Neeper, Alexander M. *Maps and Descriptions of the Election Districts in the Cities of Pittsburgh and Allegheny.* Pittsburgh: W. V. Dermitt, 1886.

Nevin, Adelaide Mellier. *The Social Mirror.* Pittsburgh: T. W. Nevin, 1888.

Ohler, Samuel R. *Pittsburgh Inclines.* Pittsburgh: Pickwick-Morcraft, 1972.

Pankey, William Russell. *History of the Churches of the Pittsburgh Baptist Association.* Philadelphia and Chicago: Judson, 1939.

Parke, John E. *Recollections of Seventy Years and Historical Gleanings of Allegheny, Pennsylvania.* Boston: Rand, Avery, 1886.

Pennsylvania Railroad, Pittsburgh, Fort Wayne, & Chicago Railway Company. *Corporate History of the Pittsburgh Fort Wayne and Chicago Railway Company: Together with the Mortgage, Leases, Deeds, and Agreements of That Corporation Assumed by the Pennsylvania Company and in Force August 1, 1875.* Pittsburgh: Stevenson and Foster, 1875.

Pittsburgh Chamber of Commerce. *The Mercantile, Manufacturing and Mining Interests of Pittsburgh, 1884.* Pittsburgh: Wm. G. Johnson & Co, 1884.

Pittsburgh City Planning Commission. *City of Pittsburgh, Pennsylvania, Figures and Data Compiled for the National Conference on City Planning Held at Pittsburgh, May 9th, 10th and 11th, Nineteen Hundred Twenty-One.* Pittsburgh: Sutton, 1921.

Pittsburgh Cyclorama Co. *The Battle of Gettysburg: As Exhibited by the Pittsburgh Cyclorama Co.: Giving a Succinct and Accurate Account of the Great Battle, with Key Explanatory* [sic] *of the Painting.* Pittsburgh: Shaw Brothers, n.d.

Pittsburgh Flood Commission. *Flood Prevention, Reforestation, Navigation.* Pittsburgh: Pittsburgh Flood Commission, 1923.

———. *Safeguarding Pittsburgh from Floods.* Pittsburgh: Pittsburgh Flood Commission, 1911.

Pittsburgh Gazette Times. *The Story of Pittsburgh and Vicinity.* Pittsburgh: 1908.

Pittsburgh Press Club. *Prominent Men of Pittsburgh and Vicinity: Members of Pittsburgh Press Club, 1912–1913.* Pittsburgh: Pittsburgh Press Club, 1913.

Playground and Vacation School Association. *Annual Report of the Playgrounds and Vacation Schools of North Side, Pittsburgh, Formerly the City of Allegheny.* Pittsburgh: 1910.

St. Anthony's Chapel. *St. Anthony's Chapel, Pittsburgh, Pennsylvania.* Pittsburgh: St. Anthony's Chapel, 1978.

St. Cyprian Parish. *St. Cyprian Church, 1920–1970: Golden Jubilee Observance Day, Sunday, October 11, 1970.* Pittsburgh: 1970.

St. Gabriel Archangel Parish. *St. Gabriel Archangel Slovak Church, N.S., Pittsburgh, Pa.: Dedication, Sunday, April 30, 1972.* Pittsburgh: 1972.

St. Gabriel Parish. *PamäTníK ZlatéHo Jubilea Slovenskej RíMsko KatolíCkej Osady Sv. Gabriela, N.S., Pittsburgh, Pa., Roman Catholic Church, N.S., Pittsburgh, Pa. 1903–1953: Souvenir of the Golden Jubilee of St. Gabriel's.* Pittsburgh: 1953.

Sanborn Map Company. *Fire Insurance Maps of Allegheny, Pa.* New York: Sanborn Map Company, 1906.

———. *Fire Insurance Maps of Pittsburgh.* New York: Sanborn Map Company, 1925.

———. *Fire Insurance Maps of Pittsburgh and Allegheny.* New York: Sanborn Map Company, 1884.

Sanborn-Perris Map Company. *Fire Insurance Maps of Allegheny, Pa.* New York: Sanborn-Perris Map Company, 1893.

Smith, Percy Frazer. *Memory's Milestones: Reminiscences of Seventy Years of a Busy Life in Pittsburgh.* Pittsburgh: Murdoch-Kerr, 1918.

Swift, Elliot Elisha. *History of the First Presbyterian Church of Allegheny.* Pittsburgh: Nevin, Gribbin & Co., 1876.

Thurston, George H. *Allegheny County's Hundred Years.* Pittsburgh: A. A. Anderson & Son, 1888.

———. *Pittsburgh and Allegheny in the Centennial Year.* Pittsburgh: A. A. Anderson & Son, 1876.

Ubelaker, Douglas, Erika B. Jones, and Diane Beynon Landers. *Human Remains from Voegtly Cemetery, Pittsburgh, Pennsylvania*. Washington, DC: Smithsonian Institution Press, 2003.

United States Bureau of the Census (and predecessor organizations). Population, manufacturing, and agricultural schedules. 1830–1930.

University of Pittsburgh Digital Research Library. *Historic Pittsburgh City Directories, 1815–1945*. http://digital.library.pitt.edu/p/pitttextdir/.

Van Trump, James. *Landmark Architecture of Allegheny County, Pa*. Pittsburgh: Pittsburgh History & Landmarks Foundation, 1983.

Walker, Susan Cooper. *When I Look Back and Think*. Maryville, TN: privately printed, 1943.

Yanosko, James W., and Edward W. Yanosko. *Around Troy Hill, Spring Hill, and Reserve Township*. Chicago: Arcadia Publishing, 2011.

INDEX